Liverpool Territorials in the Great War

Liverpool Territorials
in the Great War

Paul Knight

To Graham

Hope you enjoy the book

Paul Knight

3 August 17

Pen & Sword
MILITARY

First published in Great Britain in 2017 by
Pen & Sword Military
an imprint of
Pen & Sword Books Ltd
47 Church Street
Barnsley
South Yorkshire
S70 2AS

ISBN 978 1 47383 404 0

A CIP catalogue record for this book is available from the British
Library

Typeset in Ehrhardt by
Mac Style Ltd, Bridlington, East Yorkshire
Printed and bound in the UK by CPI Group (UK) Ltd,
Croydon, CR0 4YY

Pen & Sword Books Ltd incorporates the imprints of Pen & Sword
Archaeology, Atlas, Aviation, Battleground, Discovery, Family
History, History, Maritime, Military, Naval, Politics, Railways, Select,
Transport, True Crime, and Fiction, Frontline Books, Leo Cooper,
Praetorian Press, Seaforth Publishing and Wharncliffe.

For a complete list of Pen & Sword titles please contact
PEN & SWORD BOOKS LIMITED
47 Church Street, Barnsley, South Yorkshire, S70 2AS, England
E-mail: enquiries@pen-and-sword.co.uk
Website: www.pen-and-sword.co.uk

Contents

Acknowledgements

This work has only been made possible with the assistance of a large number of people, whether they knew it or not. While writing the book, I was employed by the British Army as the First World War project officer (Operation REFLECT) at Headquarters 42nd Infantry Brigade and HQ North West. This post gave me the opportunity to discuss my ideas and explore the issues of the British Army during the Great War. The Merseyside Branch of the Western Front Association also provided opportunities for exploring and discussing the Territorials and the Western Front, especially during the tour of the Western Front in April 2016. Of particular note were: the Chairman, Peter Threlfall, Judith Beastall, Neil Olsson and Bob Dixon.

Mireille Surridge receives a particular mention for realising that I would be interested in *To Answer Duty's Call*, and for giving me her copy of the book.

Of the museums, Karen O'Rourke (also a WFA member) of the King's Regiment Collection at the Museum of Liverpool and Ian Riley of the Liverpool Scottish Collection have been most helpful. Also, staff at the Canadian War Museum, the Royal Artillery Museum, the Royal Signals Museum and the Royal Logistic Corps Museum have been helpful with answering questions on their specific armies and corps.

The staff of the Imperial War Museum and The National Archives offered great assistance with primary source research.

Thanks should also go to Captain Harry Smedley of 103 Regiment Royal Artillery, who received the Thomas Westwell papers and passed them onto me, which are now with Major Bob Dobson at 33 Signal Squadron. Judith Beastall conducted the additional research on Serjeant Westwell and the author's great uncle, Corporal John Service. Ken Lees (for his research into 9th King's) and Kathy Donaldson from the Liverpool First World War Research Committee are also thanked for providing a press photograph and further background information into Service's award of the Military Medal.

List of Maps

Chapter 1

Introduction

In August 1914, the War Office very quickly grasped the scale of the unfolding conflict and set about expanding Britain's small peacetime army. They went about this in two ways. Firstly, they raised new infantry battalions for the duration of the war – Service battalions – which would include the famous Pals battalions. The King's (Liverpool Regiment) raised eight Service battalions that served overseas, the 11th to 14th and 17th to 20th Battalions, the last four being the famous Liverpool Pals. Secondly, they approached the part time Home Defence soldiers of the Territorial Force. At the outbreak of the war, the Territorial infantry of the King's Regiment consisted of six battalions, and they quickly volunteered for operational service overseas: the Liverpool Scottish fought in Flanders before Christmas 1914, and all battalions were fighting there by early 1915. The Territorials also included a full range of other arms: the Royal Field Artillery (RFA), Royal Engineers (RE) and Royal Army Medical Corps (RAMC); a RE field company and a RAMC field ambulance would serve at Gallipoli from mid-1915.

Crucially, the Territorials had only been trained to defend the UK mainland (legally, they could only be compulsorily mobilised for Home Defence) from 1908, or back to 1859 if you include their previous incarnation as Volunteers.

There were normally two Regular Army battalions in each regiment; one on imperial garrison duties overseas and one on Home Service duties in the UK. When the Home Service deployed overseas (for example, the 1914 British Expeditionary Force), the role of the Territorials was to fulfil their Home Defence role. They were never trained or equipped to fight in a major continental war. And yet large numbers volunteered for just such a task. However, if the Territorials were fighting overseas, who would perform the Home Defence role? While preparing for overseas operations, the Territorials also doubled in size, creating Second Line Territorial units: the invasion threat kept Liverpool's Second Line Territorials in the UK until 1917.

STILL WITH THE BRIGADE.

Group taken at Larkhill Camp, 1922   [*Photo by Bassano*]

Names (reading from left to right).
Back Row – Saddler Sergt. Cunningham, Dr. Robinson, Dr. Daniells, Dr. Lunt, Gnr. Wallace, Sergt. Eisenberg, B.S.M. Lewis, M.M.,
Sergt. Humphreys, L/Sergt. Davies, Gr. N. Jones, L/Sergt. McCarrick, Sergt. McCausland, M.M., Sergt. Kirby, Sergt. T. A. Jones.
Centre Farrier-Sergt. Duff, Br. Doran, Sergt. Jones, Br. Brown, B.S.M. Parry, Sergt. Budd, M.M., Sergt. O'Dowd,
Q.M.S. Armson, M.M., Lt-Col. C. N. Cross, M.C.
Right of Gun – S.S. O'Donnell, Dr. J. Ward, Sergt. Blackburn, Farrier Bennett, Br. Hill, Sergt. Jaycock, Q.M.S. Gerrard, Q.M.S. Seed.
Seated – Farrier-Sergt. Mason, Farrier-Sergt. Wright, Sergt. Perrin, L/Sergt. Fallon, L/Sergt. Clark, Br. O'Brien, Br. Hutchinson,
Sergt. Jameson, L/Br. Daley, L/Br. McGuinness, L/Br. Hughes, Dr. Banks.

Still with the Brigade, 1922. Veterans of the Great War still serving with the Brigade. (*Wadsworth*)

Volunteers had served in Overseas Operations during the Boer War. The Territorials are still training in the City today, under their new name of Army Reserve, and they are still volunteering for Home Defence (or UK Ops, like the Cumbria and Lancashire Floods of 2015/6, or the London Olympic Games) and Overseas Ops, in the Balkans, Iraq and Afghanistan.

Yet Liverpool's Territorial Force has no memorial of their own in their City in the Derby Transept of the city's Anglican Cathedral, out of the way and high up so it is easily missed (and, indeed, on the author's first search for it, none of the Cathedral staff knew of its existence) is a memorial to the 55th Division. If you look closely on the Cenotaph on St George's Hall Plateau, you will see headstones with a range of infantry capbadges (but none of the other arms), alongside those of the RN and RAF; there are also Christian and Jewish graves side by side. To the rear of St George's Hall, near the memorial to the King's Regiment, are smaller memorials to the Liverpool Scottish (they also have a memorial tucked away inside the Hall – and one

Details from the
Cenotaph, Liverpool.
A girl laying wreath at
a headstone with the
Horse of Hannover
capbadge, next to
a Liverpool Pal;
Liverpool Scottish next
to a South Lancashire;
Liverpool Irish and
Liverpool Rifles.

Unveiling of the
55th Divisional
Memorial, 1925.

CATHEDRAL MEMORIAL TO THE 55TH DIVISION.
The 55th (West Lancashire) Division Memorial has been dedicated by the Bishop of Liverpool in the
Cathedral of that city.   Left : Lieutenant-General Sir H. S. Jeudwine, who commanded the division
during the war, talking to Lance-corporal J. Hewitson, V.C., outside St. George's Hall, Liverpool, at
his inspection of ex-Service men before the dedication.   Right : The Memorial.

to the Lancashire Fusiliers; one wonders if they knew the 2/5th Lancashire Fusiliers served alongside Liverpool's Territorials a century ago?) In France they are remembered on the 55th Division's Memorial in Givenchy; the Liverpool Scottish Memorial at Bellewaarde Ridge near Ypres, Belgium and in St George's Church, Ypres, where brass plaques remember long forgotten battalions, like the Liverpool Rifles. The 57th (Second West Lancashire) Division has no memorial or divisional history.

In comparison, there are three memorials in Liverpool to the Liverpool Pals, including a frieze in Liverpool Lime Street Station, from where the Pals departed, opposite the St George's Hall Plateau where they paraded before leaving Liverpool (as, in fact, did many other units), and where the city's war memorial stands today. The Pals concept was one which the City of Liverpool can be justly proud – it was the creation of Lord Derby, the Liverpool's aristocratic patron, and would be adopted across the industrial cities of the UK: "This should be a battalion of Pals, a battalion in which friends from the same office will fight shoulder to shoulder for the honour of Britain and the credit of Liverpool." In France, the Liverpool (and Manchester)

Pals are commemorated at the 30th Division memorial in Montauban, the location of not only their greatest achievement but also the most successful attack on 1 July 1916; just over two miles away, in Guillemont church, is a new plaque to the dozen battalions of the King's Regiment who fought there from July to September 1916, but only the four Pals battalions warrant a special mention. The achievements of some units persist, while others are lost to posterity.[1]

55th Divisional Memorial, Givenchy.

As a concept, the Pals idea was short term, limited in numbers and limited in military scope. The Liverpool Pals only raised four battalions, of which two were broken up before the end of the war. The remaining battlions only survived by absorbing the Lancashire Hussars (first raised in 1798, they were part of the Territorial Force), which dismounted and retrained as infantry and 14th King's, one of the regiment's service battalions. Those four battalions would go into action for the first time on the First Day of the Somme, almost half way through the war. Other arms raised under the same scheme were not honoured with the 'Pals' title. The Royal Field Artillery batteries and RAMC field ambulances, for example, were entitled 'County Palatine' in honour of their home county, but they were not Pals: the 98th (County Palatine) Field Ambulance, RAMC which supported the Liverpool Pals in 30th Division throughout the war was actually a pre-war Territorial unit, the 2nd (West Lancashire) Field Ambulance. Furthermore, the Pals sit within the wider category of Service battalions, wartime only units. The Liverpool Pals were the 17th, 18th, 19th and 20th (Service) Battalions, The King's (Liverpool Regiment), yet the first of the Service battalions raised in Liverpool was a pioneer battalion, the 11th, and landed in France almost six months ahead of the Pals. The story of Liverpool's Service battalions, the 11th to 14th, still needs to be written: Sergeant David Jones, 12th King's, won the Victoria Cross on 2 September 1916 at Guillemont, a battle more closely associated with the Territorials and Pals.

At the outbreak of war, the territorial infantry of the King's Regiment was 50 per cent larger than the Pals would ever achieve. And then there were the other arms. The Territorial Force was then doubled in size about the time the Pals concept was created: Liverpool provided the core of two divisions of the Territorial Force.

This book aims to chart the Liverpool Territorials, of all arms and capbadges, who had not trained for but who voluntarily entered the maelstrom which would be the First World War; their descendants in the Army Reserve still train in the city today. This book will also show that the Territorials were the precursors of the Pals concept, with battalions and regiments raised from the same communities and work places all serving together.

This book explores the role of the Liverpool Territorials during the First World War. The core of what would become the 55th (West Lancashire) and the 57th (Second West Lancashire) Divisions TF were raised in Liverpool; but not all the units that made up the divisions were raised in Liverpool. Many Liverpool raised units would not serve in those divisions, while non-Liverpool units were posted into them.

When the Territorial Force was created in 1908, it formed fourteen infantry divisions, fourteen mounted brigades, unassigned Army Troops and non-deployable units, like General Hospitals and the Royal Garrison Artillery. In Lancashire, there were two infantry divisions, the West Lancashire Division based in Liverpool and the East Lancashire Division based in Manchester. The foundation members of the West Lancashire Territorials were:

- The Lancashire Hussars
- 1st, 2nd, 3rd and 4th Brigades, Royal Field Artillery
- West Lancashire Heavy Battery, Royal Garrison Artillery
- Lancashire and Cheshire Companies, Royal Garrison Artillery
- 1st and 2nd Field Companies, Royal Engineers

- Divisional Telegraph Company, W.T. Company, Cable and Airline Companies, Royal Engineers
- Works and Electric Light Companies, Royal Engineers
- Divisional Transport and Supply Column, Army Service Corps
- 1st, 2nd and 3rd Field Ambulances, Royal Army Medical Corps
- Western General Hospital, Royal Army Medical Corps
- 4th and 5th Battalions, The King's Own (Royal Lancaster Regiment)
- 5th, 6th (Rifle), 7th, 8th (Irish), 9th and 10th (Scottish) Battalions, The King's (Liverpool Regiment)
- 4th and 5th Battalions, The Prince of Wales' Volunteers (South Lancashire Regiment)
- 4th and 5th Battalions, The Loyal North Lancashire Regiment.[2]

The Works and Electric Light Companies RE, is sometimes listed as the Lancashire Fortress Company RE, whose headquarters were originally in the Mersey Dock Board Office, but then moved to Tramway Road, Aigburth, in 1911 to be with one works company (No. 1) and two of electric lights (Nos. 2 and 3). Although the company would not serve overseas in the war, its members did. Second Lieutenant Bogle would join 1/2nd (West Lancashire) Field Company RE in Gallipoli while Sapper Clark, who enlisted on 8 August 1914, died in Templebreedy, Cork, apparently by falling off a cliff. Lieutenant Wright joined the Company while an engineering undergraduate at the University of Liverpool. He graduated in 1914 and was commissioned into the Royal Garrison Artillery, then served in France with 55th and 57th Divisions before being killed on 10 April 1917 while attached to the Canadian artillery as a Forward Observation Officer (FOO) at Vimy Ridge. He was fatally wounded by machine gun fire while fixing a broken telephone cable.[3]

The most obvious units that will not be covered in this book are those infantry regiments other than the King's Regiment, as they were raised elsewhere in Lancashire. As the war progressed, the idea that local units would recruit local men began to break down and, although there was a strong correlation, it cannot be guaranteed that only Liverpool men served in Liverpool units. However, for practical reasons, boundaries have to be drawn, even if they are somewhat artificial.

Not all of these units were part of the West Lancashire Division, in particular the Royal Garrison Artillery, whose main role was coastal and port defence. It would also be impractical to exclude some units that were not raised in Liverpool but worked closely with Liverpool units. In particular, of the three Field Ambulances, the 1st and 2nd were raised in Liverpool, while the 3rd was from St Helens. It would be difficult to exclude the 3rd Field Ambulance when writing about the TF Field Ambulances as a whole. The Royal Engineers were similarly divided between Liverpool and St Helens and it would be difficult to write about some, but not all, of those Companies.

During the war this organisation naturally changed. A third Field Company Royal Engineers was added, a Divisional Ammunition Column was formed from Brigade Ammunition Columns, and a contingent of Veterinaries were raised.[4]

RE Fortress Company. Sapper J. W. Philipson, Lancashire Fortress, Royal Engineers, unfortunately not dated.

I will not be covering units created during the war, such as machine gun or trench mortar battalions (which were initially raised by detaching infantry who had trained on these weapons into specialist units), or the role of higher formations. Space is finite and to attempt to cover everything is simply impractical.

The sources available for this book are disjointed. The Reverend JO Coop's *Story of the 55th Division* starts from January 1916 when the division was reformed. His history was one of the first to be published, so it is not without its problems. It was published soon enough after the war for recently demobilised soldiers to buy as a souvenir of their time in the division, which is in line with the strong idea of a corporate identity fostered by the division's only wartime General Officer Commanding (GOC), Major General Sir Hugh

Jeudwine. Coop was the division's senior chaplain. The most common source are the War Diaries, but these usually only commence when a unit was ordered to deploy on active service, not from when it was mobilised. For most of the infantry, they commence in the winter of 1914/15 and for the other arms in early 1916. The War Diaries do not cover the period in the UK and Wyrall, who wrote the history of the King's Regiment and who largely relied on the War Diaries, commenced the story from when those battalions arrived in France. The content and quality of the War Diaries vary from unit to unit and from author to author. They often appear as monthly summaries and so a quiet month can take up less than a page. Elsewhere, they can be much more detailed. Details of casualties, changes of commanding officer, awards and decorations, and officers going on leave are commonplace. The extent to which the soldiers are included, or even named, is variable. Unfortunately for the historian, a great deal of the day-to-day detail is covered in a few words; the modern equivalent would be NSTR, ie Nothing Significant To Report.

Published battalion histories are more helpful, and the three used here are McGilchrist's *Liverpool Scottish*, Roberts' *9th Kings* and Wutzburg's *2/6th (Rifle) Battalion*; but these are still only three histories for the twelve battalions that served overseas. Clayton's *Chevasse Double VC* (10th King's), McCartney's *Citizen Soldiers* (6th and 10th King's) and Gregson's 2004 PhD thesis on 7th King's do help to fill in the gap. The fate of the arms in divisional histories is summed up by Captain Stair Gillon (late KOSB) who wrote that in the 280 page history of the 29th Division (in which a West Lancashire Field Ambulance served throughout the war): 'Little more than a passing mention can be made of the Royal Engineers, the Signals, the R.A.M.C., the machine gunners, the train, the amusements and ..... the chaplains' department'. Fortunately, the 29th Divisional Artillery published its own history to redress this imbalance. Similarly, we are fortunate that the 1st (West Lancashire) Brigade, RFA and 2/2nd (West Lancashire) Field Ambulance, RAMC published their own accounts too.[5] Gibbon's *42nd (East Lancashire) Division* and the anonymously published *East Lancashire Royal Engineers History* recorded the exploits of the 1/2nd (West Lancashire) Field Company RE for the first half of the war. The combination of the War Diary, unit histories and divisional history makes that Field Company by far the easiest to write about. In comparison, the Army Service Corps, for example, has two histories, by Young (2000) and Beadon (1931), but these histories focus on the ASC as a whole and do not permit space for the exploits of individual companies.

Within the city are records held at the Liverpool Record Office, at the King's Collection of the City of Liverpool Museum and the archive of the Liverpool Scottish Association.

For websites, there is a dedicated website to the 9th King's (www.9thkings.co.uk); Liverpool and Merseyside Remembered (www. liverpoolremembrance.weebly.com) and Liverpool John Moore's University (www.merseyside–at-war.org) both holds photographs and memoires of men, women and places associated with the war and the city. www.21stdivision1914-18.org covers the 2/2nd (West Lancashire) Field Ambulance during its operations on the Western Front.

The availability of information does mean that there is a concentration on the 6th, 7th, 9th and 10th Battalions of the King's Regiment and 1/2nd Field Company RE, but that really is as a result of the willingness or otherwise of the veterans to record the history of their units.

The Territorial Force

Who, and what, were the Territorials of 1914?

In the historiography of the First World War, the Territorial Force[6] is often overlooked, squeezed between the heroically overwhelmed Old Contemptibles of the British Expeditionary Force and the citizen army raised around the New Army divisions, composed of those Service (including the Pals) battalions that were blooded so infamously at Gallipoli and on the Somme.

In between stood the Territorials.

In many respects, 1915 is the forgotten year of the war. At the outbreak of the conflict, regular army units were brought up to strength and maintained by the Regular Reserves and the Special Reserves, but by the end of the First Battle of Ypres they were fast running out of men.[7] Battalions on imperial garrison duties were recalled as soon as replacements were available. An Indian Corps was deployed from half way around the world in 1914; but its infantry would be redeployed to the Middle East by the middle of 1915. And then there was the Territorial Force.

It was the Territorials who sent battalions in the autumn of 1914 to the Western Front to reinforce the overwhelmed regulars. It was the Territorials who sent battalions and whole divisions around the empire to strengthen its defences, thereby relieving regular battalions for service on the Western Front. All of this was undertaken while Lord Kitchener was calling for the first 100,000 volunteers – the Service Battalions. The Territorials had already mobilised several times that number.

In simple terms of infantry battalions, during the war, the regulars raised 267 battalions, the New Army raised 557 battalions, while the territorials raised 692 battalions. The territorials also raised twenty nine infantry and five mounted divisions to the New Army's thirty infantry divisions.[8]

The Territorial Force had been created as recently as 1908, based on the Volunteer Movement and as a consequence of the Haldane Reforms. The Volunteers had existed since the French invasion scare of 1859.[9] The Haldane Reforms were one of a series of reforms in the Army between 1902 and 1912 following its less than impressive performance during the Boer War.[10] The impact of these reforms was that, arguably, the individual British soldier in 1914 was the best equipped and trained in Europe, and the best that Britain ever sent abroad.

One of the questions being asked at the time was: what exactly were the Volunteers for? This question was being asked against a backdrop of economising or, in today's language, defence spending cuts; and, critically, in opposition to Continental-style conscription.[11] Haldane's reforms were also conducted against a background of British domestic politics (Haldane came to office in 1905 as part of the Liberal Government formed in that year), post Boer War army reforms and international events, like the Russo–Japanese War of 1904–05. The UK's main defence concern was India, threatened primarily by Russia, resulting in what Rudyard Kipling called 'The Great Game'; a cold war in Central Asia between Russia and the British for domination of places like Persia (Iran), Afghanistan and Tibet. Russian defeat at the hands of the Japanese in 1905, followed by the Anglo–Russian Entente of 1907, secured India.

The Russian Threat was replaced by the Prussian Threat and with concerns about a pre-emptive invasion from Germany across the North Sea against the undefended and isolated coast of East Anglia. The invasion scares were explored by novels like William Le Queux's *The Great War in*

England (1897) and *Invasion of 1910*. There was also the new spy genre, like Erskin Childers' *Riddle of the Sands* (1903) and John Buchan's *The 39 Steps* (1915, but set in the summer of 1914). Even Edith Nesbit's *The Railway Children* (1905) has a spy element. For many years before the war, Germany planned to create a navy two thirds the size of the Royal Navy, threatening both the British mainland and imperial security. In 1909, Louis Blériot flew across the English Channel, a great feat but which made it clear to the Edwardians that Britain was no longer an island that could be protected by the Royal Navy alone. Just over five years later, on the night of 19–20 January 1915, Zeppelins bombed Britain, killing four and wounding sixteen, which realised the fears of Blériot's achievement.

The defence planners of the decade before 1914 were facing an increasingly uncertain world.

Haldane's 1908 reforms were not entirely original. They included some changes which were already being implemented, such as the formation of Volunteer infantry divisions and mounted brigades. One of the key changes was to link, for the first time, the regular army battalions to those of the reserves. The concept of a multi–battalion regiment was still relatively new across the whole of the British Army. The Cardwell Reforms of 1870, which famously abolished the purchase of commissions for officers, also amalgamated the remaining single battalion regiments into two battalion regiments, redistributed the county titles and established a Regimental depot established, known as localisation.

The 8th (The King's) Regiment of Foot already had a depot in Liverpool and, being one of the senior regiments, already had a second battalion. As part of the Childers Reforms, the regiment's name was changed in 1881 to The King's (Liverpool Regiment) and it commenced an association with the region's volunteers and militias. However, there was still no formal system of reserves to support the small Regular Army during protracted campaigns. This weakness was highlighted during the Boer War.

Haldane linked, for the first time, the Regular and the Reserve battalions, although there was still no expectation that they would serve together. Even the Regular sister battalions were unlikely to serve together. In the case of the King's Regiment, the 1st Battalion served on the Western Front throughout the war, while the 2nd Battalion remained in India. The reforms established

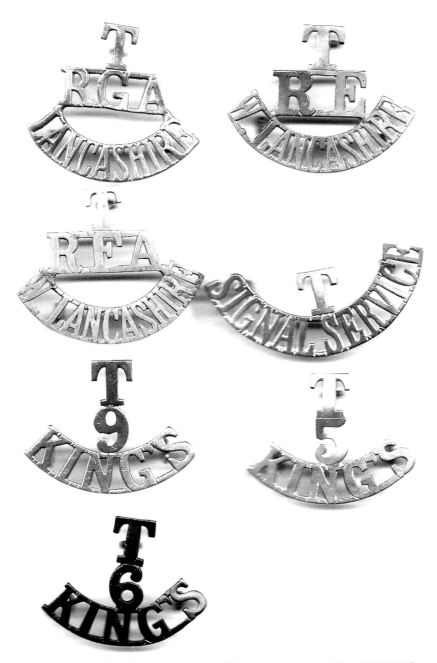

Territorial shoulder titles. West Lancashire's RFA and Lancashire RGA; RE Field Company and Signal Service; 5th, 6th and 9th King's.

a Special Reserve battalion, the 3rd Battalion, and in larger regiments like The King's, a 4th Battalion, the Extra Reserve, both from the old Militia. The 3rd Battalion was not expected to be mobilised and serve as a formed unit; rather it provided a trained reserve of soldiers and officers to bring the regular battalions up to a wartime establishment and to provide drafter for the active battalions. The 4th Battalion was intended to replace a regular battalion in an imperial garrison to relieve the regulars for a warfighting role. These battalions were composed of either ex-regulars or volunteers, who undertook a period of full time service before undertaking a part time military commitment. This scheme did provide reinforcements to the regular battalions, but was not considered to be a great success and when the reserves were reformed in 1920 the special and extra reserve battalions were not reconstituted.

Haldane's Territorials were administered through newly formed County Associations. There were, theoretically, fourteen deployable infantry divisions and fourteen mounted brigades, complete with supporting arms, in addition to the non-deployable units like General Hospitals. In Lancashire, there were two County Associations, West and East Lancashire, based in Liverpool and Manchester respectively. Within each TF division, the TF infantry battalions belonging to the same regiment would serve together. The brigading of Territorial battalions from the same regiment meant that, uniquely, they would serve together. In many Continental armies, the regiment has a similar role as the brigade in the British Army, with the 1st, 2nd, 3rd and 4th battalions of a regiment serving together. This meant that when the battalions, brigades and divisions suffered heavy casualties, the impact of those losses were concentrated in the communities where they recruited from. This localised recruiting is a characteristic usually attributed to the Pals battalions, but is clearly in place from 1908. In the case of the King's Regiment, there were six TF battalions, numbered 5 to 10. Four were brigaded together in the Liverpool Brigade and two more in the South Lancashire Brigade with 4th and 5th Battalions, The South Lancashire Regiment. Some of these battalions had a lineage going back to the Volunteer movement of the mid-Victorian period, although the most junior battalion, the 10th, was only raised in 1900. These battalions were entirely made up of territorials, with the regular component limited to adjutants and sergeant instructors. At brigade and divisional level, commanders and staff officers were regulars.

The reserves system was planned to mobilise, at full strength, about 500,000 men, of whom 302,199 were territorials; this compared with the 250,000 men of the Regular Army. Many of the Regular Army units were distributed around various imperial garrisons and so were not immediately available for European service. For various political reasons, the territorials were only intended to serve in Britain. They could volunteer for overseas service, for which the Territorial Force Imperial Service badge was awarded and worn on the right breast. By 1912, some 7 per cent of territorials had volunteered, or 17,621 men, which is similar to the 6 per cent of the old Volunteers who had served in the Boer War. As well as individuals, five complete units had also volunteered.[12]

The West Lancashire County Association was responsible for the West Lancashire Division:

Lancashire Hussars
    Artillery
        I (West Lancashire) Brigade, Royal Field Artillery
        II (West Lancashire) Brigade, Royal Field Artillery
        III (West Lancashire) Brigade, Royal Field Artillery
        IV (West Lancashire) (Howitzer) Brigade, Royal Field Artillery
    Royal Engineers
        1st (West Lancashire) Field Company
        2nd (West Lancashire) Field Company
        West Lancashire Divisional Signals Company
    Royal Army Medical Corps
        1st (West Lancashire) Field Ambulance
        2nd (West Lancashire) Field Ambulance
        3rd (West Lancashire) Field Ambulance
    Army Service Corps
        West Lancashire Divisional Train, Army Service Corps

North Lancashire Brigade
    4th Battalion, The King's Own (Royal Lancaster Regiment)
    5th Battalion, The King's Own (Royal Lancaster Regiment)
    4th Battalion, The Loyal North Lancashire Regiment
    5th Battalion, The Loyal North Lancashire Regiment

Liverpool Brigade
   5th Battalion, The King's (Liverpool Regiment)
   6th Battalion, The King's (Liverpool Regiment)
   7th Battalion, The King's (Liverpool Regiment)
   8th Battalion, The King's (Liverpool Regiment)

South Lancashire Brigade
   9th Battalion, The King's (Liverpool Regiment)
   10th Battalion, The King's (Liverpool Regiment)
   4th Battalion, The Prince of Wales's Volunteers (South Lancashire Regiment)
   5th Battalion, The Prince of Wales's Volunteers (South Lancashire Regiment)[13]

The deployable division did not include all of the territorial units, like the 1st Western General Hospital or the Royal Garrison Artillery. The author has found no evidence that the Lancashire Company RGA deployed to France but did find the graves of three soldiers serving with 1/1st (Lancashire)

Lancashire Company Royal Garrison Artillery in France. Headstones of Gunner Magill from Liverpool and A/Bombardier Taylor.

Heavy Battery, RGA. 1282 Gunner WA Magill, son of Mr and Mrs W Magill of 4 Dorothy Place Fleet Street Liverpool, was killed in action on 17 July 1916. In the same row in Dantzig Alley British Cemetery, Mametz are also buried 1447 Acting Bombardier W Taylor and 299 Gunner Foot, all killed the same day, but there is no further biographical detail. There is, however, a statement of effectiveness of the Lancashire Company RGA in the War Diary of 1/4th (West Lancashire) (Howitzer) Brigade. It may have been that the Lancashire Company absorbed into the Howitzer Brigade in 1915?[14]

Infantry

The 5th, 7th (Irish) and 9th Battalions of The King's Regiment recruited 'respectable' working classes while the 6th (Rifles) Battalion recruited from the middle classes: Rifleman Ellison claimed that the 6th only recruited 'clerks, solicitors, accountants and shop assistants', with recruits accepted based on their education, sporting activities and profession. Helen McCartney found this professional class linked the recruiting practices of the 6th and 10th (Scottish) Battalions. The author made a special visit to the grave of Captain William Sproat Montgomery, OC D Company 6th King's, because he exemplified what have been called 'collar and cuff' battalions. Montgomery was a pre-war Territorial who lived in Bromborough and was a partner in, and manging director of, a Liverpool firm. He was worth some £2 million in today's money but unfortunately survived less than a month in France before being mortally wounded. KW Mitchinson's study of the 5th Londons (London Rifle Brigade) found exactly the same practices. What this does mean is that the territorials were drawn from men who worked together, which is usually considered to be a characteristic particular to the Pals.

Trevor Hildrey, in his tribute to the Old Crosbeians (OCs) from Merchant Taylor's School, Crosby during the war, identified a strong correlation between the school and 6th King's, despite being located at opposite ends of the city. Of 731 OCs known to have served, he established a link with the 6th on sixty three occasions, making it the 'school's battalion'. When a school cadet corps was established in 1915, the West Lancashire County Association approved its affiliation with the 6th, although this link was already established from the outbreak of the war, if not before. Of 155 OCs known to have died and have been recorded in Hildrey's book, forty seven can be identified as serving in a West Lancashire Territorial unit (including one who served with 2/5th Lancashire Fusiliers, part of the 55th Division from January 1916) and of those, half, twenty four, served with the 6th before or during the war. Of those twenty four, where a pre-war occupation or status is given, eleven were clerks or a similar professional position at, for example, Royal Insurance or the Mersey Docks and Harbour Board. Bearing in mind that boys leaving school in the summer of 1914 onwards would not have the opportunity to develop a civilian career, this sample supports McCartney's assertions of a battalion recruiting from the professional classes. Furthermore, of the twenty four, twelve would obtain a commission, although usually not in

The author at the grave of Captain William Sproat Montgomery, Ypres Ramparts CWGC.

the 6th and usually after a period in the ranks. This further supports the idea of a class battalion ethos by providing the 'right' material for commissioning.

Lieutenant Norman Bark is one such story. After leaving school in 1913, he joined an accountancy firm and enlisted in 6th King's. He was commissioned into the King's Own Scottish Borderers in August 1916. Having recovered from wounds received on Vimy Ridge, transferred to the Royal Flying Corps, in which he was killed on 1 October 1918. Rifleman Harry Liversidge left school in 1913 and must have joined the 6th as soon as war broke out, because he was killed while on railway guard duty on 10 September 1914. He is buried in Anfield Cemetery (which has a CWGC section). Liversidge's short and particularly unfortunate military career curtailed a career that

Rifleman Harry Liversidge. Killed on duty guarding a railway 10 September 1914. He was the first of 365 Army burials in Anfield CWGC.

might have mirrored Bark's. Or it could have followed that of brothers Riflemen Arthur and William Fairburn, both pre-war territorials and both clerks; Arthur with the Royal Insurance Company and William in the family firm supplying the shipping lines operating out of Liverpool. Both were killed on the same day, 5 May 1915, during 6th King's desperate defence of Hill 60.

The 10th (Scottish) Battalion also required a non-manual occupation and, like the 6th, had an attestation and subscription fee. 10th King's charged ten shillings on attestation, which enforced a degree of social exclusivity – a prohibitive sum for many of Liverpool's manual workers. Paying to join the more exclusive units was not uncommon, as Mitchinson shows with the 5th Londons, The London Rifle Brigade, especially when the regulars in their brigade could not believe that they were paying for the privilege of living in the trenches! 10th King's were not as popular amongst the Old Crosbeians, but they enlisted and some were subsequently commissioned, as is seen with Lieutenant Adrian May, who served with 6th King's but was commissioned into 5th King's on 1 January 1916 and was killed on 8 September that year. These membership fees were abolished for the remainder of the war with the introduction of conscription in 1916. Territorials paid for the privilege of serving King and Country! The 8th (Irish) and 10th (Scottish) Battalions also recruited from their own ethnic groups, or at least persons who could establish at least a tenuous link.[15]

The battalion headquarters were distributed throughout the city:

Liverpool Scottish on Parade, 1912. (*P. Threlfall*)

Anonymous Rifleman, 6th King's, in
what appears to be a winter photograph,
showing the rifles button on the great coat
and the Liverpool Rifles' capbadge, the
backing was red.

Anonymous Rifleman, 6th King's. This
portrait shows the rifles buttons and
the Liverpool Rifles' capbadge, and in
addition a woven economy shoulder title.

5th King's drill hall was at 65 St Anne Street, Liverpool, on what is today Merseyside Police's St Anne's Police Station. They styled themselves Rifles (until 1937) and so wore black rifles buttons and blackened badges. The battalion returned to St Anne Street until a new barracks was opened on Townshend Avenue, Norris Green, in 1937. The battalion survives as A Company, 4th Battalion, The Duke of Lancaster's Regiment at Townsend Avenue.

6th (Rifle) King's, the Liverpool Rifles, occupied the Princess Park Barracks on Upper Warwick Street in the fashionable Sefton Park area of Liverpool. As Rifles, they wore black rifles buttons and blackened badges. They also wore a special badge of a Lancashire Rose over a bugle horn, while the officers wore a khaki boss badge. In 1936 they were redesignated as an anti-aircraft regiment and then a searchlight regiment.

7th King's were based at 99 Park Street, Bootle, and recruited from the north of the city along the railway to Southport, with companies in Crosby and Formby. Gregson's thesis on the battalion describes a recruiting area divided between the working class poor of the dock and industrial areas of Bootle, up to the more genteel and middle class areas of Crosby and Southport. This was reflected in the increased proportion of NCOs originating in Southport rather than Bootle. They wore an all-white version of the standard bi-metal King's capbadge. In 1938 the battalion was converted to armour, as 40th Regiment, Royal Tank Regiment, and in 1967 became part of the Duke of Lancaster's Own Yeomanry, now a squadron based in Wigan within the Queen's Own Yeomanry.[16]

8th (Irish) King's, the Liverpool Irish, were based at 75 Shaw Street, which is today a vacant plot. As an Irish regiment, they wore black buttons and had their own capbadge based on a harp. The 8th were not reformed until the Second World War, during which they trained for the D-Day landings as part of 7th Beach Group. After the war, they were redesignated as Royal Artillery and today survive as A Troop, 208 Battery, 103 Regiment, Royal Artillery.

9th King's headquarters were at 57–61 Everton Road, on Everton Brow, from where today there are views across the park, city and river to Birkenhead and the Welsh hills beyond. This battalion recruited from the Everton and Anfield areas, now associated with the football clubs. According

Derelict Drill Hall of 9th King's, on Everton Brow.

to Roberts, they were the 'tradesmen and artisan classes', with the officers drawn from the 'professional class and business houses of the city'. The 9th also had a detachment in Ormskirk, from where the battalion 'drew some of its finest fighting material. Agriculturalists make good soldiers, and this was evidenced on many occasions later by the behaviour and ability of the men from this town.' The Everton drill hall still stands, but is in a sad state of disrepair, while the Ormskirk Drill Hall is still in use as the Ormskirk Civic Hall. The battalion had raised a company for service in the Boer War and those men then used their experiences usefully in raising standards on the inter-war annual camps. Exactly how useful or relevant those lessons were by 1914 is unclear, but it was clearly better than nothing.[17]

10th (Scottish) King's, the Liverpool Scottish, were at 7 Fraser Street, Liverpool, a short distance from Liverpool Lime Street station and within walking distance of the commercial district from which it recruited many members. They were a kilted battalion with the associated uniform distinctions and their own capbadge. The Fraser Street barracks were in use until 1967 but are now a car park. Although the junior battalion, in 1900 volunteers fought in the Boer War.

Of the six Territorial battalions, four were located within a mile of each other in a triangle between St Anne Street, Shaw Street to Everton Brow and Fraser Street. This area was much more densely populated than today, which is just as well as they had to recruit some 4000 men.

Yeomanry (Cavalry)[18]

The Lancashire Hussars were based in Prince Albert Road, Liverpool but also recruited around Wigan and St Helens. A Squadron was based in Ashton-in-Makersfield, with drill stations at Wigan and Liverpool; B Squadron in St Helens; C Squadron in Newton-Le-Willows; and D Squadron at Rainhill. The Hussars' distribution is similar to a modern Army Reserve distribution of sub-unit level Army Reserve Centres scattered across a region. Another point of note is that Wigan was the home of 5th Battalion, The Manchester Regiment TF, who belonged to the East Lancashire Division, whereas the Yeomanry belonged to the West Lancashire Division. Today, Wigan is the home of B (Duke of Lancaster's Own Yeomanry) Squadron, Queen's Own Yeomanry; the DLOY were the other Lancashire yeomanry regiment and part of the East Lancashire Division.

Royal Field Artillery[19]

I (West Lancashire) Brigade was based at Windsor Barracks, Spekeland Street, Edge Hill. The street no longer exists and the area is now a housing estate.

II (West Lancashire) Brigade HQ was based in Stanley Street, Preston from 1911, with batteries in Preston, Blackpool, Bamber Bridge and Lancaster.

III (West Lancashire) Brigade HQ and one battery was based at Admiral Street, Toxteth, with another battery based in 1 Earp Street, Garston and a third battery in Widness. The Admiral Street Drill Hall is now the St Silas School playground, while Earp Street is now housing.

IV (West Lancashire) (Howitzer) Brigade was based at The Grange, Edge Lane, which remained in use as an artillery barracks until the 1960s. The barracks still stand, although currently unused and empty since 4th Battalion The Parachute Regiment left in 1999.

The Royal Artillery remain in Liverpool in the form of 208 (3rd West Lancashire) Battery in Brigadier Philip Toosey Barracks (of *Bridge on the River Kwai* fame). Toosey was a pre-war Territorial for another war. The battery includes A (Liverpool Irish) Troop, descended from 8th King's and who still wear a caubeen on special occasions.

Lt Col Osborne CO 1/4th (West Lancashire) (Howitzer) Brigade RFA. (*Wadsworth*)

Royal Army Medical Corps[20]

1st (West Lancashire) Field Ambulance were based at 73 Shaw Street, Liverpool, before moving to Tramway Road in 1910.

2nd (West Lancashire) Field Ambulance were based at 19 Low Street, Liverpool, before moving to Harper Street in 1910.

3rd (West Lancashire) Field Ambulance were based at Croppers Hill, St Helens, with sections in St Helen's, Kendal and Blackpool. The Blackpool section was disbanded in 1911 and re-formed in St Helen's while the Kendal section began recruiting in Barrow-in-Furness too.

The role of the Field Ambulances (and the Western General Hospital) is now performed by 208 Field Hospital at Chavasse House.

Royal Engineers[21]

The Field and Signals companies are listed at either 38 Mason Street, Edge Hill, and returned there after the war until a new Drill Hall was built at Score Lane, Childwall, or at Croppers Hill, St Helens.

An Electric Light Company was based at Tramway Road, Aigburth, although there is no indication of a drill hall in 1908. RE were based there in

1922. The current 208 Battery, 103 Regiment RA Army Reserve Centre on Aigburth Road is adjacent to Tramway Road.

Their roles are performed today by 75 Regiment RE, based at Warrington and Birkenhead and by 33 Signal Squadron in Huyton.

Army Service Corps[22]

The formation of the Army Service Corps companies of the TF allowed 'a change from chaos to ordered progress' which, six years later, had provided 'steady and ordered progress' from the old Volunteer days where not every formation was supported by a Transport and Supply (T&S) Column. Each column was supported by a regular adjutant (not appointed until 1911) and several NCO instructors. The T&S Column for the West Lancashire Division was organised thus:

Unit	Location	Strength		Notes
		Officers	Men	
West Lancashire Div HQ Coy	Derby Road, Southport (by 1909)	8	201	
Liverpool Bde Coy	Tramway Road, Aigburth	4	97	
South Lancashire Bde Coy	Bath Street, then 46 Legh Street, Warrington (in 1909)	4	97	
North Lancashire Bde Coy	Tramway Road, Aigburth	4	112	Includes 12 2nd Line Drivers for two Infantry Battalions (Army Troops) in Cumberland and three Drivers for a Cable, an Airline and a Wireless Telegraph Company[23]
Strength		20 Officers	507 Other Ranks	527 All Ranks

Today the ASC is still based in Liverpool in the form of 156 Regiment Royal Logistics Corps, with a squadron in Allerton and another in Bootle.

Establishing the Territorial Force

The formation of the territorials required a fundamental restructuring from the old Volunteer movement. This was conducted through the County Associations, who were tasked with recruitment, providing pay and equipment, and maintaining real estate. The work started with persuading the Volunteers to join the Territorials. Many did, but some took personal affront at the changes and refused to. It could also have provided an opportunity for the 'dead wood' to be quietly retired with dignity. Recruiting was aided by the Invasion Scare of 1909, when Germany increased the tempo of the naval arms race by building dreadnoughts. Territorials signed on for a four year enlistment period, so those 1909 enlistments expired in 1913. In January 1913, the TF nationally was 16 per cent understrength, and by April 1914 it was down to 20 per cent understrength. The national strength of the TF peaked at 270,041 in 1909, but fell to 245,779 by 1913; by 1 July 1914, the strength had risen slightly, to 268,777. Within this national picture there were many successes. The Yeomanry and General Hospitals were over 90 per cent recruited, with the Yeomanry being over strength for troopers, but 12 per cent understrength for officers.[24]

Units were merged and amalgamated, and the new structure required the creation of new titles. Not all units agreed with their position in the new regimental seniority. Then there were the new units to be raised. The old Volunteers had concentrated on infantry, yeomanry and artillery, mostly garrison artillery to defend ports against invasion. The new Territorial model required deployable field formations and for this they required logistical support.

The County Associations also inherited the Volunteer's real estate, which included properties in the wrong location, the wrong size, with inadequate facilities, indebted or in need of repair.[25]

Training to the new, higher standard was difficult. Then, as now, territorials were expected to train in their spare time but, in 1908, there was less spare time available. Most men worked a six day week so a training weekend (which today is common) was rare. A fortnight was about the maximum annual leave, and many men objected to taking their whole leave allocation just to attend annual camp – nationally, the number who could attend the full fifteen day camp was around 60 per cent. To counter this, many camps were held in holiday locations, like the seaside, but this was difficult to achieve, and not always popular with divisional commanders. Major General Townshend, while commanding the East Anglian Territorials, complained:

> I could have trained them at Thetford, but am given to understand that the want of amusements (cinemas, theatres etc.) in that locality caused it to be so unpopular with the Territorials when General Byng trained there before, that it lessened the number of recruits. Lots of them would leave. Everyone, in short, seemed to be in collusion to arrange for a "good time" when out of training!

The West Lancashire Division was not immune to this pressure either: 5th King's trained at Halton Camp near Lancaster in 1910 and at Morfa Camp, Conway in 1911, while the 10th King's were at Denbigh Camp, North Wales in 1913 and at Hornby Camp in 1914.[26]

The quality of musketry amongst the infantry was a major cause for concern. The territorials were not issued the new Short Magazine Lee Enfield rifles, and would go to war with obsolete Magazine Lee Enfields. The West Lancashire County Association complained of the difficulties in obtaining leases for new ranges. For Liverpool's units, it was a quick train ride up the coast to the Altcar Ranges near Southport. Even with access to ranges, the War Office only supplied ninety rounds of ammunition per man per year, but generously offered to sell more ammunition to Associations or individuals at a reduced rate.[27]

If there were problems with the infantry, then the Horse and Field Artillery were in an even worse state. First of all, they were equipped with obsolete 15-pdr guns and 5-in howitzers when the Regular Field and Horse Artillery re-equipped to 18 and 13-pdrs and 4.5 inch howitzers from 1904. Not only were the Territorials' guns obsolete, but they were regularly issued without the complete complement of instruments. Live firing took place on alternate annual camps. Firing could take place on training weekends if there were ranges nearby, if there were no neighbours to offend and if the County Association could afford to hire the seventy-eight horses required to move a RFA battery or the 117 horses required for a RHA battery. In contrast, the Royal Garrison Artillery, who manned fixed fortifications usually around ports, were considered highly efficient.[28]

The Engineers (both Field and Signals), Medical and ASC units were judged to be as good as or, in some cases, superior to their Regular counterparts. Both relied on their civilian trades to supplement their Territorial training – Beadon, writing on the ASC from 1931, thought that there was 'little difficulty in recruitment and officering by zealous professional men'. Furthermore, by 1913, each ASC unit had experience in supplying their formation on an annual camp; and for the Annual Camp 1914 they would be conducting collective training with their formations. The ASC, in supplying its formations, performed its wartime role for real even in peacetime, otherwise there would be a lot of hungry soldiers.[29]

The County Association was also responsible for clothing and equipping the territorials, for which they received a grant per man. The County Association also inherited the old uniforms and equipment from the Volunteers. As money was limited, there was an incentive to wear out old stock first. Associations started by replacing obsolete Slade Wallace equipment with the '03 Pattern Bandolier equipment, which was issued to, but quickly rejected by, the Regular infantry, but that did mean that there were large stocks of cheap, unwanted equipment available. The West Lancashire Territorials were in the process of being re-equipped with a cheaper, commercial pattern of the

Railway Guard Duty. Rifleman of 6th King's, a dangerous post, as Rifleman Harry Liversidge found out to his peril. He wears the commercial variation of '08 Mills Webb equipment, with only three pouches each side.

new '08 Pattern Mills Webb equipment, although holding only ninety rounds rather than 150 rounds: photographs of 4th King's Own on mobilisation show them equipped with the commercial pattern of web equipment, but 5th King's Own are still wearing '03 Pattern Bandolier equipment. They were doing better than their counterparts in the East Lancashire Division, who were still wearing the old '03 Pattern Bandolier equipment when they landed at Gallipoli in 1915.[30]

But how did this actually translate into effective training?

One of the key problems facing the British Army during the war was a lack of experience in commanding larger formations. Between the end of the Boer War and the outbreak of the First World War twelve years later, there were limited opportunities for commanders (and their staff) to gain the necessary experience – when Sir John French took command of the BEF in August 1914, he had not commanded anything larger than a division except on manoeuvres. In contrast, continental generals had large conscript armies with which to exercise. While French's European counterparts may not have had operational experience for an even longer period, they did at least have large scale, regular exercises for multiple corps in which the command and control functions of the commanders and their staffs could be put through their paces.

The 1912 Army Manoeuvres was held in East Anglia – the same area covered in Le Queux's *The Invasion of 1910* – and included 47,000 men. Although this was small compared with comparable manoeuvres conducted by continental armies – one held in Germany the previous week was twice the size – it did include two TF brigades: the Liverpool Brigade and the 1st South West Mounted Brigade. Another key difference was that the continental corps were permanent formations that exercised together in peacetime and expected to fight together in wartime. Not so the British equivalent, which was an ad hoc formation brought together just for the manoeuvres without any expectation of serving together on operations.

As was traditional, there were two forces, Red commanded by Lieutenant General Haig, and Blue commanded by Lieutenant General Grierson. Of the two, Haig was considered to be the leading light on cavalry while Grierson was considered to be more scientific in his approach. Both forces contained commanders who would play a significate role in the First World War, including Allenby and Rawlinson.

Blue Force was slightly larger as it contained the less efficient Territorials: *The Times* of 17 September 1912 considered that they could hardly be expected to hold their own against regulars. The Liverpool Brigade travelled to Cambridge by train and then dug in around the city while Grierson advanced the rest of his force to locate Red Force. The Hampshire Carabineers of the Yeomanry Brigade confounded expectations by attacking a Red Force battalion in the flank and rear to capture a company and severely mauling an artillery battery. Later, with the regular Scots Greys, the Yeomanry Brigade would dismount to attack and capture the village of Camps Green.

Elsewhere, the village of Horseheath was vigorously contested not just by Blue Force's 8 Brigade (part of Rawlinson's 3rd Division) but also by a controversial umpiring decision. Into the maelstrom, Grierson decided to commit the Liverpool Brigade on the left of the 3rd Division. The territorials' arrival was delayed by congestion caused by civilian traffic and so a junior staff office decided to deploy them on the right of 8 Brigade. The remainder of the 3rd Division (7 and 9 Brigades) were also arriving on the battlefield but, according to Batten, 'the intervention of the Territorials

5th King's on Annual Camp, 1912. The battalion claimed Rifles status, as is shown by their black buttons, but their capbadges and shoulder titles are un-blackened.

transformed the situation on the north of the battlefield'. When a ceasefire was called at the end of the day, Blue Force clearly had the advantage.

Greirson was considered the winner. In 1914, he and Haig were assigned to command II and I Corps respectively. Unfortunately Grierson died of a heart aneurism on 17 August and was denied the opportunity to apply his 1912 success for real. For the Territorials, however, there was nothing but praise for their performance and potential, which destroyed *The Times'* predictions. They had, indeed, punched well above their weight, as they would do after 1914. Haig, having had his fingers burned and learnt his lesson, would write later 'I was very intimately acquainted, of course, with what the Territorials had been doing'. Haig was not the only senior commander during the war to have a positive pre-war experience of the Territorials. The first Commander-in-Chief of the BEF, Sir John French, had been the adjutant of a yeomanry regiment and had a high opinion of the territorials: he was full of praise of them for 'filling the gap' early in the war.[31]

This contrasted with Kitchener, who distrusted the territorials and would, in 1914, raise his New Armies. While those New Armies were being raised, trained and equipped, the territorials who had so impressed Haig were busy fighting, and dying, under him in France. What the manoeuvres did not show were the casualties which would been incurred in a modern battle. There were, however, anecdotal reports at the time that the 'battle' of Horseheath would have been a bloodbath on the scale experienced post-1914. One newspaper wrote, "Had it been real warfare, Horseheath village would have presented a scene of carnage terrible to contemplate"; while Sir John French, Chief of the Imperial Staff, Director of the 1912 manoeuvres and in 1914 Commander-in-Chief of the BEF, criticised both divisional commanders for fighting in a village that was overlooked on all sides by higher ground and which could be dominated by enemy artillery. Both situations, a bloodily fought over village and operating where the enemy had control of the high ground, would be recurring scenarios post-1914.[32]

If 1912 showed anything, it was that the territorials did not lack the pluck and courage for what was to come. It also showed that the evidence of likely casualties in a modern war was there for those who wanted to see it.

So despite having obsolete equipment, the complexities of the inherited Volunteer and Yeomanry heritage, financial constraints, public support mixed with apathy towards joining, and terms and conditions of service which could take up a man's entire annual leave allocation, the territorials were improving in efficiency. A great deal of work had been done in four years. The potential had been shown by the Liverpool Brigade in 1912. The real answer would only be discovered if, and when, they were mobilised.

Mobilisation

At eleven o'clock last night England declared war on Germany. We now know exactly what our position and responsibilities are in the horrible period which now has to be gone through. We must accept the position and shoulder the responsibility with British fortitude and determination. The honour, dignity, integrity and future fortunes of the British Empire are at stake to a degree never before conceived possible.[33]

The role of the territorials was Home Defence. When the regulars were mobilised and deployed overseas, it was the territorials who were to replace them in the UK. Most of the territorials were assigned to one of two roles, either Local Force or Central Force. Local Force comprised TF units based in the likely invasion areas, for example, the east and south coasts, from where they would resist the initial landings. Central Force would be a mobile reserve which could be deployed to meet the invasion, and consisted of units from areas away from the invasion areas. The two Lancashire TF divisions, however, were not part of either plan. Their wartime role was to replace the Regular Army in Ireland. They were to sail five days after mobilisation, which gave very little time to prepare. The territorials expected six months of mobilised training before being sufficiently proficient to take to the field.[34] How the West and East Lancashire Divisions were expected to deploy to Ireland within five days of mobilisation was never determined. Concerns existed about the reliability of some of the Lancashire Territorials because of the strong Irish connections. In the summer of 1914 two crisis occupied the minds of the British Government – Irish Home Rule (an Act granting home rule to a united Ireland was passed in 1914, but suspended for a year due to the war) and Suffragettes, not the Sarajevo assassination. It is fortunate that the Lancashire territorials were not sent into the maelstrom of 1914 Irish politics.[35]

The mobilisation experiences of units differed. In the summer of 1914, against the backdrop of a European crisis, the Liverpool Scottish left for Halton Camp near Lancaster for its Annual Camp. The battalion was almost at full strength, with 913 officers and men, including the young RAMC Lieutenant Noel Chavasse. He signed the leave book of the Royal Southern Hospital, Liverpool, for the period 2 to 16 August 1914 and a locum, a Dr Power, awaited his return. Having arrived at Halton Camp on the 2nd, the battalion had

Private Kaye, Liverpool Scottish. A fine portrait showing the uniform characteristics which made the battalion popular. (*P. Threlfall*)

barely unpacked when they were ordered back to Liverpool the following day. Once back at Fraser Street, the battalion was sent to their homes. Like the Liverpool Scottish, 7th King's were also on Annual Camp when war was declared, in their case in Westmorland, with a strength of some 700.[36] This would put their strength at about 70 per cent of establishment or the national average for the infantry.

McGilchrist says that the Liverpool Scottish paraded about 600 men at 2200 hours on 7 August at their Fraser Street Barracks (although this figure conflicts with 913 given above). There they received their £5 embodiment (mobilisation) grant, 10/- kit allowance and ammunition.

At 1400 hours on 6 August 1914, 9th King's reported as mobilised: just one man was unaccounted for. More pressing matters for the Commanding Officer, Lieutenant-Colonel Luther Watts V.D., were accommodation, feeding and transportation. For the first night they were accommodated in the Hippodrome Theatre (where the artists put on an additional performance) before space was found in Liverpool College. Feeding, in relays, was provided at the Newboys' Home on Everton Road.[37]

Mobilisation covered a host of duties, including attesting new soldiers to bring the battalions up to full strength. Much of this additional recruiting would have been through word of mouth, with existing members recruiting friends and colleagues eager to join up and to serve with people they knew. Nationally, the TF was 90,000 over establishment by 3 November 1914, and had doubled in strength by the end of the year. In additional to military training, they provided working parties for the docks, which must have come as a great shock to the Liverpool Scottish, as they were largely drawn from the mercantile class – clerks in shipping and insurance companies – not from the docks.[38]

In 1914 all armies were dependant on horses and mules, and the British Army was no exception. There was no guarantee that there would be sufficient of them to move both the Regular Army and the Territorial Force on mobilisation and to keep the economy working. It was estimated that the regulars required 42,000 horses and the territorials about twice that number. This was before any expansion of the army was undertaken or the replacement of horses killed or injured in battle.[39] Captain Harrison, the Transport Officer of the Liverpool Scottish, set about acquiring horses and wagons; but his first batch were taken over by another unit. McGilchrist does not mention which battalion got the horses, just that they went to a regular battalion billeted in the city's St George's Hall. The same fate befell 9th King's. The horses and transport acquired by the battalion were taken over by the Army for another unit, as

Anonymous officer, King's Regiment. His Territorial status is indicated by the T beneath each collar badge.

was the second successful collection; but on the third attempt the battalion was allowed to keep the horses and wagons. Roberts does not say where the horses and wagons went to. Transport was a matter that had vexed the territorials in peacetime. Horse and wagons were generally hired by the County Association when needed.

Patriotic employers continued to pay soldiers who had volunteered. Bootle Council agreed to pay allowances to dependents and to hold jobs open for men until their return, assuming that they were still fit to perform their duties, while Cunard paid a month's full salary and then three years' salary at half pay. One problem facing the middle class battalions, at least, was the pay differential between that of a city clerk and a private soldier.[40]

On the 10th the South Lancashire Brigade entrained for Edinburgh as part of the Forth Defences. The 9th King's and the Liverpool Scottish were off to war.[41]

Wyrall, in his history of the King's Regiment during the war, reviewed the city's contribution: 'Every profession and trade in the great city of Liverpool and its suburbs was represented amongst the officers and men of the battalions, which (with the exception of the Adjutants, who were Regular Army officers) were, in every sense of the word, formed of "citizen soldiers".'[42] This reads exactly like the 'Pals' concept.

Chapter 2

The Division Broken Up –
The Infantry in France, 1914–1915

Although the role of the Territorial Force was Home Defence, it soon became clear to the planners in the War Office that more men and units were needed for Overseas Service. Seven percent of the TF had volunteered for Imperial Service before the war, but that was not going to be enough. On 27 August 1914, the War Office announced that if over 80 per cent of a unit volunteered, then that unit could serve together as a formed body.[1] How they would be used was unclear. The first formation to be deployed overseas, early in September, the East Lancashire Division, went to Egypt to guard the Suez Canal and the following year would fight in Gallipoli.[2] There they would be joined by the Lowland, Welsh and East Anglian Territorial Force Divisions, plus yeomanry regiments. Not all TF units were part of deployable divisions. Some, like 4th and 5th Battalions, The Border Regiment, were unattached Army Troops: 4th Borders would spend the war in Rangoon on imperial garrison duties.

The West Lancashire Division was broken up. Individual units were deployed to the Western Front or Gallipoli to reinforce mostly regular army divisions and would not be reformed until January 1916. Many of the other arms units remained in the UK as they were not required overseas but were needed in the Home Defence roll.

When territorial units and formations volunteered to deploy overseas, there remained two problems. Firstly, not all territorials could, or would, volunteer. Soldiers had to be 19 to serve overseas and, while there are many tales of an official blind eye being turned to under-age recruits, it was a bit more difficult for a serving soldier. Others were overage or medically downgraded, including a number of commanding officers, like Nicolls of the Liverpool Scottish, who, having spent their volunteer and territorial careers training themselves and their unit for this moment, were prevented from leading their men to war.

Others did not want to serve overseas for family or economic reasons. It was one thing to volunteer to defend your town and family from invasion, it was another to go to war for another country. There were those who, giving up comfortable positions with good salaries, now found their families having to survive on a private's salary – Mitchinson in his study of the London Rifle Brigade found that, initially at least, patriotic employers paid the salary difference, as did Bootle Council and Cunard for the Liverpool Territorials. There were other, distinctly middle class, issues to be resolved, like whether or not insurance companies would pay out on life insurance policies under wartime conditions.[3]

The second problem was who would perform the territorials' Home Defence role? On 15 August 1914, the decision was taken to raise a second, duplicate unit, referred to as the Second Line Territorials, using those who were not serving overseas as the core. To distinguish between the First and Second Line units, they became, in the example of 5th King's, 1/5th King's and 2/5th King's respectively. In time, the Second Line would form a new division, 57th (2nd West Lancashire) Division. A Third Line would also be authorised in November 1914, which would serve as a depot for recruiting and training, and would be designated 3/5th King's. By the end of the war the Third Line battalions were rationalised into Training Battalions.[4]

That Liverpool's Territorials were able to both fulfil their contractual duties (Home Defence) and volunteer in sufficient numbers to provide more units for the Western Front and Gallipoli – for which they had not enlisted, trained or been equipped – speaks highly of their commitment.

While the territorials were expanding, Lord Kitchener, who became Secretary of State for War at the outbreak of the war in 1914, requested the 'First Hundred Thousand' of half a million men and created the New Army. Kitchener, hero of the Empire, had no knowledge of the 'Home Army', unlike French and Haig. He also thought that the TF could not expand and train at the same time. His New Armies struggled as much as the territorials. This duplication of effort did nothing to assist the war effort. According to Beckett, there is:

'little doubt that the creation of the [New Army] led to an unnecessary duplication of effort that damaged both organisations, and that Territorial associations could probably have been made an adequate basis for expansion.'

While this statement may be open for debate, Beckett cites the New Zealand experience for how the territorials could have been better used.[5]

1/10th (Scottish) Battalion, The King's (Liverpool Regiment), TF – The Liverpool Scottish

On 10 August 1914, the Liverpool Scottish left their home town for Edinburgh, where their training regime continued in earnest, presumably assisted by the removal of home town distractions. If, as appears to have become the normal practice, they paraded at St George's Hall before entraining at Liverpool Lime Street Station, they were the first in wartime to do so. An hour of physical drills each morning was accompanied by company races up Arthur's Seat, which developed both fitness and inter-company rivalry. Battalion drills ended at 4:30 pm, but lectures afterwards were not unknown.[6]

In response to the War Office's call for volunteers, all of the officers and over 800 other ranks volunteered. To make up the shortfall, Major Blair and Captain Anderson returned to Liverpool with permission to recruit a further three hundred men. They achieved this within three days and could have recruited twice that number. The three hundred joined the battalion and commenced training, while those who were not going overseas were formed into two new companies, I and K. The battalion, in common with the rest of the territorial infantry, was still using the old eight company structure, in this case Companies A to H, whereas the Regular infantry had changed to a four company structure. Companies I and K formed the basis of 2/10th King's.[7]

In Edinburgh, the Regimental Medical Officer, Lieutenant Chavasse RAMC, vaccinated over 1000 men against typhoid; and the men reacted badly. They were also susceptible to 'sickness, colds and influenza', which he attributed to the solders being clerks and so 'unused to roughing it and unused to kilts'.[8] It would not be the last time that either the unsuitability of the kilted uniform or the comfortable living of the middle class clerks would cause problems for the young doctor or the men.

Their stay in Edinburgh was short lived and on 9 October the battalion moved to Tunbridge Wells, where they expected to be in training until the spring, but they spent just three weeks there before sailing to France. Before deploying, McGilchrist writes that all leather equipment was withdrawn and 'full web equipment' was issued. The leather equipment was probably the new emergency 1914 Pattern as the pre-war photographs do not show the King's territorials wearing 1903 Pattern Bandolier equipment. The reference to the 'full web equipment' may be the issuing of regulation '08 Pattern Mills Webb equipment, with 150 round pouches, rather than the commercially bought ninety round version. They were also issued with new rifles, but photographs from France show that they were still using Magazine Lee Enfield rifles, rather than the new SMLE. Musketry courses were completed, although some 300 men who had not completed the course remained behind. McGilchrist blamed the lack of ranges in both Edinburgh and Tunbridge Wells for this (which, as mentioned, was a pre-war problem for the territorials), although he considered that their later arrival in France, when the extra numbers were most needed, was a blessing. Also remaining behind was Lieutenant Colonel Nicholl, whose health was insufficiently robust for what was to come. He handed command to Major Blair, but it was a blow to the man who had trained the battalion for operations over so many years and was not able to be with them when they deployed.[9]

In a letter to his parents, Lieutenant Chavasse described how parents travelled to Tunbridge Wells to see their sons off, taking them to restaurants in taxis for a final feeding.[10] It was also the last time many of those soldiers would see their parents. Chavasse wrote about the same time to his sister Dorothea to thank her for a parcel of clothes for some of his medical orderlies, being 'poor boys and are not well off like most of our Liverpool Scottish'. They were, in fact, attached from the St Helens based 1/3rd (West Lancashire) Field Ambulance TF; the contrast between the middle class dominated Liverpool Scottish, whose parents were able to travel across the country to dine with their sons, and what appears to be working class medical orderlies relying on charity cannot be clearer. Chavasse was fatally wounded in 1917 and buried in Brandhoek New Military Cemetery No 3. Not far away is the grave of his solider-servant, Private Rudd from St Helens.[11]

Twenty-six officers and 829 men left Tunbridge Wells on 1 November 1914; but the link with Liverpool was not quite severed yet, because they sailed on the SS *Maidan*, a liner of the Liverpool based Brocklehurst Line, with which a number of the soldiers had pre-war connections. On board was another Territorial battalion, the Queen's Westminster Rifles, (1/16th Londons).[12]

The honour of being the first territorial battalion in France goes to the London Scottish (1/14th Londons) but McGilchrist is clear in his pride at being amongst the first territorials in France:

[But] they were specially selected, along with twenty-two other Territorial Battalions, on account of their record and their progress since mobilization, to assist the sorely-tried Regular Army to hold the line during the first winter campaign while the new armies were being raised and trained. It speaks volumes for the pre-war efficiency of the officers and the keenness of the men that the junior Territorial Battalion of Liverpool should be the only one selected to go overseas in 1914.[13]

Once in France, the battalion's first official duty was to provide an honour guard for the funeral cortège of Field Marshal Lord Roberts who, having visited Indian troops in the field, caught a chill and died of pneumonia. The battalion also lost a second CO, Major Blair, on health grounds. The new CO, Major J R Davidson, was an expert in drainage in his civilian profession, which would be highly beneficial to the battalion during their time in Flanders.[14]

On 5 November the battalion finally reached its first French billets, at Blendecques, after a seventy two hour, 200 mile journey in French cattle-trucks followed by a three mile march in the pouring rain. Training in trench digging and practice attacks followed, but in atrocious weather that tried the men – they were living in barns without adequate drying facilities. McGilchrist says that when the battalion was ordered to move on, only twenty 'broken down' men had to be left behind. The First Battle of

Ypres was fought while the battalion was at Blendecques and, although not required, lorries were on stand-by to rush them to the front should they be needed.[15]

The battalion was judged fit for the front line on 19 November and received new boots and puttees. These replaced the shoes and spats which were unsuitable for the trenches but there was no opportunity to wear in the boots. After a two day march in wintery conditions, during which the impracticality of the kilted uniform was again highlighted, the battalion reached Bailleul on 21 November. Woollen underwear was issued, but the kilts froze, with the creases becoming sharp with ice, cutting the men's legs. In his audio interview, Corporal McLeavy explained how the problem of sharp creases was not limited to cold weather as dry mud had the same effect as the kilt swayed. They reduced this by sewing up the inner pleats of the kilt.[16] When the kilts defrosted in the warmth of overnight billets, the lice became active and their bites made sleeping impossible. In 1917, kilts caused frostbitten knees. When the Germans introduced mustard gas, which afflicted the more sensitive parts of the body, the drawbacks of the kilt were yet again evident.

In the winter of 1914/15 trench foot became a major problem:

Just now we have several cripples with an interesting complaint of the feet, brought on by the men having their feet in water and mud for days at a time. The feet are very tender, and the men cannot walk, then when they take their boots off their feet swell like balloons. It is some circulatory trouble, and I think it is the beginning (or threatening stage) of a gangrene of the feet which was noticed in the Balkans wars, and which was probably some of the so-called frostbite in the Crimean War.

In the winter of 1915/16, when trench foot returned, whale oil was available to be rubbed into men's feet and the effects of the condition were greatly reduced. Rubber thigh boots were also issued but kilted battalions lacked trouser buttons to hold them up.[17]

The Liverpool Scottish were brigaded with 1st Lincolns, 1st Northumberland Fusiliers, 1st Royal Scots Fusiliers and 4th Royal Fusiliers, in Brigadier General W Douglas Smith's 9 Brigade, part of Major General A Haldane's 3rd Division. The Liverpool Scottish prepared to enter the trenches for the first time on 27 November 1914 by removing their cap badges and shoulder titles; they relieved a battalion of the Highland Light Infantry, who had spent forty eight hours there without loss. Their section of trench was 400 yards long and manned by 150 men in the front line, a hundred in the support trench and two platoons in local reserve. At this time the battalion changed from the eight company to the four company model and adopted the letters V to Z.

The Liverpool Scottish also saw, for the first time, regular soldiers leaving the trenches and gained an understanding of the reality of warfare on the Western Front. As soldiers of all eras will know, there is a vast difference between peacetime spit-and-polish and campaigning:

> The first sight the Battalion had of a company of regulars on the march was something of a shock. Many of the men had beards, their clothing was stained and muddy, and quite a number were wearing cap-comforters instead of the regulation flat cap. Anything more unlike the traditional smart Tommy it would be impossible to imagine. But there was one thing about them that did particularly attract the eye. Every man's rifle was absolutely spotless, not a bad illustration for civilian soldiers of the distinction between the superficial and the essential.

Y Company, commanded by the Senior Captain, Arthur Twentyman, had the honour of being first into the trenches. Unfortunately, he was also the first of the officers to die, after just twenty four hours. According to Lieutenant Chavasse, Twentyman was 'overrash – he was screened by a hedge, but not sufficiently'. Twentyman had become concerned about a German sniper who was opposite a sap-head and so went to get a jam-tin bomb from the RE. On his return, he went over the top of the trench instead of through it, relying on the protection of a thin hedge. Twentyman represented the pure Territorial of the early war. Thirty-seven years old, born in Liverpool, privately educated at Liverpool College, and with a white collar occupation, he worked before the war as a cotton broker at F D Clarke & Co. He is buried in Rue-Petillon Military Cemetery.[18]

After seventy two hours in the trenches, the battalion was relieved. Lieutenant Chavasse:

Our men have had a terrible experience of 72 hours in trenches, drenched through and in some places knee-deep in mud and water. To see them come out, and line up, and march off is almost terrible. They don't look like strong young men. They are muddied to the eyes. Their coats are plastered with mud and weigh an awful weight with the water which has soaked in. Their backs are bent, and they stagger and totter along with the weight of their packs. Their faces are white and haggard and their eyes glare out from mud which with short bristly beards give them an almost beastlike look. They look like wounded or sick wild things. I have seen nothing like it. The collapse after rowing or running is nothing to it. Many, too many, who are quite beat, have to be told they must walk it. Then comes a nightmare of a march for about 2 or 4 miles, when the men walk in a trance.[19]

The descriptions of men coming out of the trenches by both McGilchrist and Chavasse are much the same and describe exhausted men after only days in the trenches. McGilchrist described the trenches in the winter of 1914–15:

The trenches themselves were far from being the comfortable homes that they became later in the war. There were no dug-outs, no duck-boards, no pumps, and all material required for revetting had to be improvised from planks and lumber taken from ruined houses. Even sandbags were rare and were mostly the special perquisite of the R.E. The state of these trenches after heavy rain or during a thaw is indescribable. Men had frequently to be dug out of the mud by their friends, being quite incapable of movement unassisted.

Sanitation.... was a dead letter, and the condition of the ground behind the trenches and indeed of the trenches themselves must be left to the imagination.

The trenches that they occupied on their first tour were simply a series of pits, each capable of holding three or four men each who could not sit upright without exposing their head, interconnected by shallow trenches.

These were further excavated with entrenching tools so that, eventually, it was possible to pass along without leaving the trench.

The battalion's strength fell from twenty six officers and 829 men in November to 370 all ranks by early January, with only thirty two battle losses – a lot of the sickness was blamed on the lack of hot food and drink in the trenches. Hot tea was sent up to the front line at night but, after being carried a mile and a half in the dark and over bad ground, much of it was lost and what was left was not very hot. Hot food was similarly unavailable, as they did not possess field cookers to prepare food and drink close to the trenches, or hay boxes to keep them warm during the transport to the men. The lack of water in the front line did at least mean that men did not have to shave. Each man's allocation was the waterbottle he took into the trenches for seventy two hours and whatever tea could be carried up to them.

Wet, dirty clothing also contributed to illness; and even when out of the trenches the men found it difficult to dry their only suit of clothing. Officers managed better as they usually at least had a spare uniform to change into.

Even the rifle gave them problems. The Magazine Lee Enfield rifles were not only older, slower to fire and longer (the exposed muzzle apparently made it more prone to filling with soil), they could not use the new, more powerful Mark VII ammunition because the bolt was not strong enough. Old stocks of Mark VI ammunition had to be carried into the trenches. SMLEs started to arrive early in 1915, but drafts, the wounded returning from hospital and those returning from attachments continued to carry the older rifle for some time yet. It would be the summer of 1916 before the battalion was uniformly equipped with the SMLE.[20]

Christmas found the battalion out of the trenches, which enabled them to enjoy the day in relative peace and quiet. The soldiers were well supplied with food parcels from their families and Liverpool in general. Middle class battalions were fortunate in the support that would not have been so readily available for regulars or battalions recruited from working class districts. A bigger present arrived on 30 January 1915 in the form of four officers and 302 other ranks to reinforce the battalion. These were the men left behind in Tunbridge Wells.[21]

Early 1915 saw the deaths of two more platoon commanders which, like that of Twentyman, encapsulated the death of the Edwardian middle class.

Lieutenant Fred Turner was killed on 11 January and on the 24th, Second Lieutenant P D 'Togge' Kendall was wounded and subsequently killed by a ricocheting bullet. Both were pre-war international rugby players: Turner had captained Scotland and Kendall played for England. Turner had been an undergraduate friend of Lieutenant Chavasse, himself an Oxford 'blue'.[22]

On 15 February, 9 Brigade was ordered to move to Ypres to replace 85 Brigade in 28th Division. The Liverpool Scottish, however, remained behind and joined 85 Brigade. The disappointment of leaving the brigade was clear from both sides, as Brigadier General W Douglas Smith wrote:

> The G.O.C. 9th Infantry Brigade hears with great regret that the 10th (Scottish) Battn. The King's Liverpool Regt. is leaving his command. He would like it placed on record that the Battalion since it joined this Brigade has throughout a most trying time in the trenches carried out its duties in a most efficient manner, and he has nothing but praise to bestow for the hard work it has done and cheerful spirit in which that work has been conducted. He wishes Lieut.-Colonel Davidson and all ranks success and he feels sure that the Battalion will always maintain its present reputation for good discipline and fine soldierly qualities.

After one tour in the trenches the battalion was relieved by 1/4th South Lancashires, fellow West Lancashire Territorials from Warrington. Also arriving in France in February was 1/6th King's and, as they and the Liverpool Scottish were both middle class battalions, there were most likely friends and colleagues whom they had not seen in the months since leaving Liverpool.[23]

On 28 February the Liverpool Scottish were informed that they were returning to 9 Brigade, 28th Division. The battalion arrived in the Ypres Salient on 10 March, a theatre that became synonymous with the suffering of the Tommy. Their first tour in the front line was opposite Hill 60, which became closely associated with tunnelling. On the 12th, a German mine was blown, disabling an entire platoon. The mine actually detonated under a ruined house and falling bricks, rather than the explosion, caused thirteen casualties amongst the Liverpool Scottish. The explosion also left a big hole in the line, but this was plugged by Captain McKinnell, the Machine Gun

Officer, who placed a gun on the lip of the crater while others attempted to rescue the buried. The Germans did not follow up the explosion with an attack: McGilchrist explains this by saying that the blast damaged their own trench. Evidently the miners miscalculated the charge required. After twelve days, the Liverpool Scottish were relieved by the Liverpool Rifles, on their first tour in the trenches.[24]

On 14 April, the Liverpool Scottish were again close to a mine explosion, this time under the Northumberland Fusiliers, which buried thirty five. Men from Y and V Companies went to their aid, digging them out and treating the wounded, all the while under fire. Captain McKinnell, again, set about organising the defence and rebuilding of the trench. There were three Mentions in Dispatches, two of whom, both privates, were awarded the Military Medal when it was established the following year. McKinnell was awarded the Military Cross. An anticipated German attack was disrupted by the initiative of two privates of the Signal Platoon. One, McDonald, immediately sent an SOS to Battalion Headquarters, just moments before German artillery fire cut the wire. The second, Thomson, then climbed out of the relative security of the trench to locate and repair the break. Alerted, the battalion called for artillery support, with the result that the German attack never got out of their trench.

Just over a week later, the Germans made their first use of gas on the Western Front – the Russians had already experienced this new weapon – and although the battalion was too far from the focus of the attack, gas was carried on the wind and effected the men's eyes. This led to a great deal of speculation as to what the irritant was for a couple of days before the cause was announced.[25]

3148 Lance Corporal B L Rawlins, 1/10th King's, buried at Ypres Ramparts, with an unusual family epitaph.

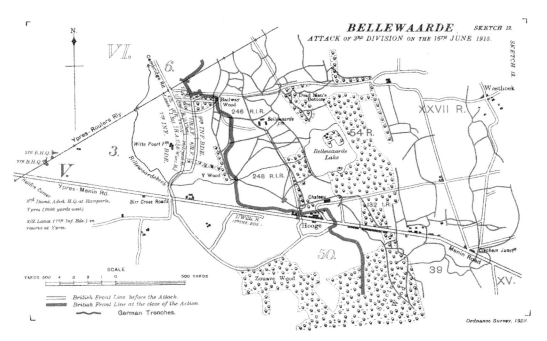

Bellewaarde Ridge, where the Liverpool Scottish and 1/4 South Lancashires went into action for the first time. (*Official History*)

The battalion spent an uneventful tour in the trenches east of Zillebeke from 2 June. When they were relieved on the 6th, they moved back to Vlamertinghe and four days later the whole division was ordered further back into the rear area for ten days' rest. It was even hoped that leave would be granted. These hopes were soon dashed, and they moved to Busseboom to commence specialist training in hand grenade throwing and wire crossing. Whatever was planned, it was more than normal trench routine.

The Liverpool Scottish's first battle was near Hooge, the First Attack on Bellewaarde, on 16 June 1915. The division's objective was the enemy trenches between the Menin Road and the Ypres-Roulers railway. 9 Brigade would attack in two waves, with the Liverpool Scottish and Lincolns being in the second wave, passing through the captured German front line trenches to take the second line trenches. The first wave would then pass through the second wave to capture a third line of trenches. The right flank would be secured by 7 Brigade and the left by the Northumberland Fusiliers. The

Hooge. This famous photograph of the Liverpool Scottish in action, shows casualties in the foreground and artillery panels in the background. (*Liverpool Scottish Trust*)

Liverpool Scottish's dispositions were V, Y and X Companies (from left to right in line) with Z Company in reserve.

Each man carried 200 rounds of ammunition, an extra day's ration plus emergency rations, and two sandbags carried in their belt. McGilchrist mentions that the 'pack' (presumably the large pack) was marked with the soldier's name and left behind, with the haversack worn on the back. The battalion went into the attack with 400 bombs (including 150 of the new Mills bombs), 125 pairs of wire-cutters, fifty one shovels (carried by one platoon per company) to rebuild and consolidate the captured trenches, six signalling screens and ten flags to indicate the positions of bombers. The signalling screens were canvas, six feet long by three feet, red and yellow, and supported by two poles and designed to indicate to artillery observers the progress of the attack. According to McGilchrist, they were 'singularly ineffective' in the smoke, dust and morning haze.

The battalion marched eight miles to the trenches, with the pipes playing and the men singing for the first four miles. But it was not all positive: Lieutenant Chavasse's stretcher bearers (SBs) were increased to twenty four in anticipation of the casualties. McGilchrist also thought that the Germans were anticipating an attack. There were new trenches to support it and, as a result, German artillery fired spoiling missions that inflicted casualties on the infantry as they moved to the assembly trenches.

Twenty three officers and 519 other ranks would go into the attack.

A preliminary bombardment commenced at 2.50 am until 4.15 am, with three pauses, at 3.10 am, 3.40 am and 4 am, to confuse the enemy and entice them onto the firesteps, where they were vulnerable. The artillery, for all the difficulties they were encountering adjusting to the new style of warfare and the shell crisis of that year, were, at least, trying different tactics to neutralise the enemy.

The first wave attacked at 4.15 am and secured their objectives. As soon as the Liverpool Scottish and Lincolns realised this, they moved forward to the edge of the former German front line trench to reorganise. V Company on the left was held up by a German machine gun until reinforced by Z Company and together they rushed and took the position, bayoneting those who resisted and taking about forty prisoners. Meanwhile, another German machine gun remained active in Y Company's sector. Three men made their way down the trenches and captured it. Corporal S Smith was awarded the Distinguished Conduct Medal (DCM) for this action.

When the artillery moved onto the second objective, the battalions of the second wave moved forward and secured them, with the only difficulty being machine gun fire from the vicinity of Railway Cutting. The second objective trench, however, was shallow, only two or three feet deep and would have required extensive work to be made into a defensible position against a German counter attack. Lieutenant Colonel Thin decided that the best option was to join the attack on the third and final objective, which was successfully taken and consolidation commenced.

Unfortunately, not all of the Liverpool Scottish resumed the attack; and those who stayed on their objective suffered severely from German counter fire. At the same time, not all of the Liverpool Scottish halted on the third objective, with some pushing on to Dead Man's Bottom, none of whom returned.

For some reason the third line, in reserve, rushed forward with the Liverpool Scottish. The *Official History* was critical: 'The spirit which prompted the movement was excellent, but the result was disastrous'.[26]

From about midday, German counter attacks developed on both flanks. With the Liverpool Scottish out of bombs, they were forced back to the German first line trenches. German counter attacks supported by artillery

Ypres from Bellewaarde Ridge. Taken from near the Liverpool Scottish Memorial, the objective of their first action.

failed; but further attacks by 7 Brigade failed to advance the line. By 11.30 pm, when 8 Brigade relieved 7 and 9 Brigades, the new front line was holding.

In the final review, the gains did not really justify the losses: of twenty three officers and 519 men, only two officers and 140 men were unscathed, and even then one of the surviving officers suffered from concussion. Four officers and 75 other ranks were killed, with another six officers and 103 other ranks missing, later posted as killed in action.

The battalion had effectively ceased to exist as a functioning unit, but had established its reputation as a fighting battalion in a regular brigade.

Meanwhile, the often unsung heroics of the RAMC and stretcher bearers went on throughout and after the battle. An hour after the attack commenced the first casualties arrived for Lieutenant Chavasse, including another rugby playing international, Lieutenant Lloyd, who played for Ireland. The Commanding Officer was also brought to the Regimental Aid Post (RAP) with an artery bleeding in his head that was difficult to stop. Unfortunately, the medical evacuation procedures failed to ensure the effective evacuation of the wounded from the RAP. This meant that the wounded remained in the small forward facility, congesting it and preventing the newly arrived wounded receiving the more specialist treatment that was available further down the evacuation chain.

Lieutenant Chavasse was awarded the Military Cross and a stretcher bearer, Private Bell, received the DCM.

Amongst the dead was the diarist Bryden McKinnell, who had been awarded the Military Cross for his work around Hill 60; whilst McGilchrist, who would write the battalion's history, was wounded. Major General Haldane was very complimentary in his Special Order, acknowledging that it was disappointing that the ground taken could not be held.

McGilchrist's father provided an anecdotal account of the battalion's performance that day. He was sharing a train journey with a Gordon Highlander returning home on leave who, unaware of his fellow traveller's connection with the Liverpool Scottish, recounted that day at Hooge:

> I've come from Wipers, Sir. My division has just been over the top at Hooge. We were in reserve close behind and I saw the finest sight I'll ever see. I saw the Liverpool Scottish make their attack and they went over just as if they were on parade.[27]

It was vital that the battalion received drafts from the 2nd or 3rd line battalions; but at this critical moment there were none available. The 2/10th were training to fulfil the home defence role while the 3/10th had only been formed a few weeks before. Six officers did arrive; but it would be September before the first draft of 105 men arrived.

As 1915 progressed it was becoming increasingly difficult to find recruits to replace casualties. Not only was the initial enthusiasm drying up, but there was increasing competition from the New Armies. By 1918, this massive expansion in the number of battalions was unsustainable and early in that year a wide scale reduction was undertaken. Also, the different expectation could be quite distinctive: 'Class' battalions, like the Liverpool Scottish (and also the Liverpool Rifles and the London Rifle Brigade), had a distinctive character that they wished to maintain. This influenced the type of recruits they would accept. The territorials had already proved themselves in action, while Kitchener's men had been training safely at home. So, when a platoon from a New Army Service battalion, 12th Manchesters, was attached for training, and felt insulted at being trained by territorials, one of their number made an ill-judged remark about the calibre of the territorials to a Lincoln. The strength of the Manchesters was temporarily reduced by one.

These sentiments worked both ways. When five replacement officers from 16th King's (another New Army Service battalion) arrived, Lieutenant Colonel Davidson expressed his dissatisfaction at receiving 'khaki' officers into a 'kilted' regiment, especially as the middle class professional roots of his battalion provided no shortage of officer material. The five remained, although the War Office was careful not to repeat the exercise. As will be discussed below with regards to 1/9th King's, who received more officers from the 15th and 16th King's, these transfers took place after those battalions had been reduced in status to reserve battalions and so there was a surplus of young officers at home when there was a shortage overseas. Mitchinson found similar tensions in the London Rifle Brigade, where there was plenty of officer material in the ranks. COs did not wish to lose their men to commissions in other battalions, or to receive officers who were not brought up in their traditions. Another middle-class Territorial battalion, the 28th Londons, the Artist's Rifles, became an officer training regiment.[28]

On 25 September, 8 Brigade launched an attack about Sanctuary Wood. The Liverpool Scottish were in divisional reserve. The machine gun section provided supporting fire and (the now) Captain Chavasse with his medical orderlies worked throughout the night for the Gordon Highlanders. In response to a German counter attack on the 29th, carrying parties were provided. This tour ended on 19 October. They were back in the trenches on 21 November, by which time the weather had turned cold; but fortunately the Germans opposite were Saxons and this tour was relatively quiet – the only sniper casualties were from oblique fire coming from Prussian units either side of the Saxons. On the 29th, they were relieved by the London Rifle Brigade. The final tour with 3rd Division started on 13 December, around Reninghelst and Dickebusch, and was spent reclaiming and rebuilding old trenches at St Eloi, digging and carrying. The cumulative effect of these two tours in cold, wet trenches meant that trench foot returned. Whale oil was available and its application limited the impact, so that just three cases were sent to hospital.

However, to be effective, the men had to daily rub it into their feet, which was hardly a pleasant task in the December cold; and then there was the added discomfort of putting back on wet socks, boots and puttees. It seems to have worked in largely eradicating a potentially debilitating condition. Fortunately, the battalion was in billets for Christmas and was able to enjoy the relative comfort, aided by food packages from home.[29]

On 1 January 1916 the Liverpool Scottish were ordered to 166 Brigade of 55th (West Lancashire) Division TF, to rejoin their colleagues of the old West Lancashire Division. Brigadier General Smith was sad to lose the battalion:

> I know I shall miss you very much in the future. There is a lot of hard work before us and when I look around for the Liverpool Scottish and find them gone, I shall miss them very much. I wish you all the very greatest luck, and when you come across the Germans again I hope you will give them what you did on 16 June. You were always to the fore and never behind on that day. Few people have not heard of the Liverpool Scottish…. You have always been well behaved, which is a great thing in a country like this, where there are so many temptations.[30]

However, Captain Chavasse had reservations about the move. There had been a disagreement some years before between 55th Division's senior chaplain (and formerly chaplain to 1/4th (West Lancashire) Brigade, RFA), the Reverend JO Coop, of St Catherine's Church in Abercromby Square, Liverpool (where the University of Liverpool's Sidney Jones Library now stands) and the Bishop of Liverpool, whose palace was also in Abercromby Square. As a result, the Chavasse family worshipped not at St Catherine's, but at St Saviour's Church, in Falkner Square.[31]

1/5th Battalion, The King's (Liverpool Regiment), TF

Despite being the senior battalion, 1/5th King's was the second to deploy overseas and left Canterbury for France on 21 February 1915, Lieutenant Colonel JM McMaster commanding. They were equipped with what Wyrall calls 'fur coats', most likely the goatskin jackets synonymous with the first winter of the war. At Béthune, they joined 6 Brigade, part of 2nd Division.

Within the brigade were the regulars of 1st King's, 2nd South Staffords, 1st Royal Berkshires and 1st King's Royal Rifle Corps. Between March and September 1915 they would also be joined by 1/7th King's, so there was a significant Liverpool contribution to the brigade. From the 25th, the companies started 48 hour rotations in the front line under the guidance of 1st KRRC. Details are few, except that, on the 28th, two men were wounded.[32] 1/5th King's were in the war now.

Their first experience of an offensive, rather than trench holding, came in March, when 2nd Division attacked at Neuve Chapelle. The battalion was split up into companies to provide garrisons and covering fire to the attacking battalions. Whether the territorials were not considered strong enough to participate in the attack, or whether it was simply that there were enough regular battalions for the attack and so the territorials were given the supporting role, is not recorded. Regardless, they provided an important function with fire support and securing the front line trenches. The attack was, unfortunately, a failure, with 1 King's alone losing nine officers and 216 other ranks killed, wounded or missing. The 1/5th recorded that in their 'baptism of fire, all ranks behaved as we expected would be the case, showing the utmost calmness under a very heavy fire and an absolute disregard of personal danger'; while B and D Companies, attached to the KRRC, were also complimented by the regulars – when the KRRC was withdrawn, the 1/5th remained and held the front line trenches.[33]

The 1/5th appear to have conducted the tasks asked of them with success, although it must have been galling for them to watch the attack without participating and then to watch the pitiful casualties struggle back into and through the trenches.

Aubers Ridge on 9 May would be the BEF's next attempt to penetrate the German lines. For this attack, the 1st and the 1/5th were joined by 1/7th King's; but 2nd Division was held in Corps reserve and, although 'at readiness', they were not called upon.[34]

A week later there was another opportunity, at the Battle of Festubert (15 to 25 May), in which 2nd Division was to secure and hold the Festubert – La Turelle Road. 6 Brigade's assaulting battalions were, from left to right, 1st KRRC, 1st Royal Berks, 1/7th King's with 1st King's and 2nd South Staffordshires in support. 1/5th King's were held in Brigade Reserve.[35] It must have been trying on the character of the 1/5th to be in a reserve role, yet again, especially when the 1/7th were taking a supporting role, a battalion which had arrived in France after them. Although it is entirely speculative because of the lack of information, it is possible that 1/5th King's was a less effective battalion than the 1/7th.

The 1/5th's supporting role included digging trenches, which was not a particularly safe activity. A and B Companies moved up to commence digging. The RE officer in charge was wounded, so that the infantry were left waiting in the forward trenches, during which time they suffered casualties. When a Sapper NCO arrived to take charge, they entered No Man's Land but immediately came under rifle and machine-gun fire, resulting in yet more casualties. At dawn they withdrew, having achieved very little.

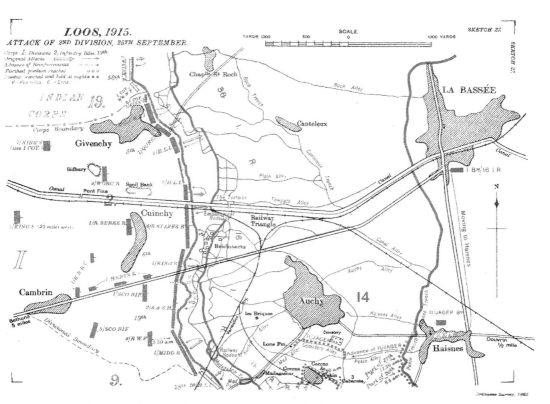

The opening of the Battle of Loos, showing 5 and 7 King's positions, not far from the scene of their 9 April 1918 action. Were any of them in both actions? (*Official History*)

Meanwhile, at 4 am on the 16th, C and D Companies were ordered forward to support two companies of 1st King's who had yet to cross into No Man's Land. They suffered casualties during the move forward, but were not ordered into the attack.[36]

The attack resumed at 10 am on the 17th, with 1/5th and 1/7th King's holding the trenches while watching 1st King's attack. The Germans did not leave the territorials alone. When the trenches were shelled they suffered yet more casualties. 1/5th King's moved forward to occupy the German trenches later in the day, with C and D Companies reaching the former German second line positions. News was received that the 1/5th would be relieved on the night of the 17th/18th by 4th King's of the Sirhind Brigade of the Lahore Division, but the 4th got lost in the trenches and the 1/5th were not relieved until the 18th. When they finally reached billets in Le Touret, the casualties were given as thirteen officers and 341 other ranks, about a third of the strength that had left Canterbury the previous February.[37]

In May 1915, 2nd Division moved to the Loos and Vimy sector and took over from the French 58th Division. As the British Army grew, it also took over more of the Western Front to relieve the pressure on the French. Compared with Flanders, this area of the front was chalk and so better drained and drier. On 2 August they and the 1/7th were ordered to report to the Commander Royal Engineers (CRE)[38] and were to re-train as pioneers (Mitchinson, in his study of the London Rifle Brigade, found that battalion was extremely displeased at being redesigned as pioneers too).[39] Each division received a thirteenth battalion as pioneers, who were trained to support the RE with the insatiable demands of siege warfare. The departure of the two battalions made it difficult for the brigade to hold the line; their efforts were appreciated. The Brigade's War Diary noted: 'The two Territorial Battalions have done sterling work since they joined the Brigade six months ago, and we are very sorry to lose them'. A month later the battalion re-joined 6 Brigade. As pioneers, the battalion did not fight with the brigade on the first day of Loos, but the following day, 26 September, A and C Companies joined 2nd South Staffordshires in the trenches. B and D Companies were held in reserve to support 1st King's. They do not appear to have been acting as pioneers. On the 30th, the brigade was relieved and moved into billets in Béthune.[40]

Early in October the Germans in the Loos sector went on the offensive. The 1/5th were in support trenches, formerly the British front line trenches, with 1st Hertfordshires (an all territorial regiment). On the afternoon of the 3rd, the Germans attacked following a two hour bombardment, but failed to break through: the 1/5th escaped with just four wounded. They were back in the trenches again on the 8th, when the Germans again attacked, but again were not engaged.[41] November appears to have been a quiet month for the battalion. They were in the trenches on the 30th until 4 December, when they emerged 'up to the ears in mud'.[42]

December was a month of change. First, they were transferred from 6 to 99 Brigade, with 1st KRRC, 1st Royal Berkshires, 22nd and 23rd Royal Fusiliers. The new brigade remained in 2nd Division. The battalion enjoyed Christmas out of the line, which was fortunate for them on their first winter in France, and they even had the afternoon off for Christmas dinner.[43]

1/6th (Rifle) Battalion, The King's (Liverpool Regiment), TF – The Liverpool Rifles

The Liverpool Rifles had, like the 1/5th, been completing their training in Canterbury until 25 February 1915, when they were ordered to France. Unusually, their War Diary began on 1 February 1915, and recorded the pre-deployment training including, for example, six NCOs and 112 other ranks departing to Sandwich on a musketery course, and two officers and sixty five other ranks departing on a machine-gunnery course. C Company also returned from leave. When the battalion was warned for France on the 22nd, the surplus stores were returned to Liverpool for use by the 2/6th. The relationship with the second line battalion was well established: on 26 March a Captain Hershall from the 'reserve battalion' joined them, and on 15 May a further five officers arrived. On 8 August, 117 other ranks joined the battalion from England and, although their origin is not stated, at this stage of the war it is likely that they came from the 2/6th.[44]

Major H Davidson led thirty one officers and 1094 other ranks to France, where they joined 15 Brigade in the 5th Division. They arrived in Vlamertinghe where, on 5 March, A Company entered the trenches under instruction from 1st Cheshires. When they were relieved on the 6th, they had suffered three men wounded. B Company entered the trenches and were less fortunate, with two killed and seven wounded: twenty year old Rifleman Henry Clarke from Wesley Street and twenty nine year old Rifleman Robert Fisher from Princess Avenue are both remembered on the Menin Gate in Ypres. Both were single and from Crosby, to the north of Liverpool, which was 7th King's recruiting area; but, as Hildrey has already established, there was a strong connection between Crosby and 6th King's. C Company had three more wounded, but D Company were unscathed. The Liverpool Rifles had survived their first experience in the line.[45]

The 5th Division held the southern end of the Ypres Salient during the Second Battle of Ypres of April and May 1915. The memory of those early days near Ypres was recorded by one unnamed company commander:

Imagine the company, in Indian file, feeling its way in the pitch dark, burdened with ammunition boxes and stores, in addition to pack, goastskin coat and rifle, stumbling into shell-holes, checking at every ditch and hedge and running to catch up in between, bogged in mud like treacle, with guides ignorant of the way and an utter uncertainty of what lay before. Now and then the flash of a bursting shell or the flares of a star-light would show up a ruined farm house and the great shell-holes on every side, filled to the brim with slimy water. Presently bullets begin to whistle, and one can hear their flick into the mud. A man is hit – there is a call for the stretcher-bearers. Never mind, press on, it is worse than useless to halt. Another is hit, then another. At length, it seems ages (it is, in fact, hours), we see before us, in a low rise among some splintered trees, a few lights, apparently coming from burrows in the earth facing towards us. Weary beyond description and dripping with sweat, we are told off in small parties to each of these burrows, which constitute the shelters of the supports, and are but a few yards behind the front line. The rifle and machine-gun fire is incessant – the bullets make loud cracks as they strike the trees overhead. The firing goes on all night and increases in intensity just before dawn. The burrows, damp and evil-smelling as they are, seem to afford security, which they do not really possess.[46]

The War Diary records a steady flow of casualties, such as Captain WS Montgomery, who died of his wounds on 13 March and is buried in the Ramparts Cemetery, Lille Gate, Ypres. He at least has a grave, unlike so many of his colleagues who are remembered on the panels of the nearby Menin Gate.[47]

On the 21st, the 5th Division entered the line at Ypres and the Rifles replaced the Liverpool Scottish. At the end of the month the battalion also won their first gallantry awards. Davidson, now promoted to lieutenant colonel, sent eight riflemen to rescue a wounded sapper on the railway line near Zillebeke Halt. Two, Crafter and Lancaster, were wounded, but were brought back by Broster and Dodsworth. The remainder, under Phillips, then rescued the sapper, and he was mentioned in the War Diary for his 'especial initiative and coolness'. Phillips and Broster were awarded the Distinguished Conduct Medal for their actions.[48]

The Liverpool Rifles were not directly involved in 5th Division's attack on either Hill 60 on 17 April or on Gravenstafel Ridge on the 22nd and 23rd. They were, however, employed on carrying duties to support the assaulting battalions, which was both deadly and exhausting – three were killed and nine wounded on the 19th, and two days later another two were killed and another twenty one wounded. This dangerous, important, yet ultimately soul-destroying hard manual work must have been particularly galling for the middle class volunteers described by McCartney as being unused to hard manual labour and, at the same time, so close to but not involved in the fighting.[49]

That would change on 5 May. The previous night, the Liverpool Rifles had been relieved, a process only completed at 6.30 am. At about the same time the Germans launched their own attack on Hill 60 and, three hours after being relieved, the Rifles were ordered to Brigade HQ. The *Official History* described Hill 60 as 'a mere rubbish heap of shell and mine-torn earth, timber and dead bodies'. The Germans used gas in the attack, which the primitive respirators (cotton pads tied around the mouth) were inadequate to protect against.

A Company, under Captain B H Wedgwood, set off first, suffering a number of casualties before it reached Davidson's Dugout, the HQ of 1st Cheshires: CSM Beechley and twelve other ranks were wounded and two killed. The company was sent to trenches occupied by a mix of Cheshires and King's Own Scottish Borderers, but with no information about where the Germans were. In the evening they were reinforced by C Company and together they held and extended the trenches overnight until relieved by the Royal West Kents at 9 pm on the 6th.

B Company, under Major R Wainwright, also suffered a number of casualties while occupying their section of the front line, where they remained until relieved by 1/9th Londons (Queen Victoria's Rifles) at 11.30 pm on the 6th. It would be 6.30 am the following morning before they reached the camp.

The account of C Company (Captain Brocklehurst commanding) started off with the very soldier-like observation that, when they received orders to move, the men were already tired after twenty three days in the trenches, and few, if any, had had their breakfast. The company came under rifle fire and adopted sectional rushes of ten men, during which Lieutenant Wilson (OC 10 Platoon) was killed. What later transpired to be A Company and some Cheshires entered a forward trench from their right, which forced the Germans to retire. A noted marksman, Lance Corporal Pennington from 12 Platoon, was preparing to engage a machine gun position when it was withdrawn. However, Germans were still occupying a rise above the position now occupied by A Company, which prevented C Company from returning fire, so the company dug in. At dusk the company advanced and joined up with A Company. From that time, their actions were the same as for A Company. The engagement

Lieutenant Westby, 6th King's. Lieutenant, later Captain, Westby, was a pre-war Territorial, as shown by his old style tunic. The photograph is taken in the back garden of 29 Sefton Park Road, situated between Sefton and Princes Parks, and which fits with the middle class background of the battalion.

resulted in fifteen dead and forty five wounded; the dead including Captain Brocklehurst who, like Captain Westby, was a resident of the affluent Sefton Park area of Liverpool. Brocklehurst was a member of the Liverpool-based shipping family.

D Company, under Captain EWK Bennet, was ordered into the trenches at 1 pm, with instructions to link up with C Company, which seemed to be easier said than done. Two patrols returned without success. Finally, Lieutenant Buckley took his platoon and located some of C Company's wounded, who directed them to Captain McKaig, in command after Captain Brocklehurst's death.

The Liverpool Rifles lost two officers and twenty other ranks killed, three officers and seventy two other ranks wounded. Despite repeated counter attacks throughout the day, the Germans gained and retained the high ground and would not be evicted until the Battle of Messine Ridge, in June 1917. When relieved the battalion remained at Ouderdom until 15 May, on which date its strength was given as twenty five officers and 699 other ranks. After three months in France, the Rifles had suffered six officers and 395 other ranks as casualties.[50]

On 24 May the War Diary reported 'Gas noticed. Respirators adjusted' but mentions no casualties. Another gas entry the following day reported no casualties. The entry for the 24th does mention stragglers from various regiments making their way from the front line, so not all units were as fortunate in avoiding the gas.[51]

The Liverpool Rifles appears to have had a quiet summer. At the end of July 1915 5th Division entrained to take over a quiet sector on the Somme. The next incident of note did not occur until the end of September. A series of patrols found no signs of hostile patrols and Wyrall speculated that the Germans holding their sector of the line were recuperating from Ypres. However, a patrol, led by Second Lieutenant Greenhalgh, comprising nine soldiers, in the afternoon of 25 September approached a wood from which shots were fired at them. They went to ground in extended order but did not return fire until the Germans emerged from the wood. The patrol opened fire and forced the Germans back into the wood, then began to retire. The patrol now regrouped and found that Greenhalgh, the Scout Sergeant, a lance corporal and a rifleman were missing. Reinforcements had already been despatched under Lieutenant Blackledge. The mortally wounded Greenhalgh and the bodies of the Scout Sergeant and the rifleman were recovered; but the lance corporal was never found. German casualties were not recorded, but in their retirement they did leave quantities of material. That sector of the front then resumed its quietness.[52]

The last months of the year were tranquil. October's War Diary entries were all very similar – all quiet and patrols. During November there were observations on German activities as well, when the mist permitted it, which described a much less destructive war than is usually imagined, but then this was 1915. On 9 November, for example, a long train was observed in the distance, and the following day two squadrons of German cavalry were observed undergoing drill, followed by a section of infantry.[53]

1/7th Battalion, The King's (Liverpool Regiment), TF

Lieutenant Colonel WH Stott's battalion left Canterbury on 7 March 1915 and arrived in 6 Brigade of 2nd Division on the 12th, where they joined up with the 1st and 1/5th King's.[54]

March was spent learning the routine of trench warfare. The battalion was fortunate not to suffer any casualties until 4 April, when four soldiers were wounded. On the 17th the first fatality occurred, when Private Webb was killed while engaged in building a sandbag redoubt. The battalion was in the battle area during Aubers Ridge but did not participate. Orders arrived too late for the brigade adequately to prepare for an attack.[55]

However, the battalion was chosen for the assault at Festubert, despite having been in France for just over two months. The 6 Brigade War Diary thought that 'They look like a useful lot', although division thought that they and the 1/5th were only 'satisfactory'. Junior commanders required greater confidence, there was a need to improve discipline and training, but were fit for the front line nevertheless. The GOC, Major General Horne, thought that Stott was young, active, with a good command of his men, but was highly critical of the training regimes in the UK:

bearing in mind that these two battalions have been embodied for seven months, the standard of training is very disappointing ... the battalion has been employed for some months guarding railways, etc., duties entailing many detachments and leaving little room for drills and exercises … drill and manoeuvre leave much to be desired. Little attention appears to be devoted in England to cultivate a smart and soldierlike bearing and to enforce strict discipline and cleanliness. This is noticeable, not only in these territorial battalions, but in the case of drafts sent to regular battalions.[56]

The Battle of Festubert (15–17 May) was the third in a series of battles to break through in the La Bassée sector. There is also evidence that attempts were being made to learn from the lessons of, for example, Aubers Ridge. Haig, commanding First Army, while planning for a resumed offensive there, contemplated a night attack by a bayonet charge without artillery support. This would have been a divergence from what would become the norm of having larger and heavier artillery barrages into 1916 and 1917, and goes against the hypothesis put forward by Alan Clark in *Lions Led by Donkeys* of failing to adjust and adapt to the new realities of 1915. Ultimately, the lesson taken away from Aubers Ridge was that the attack failed because the artillery barrage was not long enough or heavy enough. In the end, the tactics applied at Festubert was a combination of the two: a longer, heavier barrage coupled with the first night attack of war, despite the potential for chaos arising from night operations. The assaulting troops would have to cross up to 1000 yards of waterlogged fields, trenches and wire to reach their objectives; for the 1/7th, this was La Quinque Rue.[57]

In his thesis, Gregson has argued that an aspect of the battle was the blooding of new troops. In 2nd Division the explicit method of attack was to use the raw, 'expendable' troops as live bait to draw the enemy, who could then be defeated by rested, seasoned troops waiting in reserve. Brigadier General Whigham argued that by using the fresh troops 'to encourage the enemy to attack, it will be better for us to employ them and keep our seasoned troops in reserve'. However, the initial deployment at Festubert does not support this idea of the territorials being sacrificed for a regular army victory. Brigadier General Fanshawe, commanding 6 Brigade, did employ 1/7th King's in his initial assaulting force, but this was one amongst two Regular battalions; 1/5th King's remained in the brigade rear area throughout. 5 Brigade on the left assaulted with 2nd Inniskillings and 2nd Worcesters but did not utilise its territorials (1/9th Highland Light Infantry), while 4 (Guards) Brigade, including the territorial 1st Hertfordshires, were kept in reserve. As will be shown, being in the initial assault was not only the place of honour but, in the case of 6 Brigade, the safest place during the battle. It should also be pointed out that 1/7th King's, having arrived in theatre at full strength just two months ago, would have been Fanshawe's strongest and fittest battalion. And they would also have been keen to take their place in the line and show their metal, despite being 'just' territorials.

The 1/7th were on the right of the line and assaulted with A and B Companies. 1st Royal Berkshires were in the centre and 1st KRRC on the left. 1st King's and 1st South Staffordshires were in support. The assault was delayed for twenty four hours to allow the artillery more time to cut the wire and for the assaulting troops to prepare. At 11 pm on 15 May, the assaulting battalions crept in small groups into No Man's Land, apparently undetected by the Germans. The trenches were between 300–350 yards apart. At 11.30 pm, they rose and advanced. For the first 150 yards they remained undetected, walking in silence to avoid detection, but for the last 200 yards they came under heavy fire. This was no slow deliberate walk associated with the first day of the Somme. Wyrall's account starts with the assaulting battalions advancing in 'quick time', then 'double' and finally a rush. The *Official History* gives a similar account: 'Advancing in silence at a walk with bayonets fixed, the leading half companies almost reached the enemy breastwork before a shot was fired, and secured it without serious opposition'.[58]

The 1/7th got through the wire (again, another common assumption about the war is that the wire was always uncut) and into the German trenches, but found themselves mixed up with the Berkshires. The Germans had been conducting a relief when the attack was launched, which may account for how the brigade managed to successfully cross No Man's Land. At this stage, and despite being a night attack, the attack had been a complete success for them. The War Diary simply recorded: 'A & B Companies in attack, moved over parapet about 10.45pm & waited. Attack successful. German line carried.'

Unfortunately, 5 Brigade on their left and the Indian Corps on their right were severely handled by German machine guns and the obstacle of uncut wire.

At dawn on the 16th, C and D Companies attempted to cross No Man's Land to reinforce the first wave. They were cut down by German machine gun fire and none made it to their colleagues. However, 7th (Meerut) Division, on the left of the Indian Corps, entered the German trenches and were working their way to 2nd Division's positions, which they approached about 9 am. The effect of this was that fire from the right slackened and so individual men were able to cross No Man's Land to resupply ammunition to those in the captured trenches. Throughout the day German artillery was active, but fortunately they were concentrating on British trenches, not their lost trenches. The following morning, the 17th, around 7 am, white flags were seen in the German positions over on the right. This coincided with an action by 1st King's, who were bombing their way along the German trenches from left to right. Fearing a treacherous use of the white flag, according to 1/5th King's War Diary, the machine guns of both territorial battalions were turned on the white flags; but they were raised for a second time and, on this occasion, 126 Germans surrendered.

The battalion did not move for the rest of the day, but they did provide fatigue parties: 1st King's noted that the 1/7th 'very kindly' brought up 200 waterbottles. But relief did not come until the night of 19/20 May; it was 1.35 am before the last company reached their billets in Le Coutre.[59]

The Battle of Festubert was, in the language of the *Official History*, 'tantalising': it had not been possible to capitalise on the initial successes. In contrast with the popular image of the war, 6 Brigade successfully attacked and secured its objectives despite wire and machine guns. The 1/7th's performance was commendable, and there is nothing to indicate that their performance was any better or worse than their regular counterparts. But the cost had been high. Thirteen officers and 220 other ranks were recorded as killed, wounded or missing. Wyrall, writing years after the event and without the immediate post battle confusion, gave the number killed as 109. The majority of these would have occurred in C and D Companies as they tried to reinforce their colleagues early on the 16th. Amongst those who died of wounds, although not until the 27th, was Captain Josiah Dean, a pre-war territorial who worked for a Liverpool cotton merchant as their agent in Charleston, South Carolina. These were, of course, the days when Liverpool was a global centre for the cotton trade.[60]

On 2 August, the battalion was detached to train as pioneers under the CRE 2nd Division; the Brigade War Diary complimented the territorials for their contribution: 'The two Territorial Battalions [1/5th King's left to become pioneers at the same time] have done sterling work since they joined the Brigade six months ago, and we are very sorry to lose them'. After a month of training for their new role, the battalion joined 5 Brigade.[61]

The 1/7th were not chosen as one of 5 Brigade's assaulting battalions for the Battle of Loos, but they did provide left flank protection and working parties for the brigade. Despite playing a relatively minor role, there were still one office and nineteen other ranks casualties.[62]

The remainder of the month was quiet, taken up by providing working parties for 5 Brigade, and it was not until 12 November that they returned to the trenches, this time attached to 7th Division's 22 Brigade. Intercompany reliefs took place during their ten day tour. Life in the waterlogged trenches was eased by the issue of rubber waders, but that did not remove the threat of snipers; on the 14th, two men were killed by a single shot, one immediately and one dying of his wounds later. On 5 December, the division was sent to the rear of the Somme area, to Saleux, near Amiens. At the year's end, they were at Warlus, engaged in training.[63]

1/9th Battalion, The King's (Liverpool Regiment), TF

On 13 August 1914 the battalion left Liverpool by train for Edinburgh, which was bustling with the departure of fifteen battalions for the front and then on to Dunfermline, where they reinforced the Forth Defences. The battalion was well received by the townspeople, and settled into accommodation in various institutions across the town, including the workhouse. However, there were insufficient blankets for all the men, so the Honorary Colonel, Colonel Hall Walker, gave £500 for blankets and other comforts for the troops. Training continued. The men were now away from home distractions (although Dunfermline no doubt provided many distractions of its own) and so better able to concentrate on training matters. Roberts noted that 'considering the circumstances a high standard of efficiency was attained'.[64]

In October the 1/9th entrained again, this time for Tunbridge Wells. We know from Captain Chavasse's letters that 1/10th King's departed Tunbridge Wells on the 31st, so one can almost imagine a one-for-one swap: as battalions left for the front, replacements arrived. In due course, the 2/9th would replace the 1/9th in Tunbridge Wells. Training consisted of an early morning run followed by a route march or field practice. Musketry was conducted at Sandwich and trenches and machine gun posts were dug on the inland side of the Royal Military Canal originally built, ironically, by French prisoners of war during the Napoleonic Wars. Half the battalion went to Ashford as part of the London Defences and learnt to construct 'Low Command Redoubts' under the guidance of the Royal Engineers. These were, according to Roberts, 'badly sited on forward slopes' but the experience gained proved useful in France.

Christmas was festive, made successful by the generosity of the townspeople, but may well have been overshadowed by the departure of Colonel Watts, to take over command of the new Reserve Battalion at Blackpool, the 2/9th King's. Two of Colonel Watts' sons had followed him into the battalion, leading to a heart breaking outcome. Norman was an old Volunteer, having joined in 1907. In 1916 he was promoted to major, but was killed on 25 September 1916 leading a company at Flers. A year earlier to the day another son, Thomas, was killed at Loos. Unlike his father or brother, Thomas was not a pre-war Territorial, but had enlisted on 8 August 1914 and been commissioned on 11 November the same year. Interestingly, Roberts refers to the 9th as the 'foreign service' battalion, despite the fact that the 9th's role had always been Home Service. Lieutenant Colonel JE Lloyd, VD was appointed the new commanding officer.

January saw more guard duties on telegraph cables and other 'vulnerable points' that provided distractions from military training. Overall, Roberts' accounts does seem to indicate a worrying lacking of fervour, which he himself recognised: 'Judged from later standards, the training was not as intensive as it might have been', which he attributed to the absence of a parade square and 'little, if any, assistance was afforded by higher formations'. This echoes the concerns raised about the calibre of the 1/5th and the 1/7th's pre-deployment training. Officers vied to get on instructional courses but there were too few courses and too few instructors. Internal voluntary classes on tactics were held because 'everyone wanted to know more of his new profession'. Despite this urgency, parades finished in the early afternoon 'which afforded ample time for recreation'. In one paragraph, Roberts sums up both the initial enthusiasm and the poignant reality of those heady days in Tunbridge Wells:

> Such an ardour possessed the men for the fight that in some it reached the pitch of fear lest they should arrive too late upon the battlefield and receive only a barless medal. Some actually wished to transfer to another unit so as to ensure getting out at once. When at last the anxiously awaited order came that the Battalion was to go "over there", one officer was overcome with exaltation. His intense joy at being allowed to serve his King and Country on fields more stricken than parade grounds was clearly marked. After many months of distinguished service in the field, he now rests peacefully at Montauban.[65]

Unfortunately, a search of the two CWGC cemeteries at Montauban failed to reveal any King's officers buried there, so the identity of this enthusiastic officer remains lost.

When the battalion was warned off for France, there was a period of intense administrative preparation. Pay and mess accounts were settled. The Transport Section received its full allocation of mules and wagons, no doubt a relief after the frustrations of the previous August. More equipment was issued including, ominously, wire cutters and first field dressings. Wills were prepared. The officers seem to have spent a lot of money on 'necessary' comforts for campaigning, 'which did not prove useful and were ultimately lost'.

The battalion also changed from the old eight company structure to the relatively recent four company model. Each company contained four platoons. Undoubtedly, this would have produced lots of comments of frustration. Why train in one style only to change the arrangement on the eve of deploying to war? Roberts considered the changes to be beneficial, as it was too difficult for the battalion commander to brief eight company commanders in the field. More responsibility was given to the company commanders and the subalterns as they were given a command; the platoon became a tactical unit for the first time, much more than had been the case, with the old half company. The effectiveness of the platoon now reflected on the subaltern. Roberts considered the changes to be 'exceedingly beneficial'; as they are still largely in use by the British Army today, he has been proved right. Finally, the surplus equipment was returned to the Depot.[66]

According to Wyrall, it was Major TJ Bollard who led the battalion overseas, not Lloyd, and Roberts clarifies the matter: Lloyd was invalided home from France in April. The 1/9th King's left Tunbridge Well for Southampton on 12 March 1915 and joined 2 Brigade in 1st Division at Les Facons. They were not the only territorials there, as 5th Royal Sussex had joined the previous month, and fellow West Lancashire Division battalion, 1/5th Loyals, were also present. April appears to have been relatively quiet. At Oblinghem, west of Béthune, the battalion were exposed for the first time to life in draughty, dirty barns in insanitary farms. The ploughmen worked at their fields and the miners hewed the coal, and all seemed at peace. To the east, the constant boom of artillery and flow of ambulances showed the other face of France in 1915. Initial campaigning did not seem as bad as feared. There was a plentiful supply of beer and wine and estaminets were discovered: 'Many good young men who had never taken a drop of the more invigorating liquors leant that soldiers drank them, and the cause of teetotalism began to wane'. Officers from other units lent a hand to the battalion's training and, undoubtedly, their current experience helped to close any training deficiencies from the days in Tunbridge Wells.[67]

At the beginning of April the battalion began gaining experience in the trenches. On the 6th, A and B Companies entered the trenches under the guidance of 2nd Royal Sussex and 1st Nothamptons respectively. They were relieved on the 9th by C and D Companies. A and D Companies each lost a man who died of wounds.[68]

On 16 April the 1/9th was reinforced by two new second lieutenants, Broadbelt and Parker, both from the 2/9th. They were joined on 21 July by Second Lieutenant Halliwell. Drafts of other ranks started to arrive as well: thirteen on 29 July and another forty on 20 August. The system of the second line battalion as a recruiting and training battalion for the foreign service battalion was well established. Early in November, drafts started to arrive from the 3/9th. In late August came more drafts of second lieutenants, all from 15th and 16th King's. Both battalions were originally raised as part of the New Army's 35th Division but in April 1915 became reserve battalions; these drafts of young officers were presumably as a result of this restructuring. On 28 September, Captain Stocker was transferred from 1/7th King's, but without any explanation as to why this officer should be posted from one battalion to another.[69]

The battalion held a sector of the front line, Rue du Bois at Richebourg l'Avoué, during the Battle of Aubers Ridge but did not participate directly.

2 Brigade's trenches were east of the Rue du Bois, with 1/9th King's located to the north west of it. They were to attack as part of the third wave, with 2nd Royal Sussex left and 1st Northamptons right. 2nd KRRC occupied the right support, with the 5th Royal Sussex and 1/5th Loyals in left support. 1/9th King's were to the rear of the KRRC; presumably being the newest battalion they held the 'safest' post.

Generals of the First World War are often derided as being 'chateau generals', ensconced safely behind the lines and away from the danger of battle. The GOC 1st Division at Aubers Ridge occupied an observation post in a house 300 yards north east of Chocolate Menier Corner, from where he could view the whole of the German trenches at a distance of some 650 yards – well within the range of rifles and machine guns, let alone artillery fire.

The trenches were, in some places, only eighty yards apart, yet, despite this, when the British went over the top at 5.40 am, they were swept by rifle and machine gun fire from well sited enfilade positions. Those men who did reach the wire found it uncut. At 5.30 am, the battalion had advanced up to the third line trenches, suffering casualties as it did. 2nd KRRC requested support for its attack at 6 am. By now the trenches were full of dead and wounded, and provided scant protection against the artillery and machine gun fire which was sweeping the British positions. Amongst those killed was Major Bolland, so command passed to Major JWB Hunt. He decided that, with the wire uncut, it would be useless to attack without a second bombardment. Brigade was informed of this and agreed. Another attack was planned for 11.30 am, but that was postponed and then cancelled at 12.30 pm. They held the trench until that evening, when relieved by 1st Coldstream Guards.

Although the 1/9th had not contributed materially to the battle (which in any event had not achieved anything), they had been tested under fire. An anonymous officer, recorded by Wyrall, described the day:

Though the battalion, unfortunately, accomplished little, it sustained almost a hundred casualties, but it was fortunate in that it escaped the same fate as befell four of the battalions in the brigade which were almost annihilated.

As well as Major Bolland, Second Lieutenant DG Mathwin was killed. Three other officers were wounded, as well as eighty other ranks killed, wounded or missing. Major Theodore Julian Bolland was a 45 year old retired Indian Army officer from Penzance, one of those unkindly called a 'dugout'. Exactly what his connection with Liverpool was is unknown, nor his views of being given command of a battalion of territorials, except that he led them and died with them. Today, he is remembered on the Le Touret Memorial, close to Second Lieutenant Douglas Mathwin, the 20 year old son of the widowed Mrs Harry Mathwin of Birkdale, Southport.[70]

Today, Aubers Ridge is one of the largely forgotten battles but, at the time, it was considered a great disaster by the BEF at least. It was also largely ignored in the press of the day – the previous day the report of the sinking of the *Lusitania* had broken and, according to Roberts, the casual reader would consider the battle 'quite insignificant' compared with the sinking; in Liverpool there followed anti-German *Lusitania* riots. Roberts blamed the failure of the attack on the lack of high explosive shells with which to break the German wire. 1915 would be noted for the later so-called 'Shell Scandal', which would bring down the government. Curiously, the word chosen by Roberts to describe that day was 'holocaust'. This is a word with medieval origins connected with the persecution of the Jewish people. Following the events of the Second World War, this word has a specific connotation to events in Nazi Germany and is probably in much greater circulation than when Roberts published his history in 1922; it would be interesting to know what the original readership made of that choice of word. For modern readers, the horror associated with the holocaust may be oddly juxtaposed with a disastrous 1915 battle.[71]

The battalion spent the next fortnight in billets in Béthune with their new Commanding Officer, Major FW Ramsey of the Middlesex Regiment. On 20 May the battalion returned to the trenches holding the line through to July, at either Cuinchy or Cambrin. The trenches in the former were only three feet deep and were waterlogged so breastworks had to be built upwards to provide any protection. They were close to the Brickstacks, which provided ample material to hurtle through the air, causing more casualties. The trenches were as close as twenty five yards apart, which made them ideal targets for rifle grenades by both sides. No cooking was permitted in the trenches – even if it had been practical. One of the most demanding tasks of trench warfare was that of the ration party who often had to struggle through mud filled communications trenches with their precious burden of food – if they were lucky, hot food – for the men holding the front line position. It was at least useful practice for the dreadful conditions of the Somme in 1916 and Arras and Ypres in 1917. One innovation was the introduction of shorts, made by cutting down trousers. Hosetops were initially improvised from old socks, and were later bought out of battalion funds – salmon pink became the standard colour. Again, as with the blankets in Dunfirmline, the battalion's friends in Liverpool came to their assistance. This innovation does not appear to have been a result of the hot weather, but rather of the deep, slimy waterlogged trenches – shorts were simply more practical, although Richard Trafford did not like them in the winter.

Cambrin was a better sector, recently improved by French pioneers, with deep, well constructed trenches provided for more protection than the battalion had heretofore experienced. Roberts noted that this was the first time the battalion had occupied trenches rather than breastworks.[72]

In August they were in the trenches at Vermelles, where they spent each night digging jumping off trenches for a forthcoming attack. Once out of those trenches, they spent three weeks in September in the rear areas training to participate in the Battle of Loos. One event which would have raised both the battalion's morale and their standing within 1st Division was their performance in the Divisional Horse Show. 1/9th King's won all the prizes for mules, a first for their field kitchen, and two jumping prizes, coming second overall. Roberts' delight is reserved, but clear: this was a signal honour for a territorial unit and came as a surprise to the regular soldiers who though that they were 'the people'. This demonstrated the fact that though the Battalion had but a few months' experience of active service, it had soon accustomed itself to the rigours of warfare and that the transport section at any rate had attained a high pitch of efficiency. The horse shows that were held from time to time as occasion permitted provided diversion and did much to maintain a high standard of efficiency in the first line transport.[73]

1st Division's plan for its part in the Battle of Loos was to attack with 1 Brigade left and 2 Brigade right, with 3 Brigade in reserve. 1 Brigade would attack eastwards towards La Haie, while 2 Brigade's attack was south-east towards Northern Sap and Sap 81. This divergent attack would mean the two brigades moving away from each other and leave German positions intact. To address this, Green Force, comprising the 1/9th and the London Scottish (1/14th Londons), was formed. Their first task was to meet any German counter attacks aimed at pushing in between the two brigades and then, once the two brigades had secured their first objectives, both brigades and Green Force would assault the German second line trenches together. Green Force's specific objective was a German redoubt that the two brigades would converge on once they had secured their own objectives.[74]

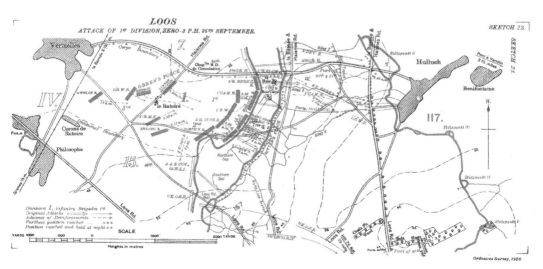

Battle of Loos, showing Green Force. Green Force in the centre, around Lone Tree. (*Official History*)

As with Aubers Ridge, Loos is perhaps not as well known today as it should be; it was both the largest British battle of the war so far and witnessed the first British use of gas. The wind on the morning of 25 September was light and hardly ideal for the effective deployment of the weapon. The gas was released at 5.30 am but, ten minutes later, the wind veered and the gas effectively hung over No Man's Land. 2 Brigade failed to reach the enemy trenches due to a combination of gas and smoke, uncut wire and the fire of the German defenders, largely unaffected by the gas. 1 Brigade fared better, as the wire had been more effectively cut and all the assaulting battalions were able to enter trenches.

At 8 am the 1/9th began to leave the assembly trenches, led by the now-Lieutenant Colonel Ramsey, and reached the front line by a series of sectional rushes. Richard Trafford spoke very highly of Ramsey, saying it was a 'pity we did not have him at the beginning'. From then on, it is not known what the battalion contributed to the battle. Division passed instructions to Green for his battalions to assist the struggling assaulting brigades but it is unknown which battalion was allocated to which task. The War Diary simply states: 'Battalion took part in attack on German lines. Captured 3-400 prisoners. Casualties 11 officers, 233 other ranks.' The German prisoners came primarily from the 59th and 157th Infantry Regiments, and provided the opportunity for the men of the 1/9th to collect the coveted pickelhaube helmets.

15th Division, on the right of 1st Division, was tasked to bomb its way northwards to relieve the pressure on 2 Brigade. While they were working their way northwards, 1/9th King's brought up a machine gun and, under cover of this, another attack was launched on the German trenches. By 3.30 pm another hundred yards of trench had been occupied.

With the British now, finally, established in the German trenches, 2 Brigade and Green Force were ordered to advance as quickly as possible. They were able to reach the Lens-Hulloch road, but that was the limit of the gains. The battalion was withdrawn to the old British front line at 4 am the following morning, but later returned to the old German positions, where more casualties were sustained, until 7 pm on the 28th, when the battalion left the line.[75]

The 1/9th King's were back in the trenches on the Lens–Hulluch road by 8 October, although in reality the trenches were just a roadside ditch. 1915 was still a period of relative movement, even if only a hundred yards or two, and it required a period of stability before the deep, well-constructed trenches of popular image could be constructed. The 1/9th's strength was given as 425, less than half the establishment strength. They were part of 1st Division's defence of the Chalk Pit and the neighbouring Guards Division of Hollenzollern Redoubt in early October 1915.

German artillery opened fire on the men in the exposed ditches about 10.30 am but did not attack until 4.30 pm on 8 October, during which time there was nothing to do but wait and suffer. Between eighteen and twenty German battalions attacked the two divisions, believing that the defenders would have been annihilated by the shellfire, but they were sorely mistaken. The battalion's two machine guns seems to have been particularly well sited and caught the enemy in enfilade fire. The Germans failed to regain any lost terrain on 1st Division's front, while temporary gains on the Guards Division sector were regained. At nightfall the 1/9th King's were relieved.

The Battalion War Diary for the day is notable for its understatement:

Enemy opened a violent artillery fire and maintained this for five hours, a heavy machine-gun and rifle-fire was sustained. Enemy advance to attack in mass, being strongly supported. Attack repulsed with severe losses to the enemy.

The battalion suffered 101 casualties of all ranks. Amongst those killed was Lieutenant Frank Milner, who was shot in the head while kneeling in the grass attending to the wounds of his orderly. He died an hour later.

Roberts pays compliments to the often unsung heroes, the stretcher bearers:

Acquitting themselves with a noble fortitude, the stretcher bearers – whose task was, perhaps, the worst of all – remained and toiled all night in evacuating the wounded. To stretcher bearers fall the most trying duties in war, but in accounts of battles little mention is made of their efforts. While the fight is on they share all the dangers of the private soldier, and often they have to remain when the others are relieved to finish their duty. The terrible sights of open wounds, bodies that have been minced by shell splinters, torn off limbs, dying men uttering their last requests, are enough to unnerve the bravest men. The stretcher bearers nevertheless continue with their task, well knowing what fate may befall them.

It is worth noting here that stretcher bearers came from two sources, members of the Royal Army Medical Corps and from the battalion itself. Triage, the process by which medical resources are allocated to victims, is usually conducted by medical professionals without emotional ties to the victims, and allocating treatment in order of need, i.e. to those with the greatest need first. The SB of the Great War also conducted triage. But his assessment was based on the best chance of surviving the journey back to the Regimental Aid Post and the care of the Regimental Medical Officer and to survive the recovery process and return to the battalion. There was no point risking life and limb to try to save someone who would not survive the journey, treatment or be able to return to the battalion. In this respect, triage is not as we would understand it today. But, in addition to making this medical assessment, the battalion stretcher bearers of whom Roberts spoke were members of the battalion and knew the men who were wounded. How do you make the choice between one soldier and another when you know them all? Roberts is right to praise the stretcher bearers, but his praise only touches the surface of what they went through and their experiences must have haunted them for the rest of their lives.[76]

The significance of 1/9th King's in holding the line that day is difficult to grasp from these figures, simple statements of fact and a brief narrative. The GOC IV Corps, to which 1st Division belonged, none other than General Sir Douglas Haig (he would not take command of the BEF until several weeks later) was impressed:

To G.O.C., IV Corps

This was a fine performance and reflects the greatest credit on all ranks.

I particularly admire the splendid tenacity displayed by our infantry in holding on to their trenches during so many long hours of heavy shell fire, and the skill with which they so gloriously repulsed with bomb and rifle the enemy's most determined onslaught.

Our gunners, too, must be complimented on their timely and accurate shooting. And lastly the Commanders, from General Davies downward, deserve praise for the successful combination of the two arms, for the handling of their units, and for the well-judged advance of the supports to the aid of those in the fire trenches.

I am very glad to hear of the great deeds of the 9th Battalion Liverpool Regiment on 8th October, 1915. They have proved themselves most worthy comrades of the 1st Liverpools, who started with me from Aldershot and have consistently fought like heroes throughout the campaign. Please convey my very heartiest congratulation to all concerned and to the 1st Division, of which I am proud to see the determined fighting spirit is as strong as ever, in spite of heavy losses.

D. Haig, General, Commanding 1st Army.
10th October 1915

To 1st Division
In forwarding Sir Douglas Haig's remarks, I desire to endorse every word he says, and to congratulate the Division on the well deserved praise it has received from the Army Commander. I hope before long to see them personally and to speak to them on parade.

H.S. Rawlinson, Lieut.-General, Commanding IV. Corps
11th October 1915

3RD INFANTRY BRIGADE
The General Officer Commanding wishes to place on record his appreciation of the steady defence made by the 3rd Infantry Brigade against the German attack yesterday afternoon. He especially wishes to commend the soldierly qualities and discipline displayed by the 1/9th Liverpool Regiment and the 1st Gloucesters, which enabled them to endure the heavy shelling to which our front trenches were subjected, and there to meet and repulse with great loss the German infantry attack.

The result of yesterday's attack again proves how powerless the enemy's artillery is against good infantry properly entrenched and the superiority of our own infantry over that of the enemy at close quarters.

The General Officer Commanding also wishes to record his appreciation of the good work done by the artillery in support of the infantry.

(*Signed*)

Lieut.-Colonel,

9th October, 1915   General Staff, 1st Division

SPECIAL ORDER OF THE DAY, BY
MAJOR-GENERAL A. E. A. HOLLAND, C.B., M.V.O., D.S.O.,
Commanding 1st Division

10th October 1915

The Corps Commander has desired the General Officer Commanding to convey to the General Officer Commanding 3rd Infantry Brigade and all ranks under his command, his appreciation of the gallant defence made by the Brigade against the German attack on the 8th instant, and especially the good work done by the 1st Battalion Gloucestershire Regiment and the 1/9th Battalion Liverpool Regiment.

(*Signed*)

B. Tulloch,

Lieut.-Colonel,

A.A. & Q.M.G.,

1st Division[77]

Ignoring 3 Brigade's assumption that German artillery was ineffective against 'good infantry properly entrenched' – the positions occupied on 8 October were described as ditches, probably enhanced roadside drainage ditches, and over hundred casualties suffered in the process, almost 25 per cent of their effective strength – the compliments paid to 1/9th King's by such illustrious commanders is most impressive.

On the 13th, 1st Division again attacked, this time the village of Hulluch, following an intense barrage and release of gas. The attack failed and although

1/9th King's was only in a supporting role it suffered more casualties from a German artillery counter barrage.[78]

CSM Byrne received the Medaille Militaire on 7 November, which is the first mention of an award or decoration in the War Dairy.[79]

From the following day the battalion enjoyed a well earned rest in Lillers until 15 November. This period even included home leave for some and light duties for the remainder. They then spent a week in Houchin – 'a dirty little village' – and then to Philosophe, near the front line, which was quiet enough except that a battery of 4.7″ howitzers fired over their billets. On the 26th, as part of 3 Brigade, they went back into the trenches again, to the same sector they had held on 8 October. This time they were holding the front line trenches, not in support, because one of the regular battalions in the brigade was too weak to perform these duties. On this occasion there was snow on the ground which had frozen hard – machine guns had to be removed from the parapets and stored by braziers to prevent the water in the jackets from freezing. The War Diary for 28 November simply says 'Freezing'. There were still no deep trenches or dugouts and the area was still under constant shelling. They were relieved on the night of the 29th, but all afternoon it rained, turning the trenches into freezing cold, water-logged ditches – the War Diary noted the misery with 'Thaw and rain', 'Mud very deep in trenches causing all movement to be extremely slow and difficult'. The conditions were such that each ration party took between three and five hours and the men then had to warm their rations as best they could in their mess tins. There was a great need for hot food. Equally in short supply were drinking and washing water – Roberts recounts men scraping the hoar frost from sandbags and taking dirty water from shell holes. The latter was very unhygienic and likely to be contaminated with residual gas. The water could be made safer (although not free of gas contamination) if properly boiled; but, as Roberts has already alluded these were difficulties in heating food, so it is unlikely that there was sufficient fuel to boil drinking water. Gumboot waders, leather jerkins and waterproof capes were issued, necessary given the weather conditions, but did not keep the men dry. They were soaked to the skin and covered in mud by the time they reached the reserve line, where they stayed until relieved on the night of the 2nd.

Roberts notes that late 1915 was also a period of innovation and change. Gas was becoming an increasing problem. Buglers were posted as gas sentries, although how they were to blow their instrument when wearing a gas hood was never made clear. 'Grenadiers', or bombers, were issued with little red flaming grenade to indicate their special role. Steel helmets were issued for the first time and considered to be a nuisance. These may well have been French Adrian helmets which were available as trench stores (that is, issued for the period soldiers were in the trenches, rather than personal issue) before the British army adopted its own Brodie helmet. Barbed wire was in place, but hardly substantial. This was not 1916: there was only a single fence to protect the battalion.[80]

1/8th (Irish) Battalion, The King's (Liverpool Regiment), TF – The Liverpool Irish

Lieutenant Colonel JA Cooney, commanding the Liverpool Irish, arrived in France as part of the Territorial Force's Highland Division during April and May 1915. The division's 3 Brigade, the Argyll and Sutherland Brigade, was replaced by the West Lancashire Division's North Lancashire Brigade on 18 April 1915, and remained until they joined the 55th Division on 6 January 1916. The 1/4th King's Own, 2/5th Lancashire Fusiliers (shortly to be replaced by 6th Scottish Rifles) and 1/4th Loyal North Lancashires were the other battalions in the North Lancashire Brigade and so it was not the pre-war North Lancashire Brigade, which had 5th King's Own and 5th Loyals instead of the King's and Lancashire Fusiliers – the last being a second line Territorial battalion from the East Lancashire Division.

The Liverpool Irish arrived in Boulogne on 3 May, and were the last of the First Line Territorials to reach France. Within a week the division was 'stood to' for the Battle of Aubers Ridge, but was not called forward. So much for very nearly being straight into the fray![81]

The Highland Division's first action was at the Second Action of Givenchy, 15 and 16 June 1915. With 7th Division on their right, the territorials were to attack towards Violaines. The Liverpool Irish were commanded by Lieutenant Colonel Neale; but as he was in the UK on sick leave command of the battalion passed to Major J A Campbell-Johnson. At 6 pm on the

15th, the Scottish Rifles (left) and Loyals (right) attacked, but on reaching Rue d'Ouvert found that most of the wire was intact. Small parties did reach the German trenches but were isolated and defeated in detail by German counter attacks.

At 6.45 pm, the Liverpool Irish were ordered up to the front line trench, by which time the other three of the brigade's battalions were committed to the fight, but without success and there was a general withdrawal about midnight. The Liverpool Irish held the line overnight. The following day would be their chance. Major Campbell-Johnson received orders at 3 pm for an attack at 4.45 pm, which gave him very little time to prepare his orders. The attack would be conducted by C, A, B and D Companies in that order. At 4 pm the artillery bombardment commenced but at 4.45 pm the German artillery shelled the

Private, Liverpool Irish, wearing the blackened buttons of a rifle regiment and the black Liverpool Irish capbadge.

British trenches. Regardless, the Liverpool Irish attacked in platoons and, in Wyrall's opinion, 'it is doubtful whether a single man ever reached the enemy's front line' because of the intensity of the fire. Some men did enter the German trenches, but in insufficient numbers to hold their gains against counter attacks. By midnight the survivors were back in their own trenches. The brigade was relieved at 4 am on the 17th and made their way out of the line.

The action cost the battalion 232 casualties of all ranks, including four officers killed and two wounded. For their efforts, the brigade was complimented: 'I desire to bring to your notice the very creditable way in which battalions of this Brigade acquitted themselves in this, their first engagement with the enemy'.[82]

Ten days later, the division entrained for the Somme front, where they relieved a French division and occupied deep, well dug trenches amongst the well-drained chalk near Aveluy, east of Albert. They manned 1800 yards of the front line, possible only because the sector was so quiet. There was little to record for the remainder of the year, expect that the Commanding Officer, Campbell-Johnson, now promoted to lieutenant colonel, was replaced by Lieutenant Colonel EA Fagan on 5 October.

The reason for the quietness on this sector was two-fold: one would become infamous the following July, and the other was due to a shortage of munitions. The Germans were not attacking, but could be heard digging every night. The Brigade Commander would have liked his subordinate commanders to attack, harass the enemy and disrupt their schemes. In an appendices to the Brigade War Dairy, the Brigadier's frustrations can be found: With reference to recent memoranda on the subject of continually harassing the enemy and, generally speaking, obtaining superiority over him, I wish again to invite attention to the fact that without the necessary munitions it is impossible to do so. As an example of this the enemy is working continuously in front of F.T. 17 and 18 [trenches]. The Battalion Commander of the sub-sector is very anxious to stop him doing so. He cannot, as a rule, be seen, but could be reached by rifle grenades, trench mortars or the howitzer battery covering that portion of the line. As, however, there are no rifle grenades, trench mortars have only ten bombs (kept for retaliation purposes) and there is no immediate prospect of getting more, and the howitzer battery not sufficient shells, the Germans continue unmolested.

Wyrall quotes from the diary of Captain RB Ross, a member of the Highland Division at about the same period: 'October 12th – 9 p.m. *Pegamata*. Not an arrow's length distant the Hun can be heard picking at his chalk. The human mole is burrowing in the tunnels of his tumulus, or he is deepening the floor of its approach, or he is strengthening its ramparts. Our own men have crept to their shelters to shiver themselves to sleep. They are mud-stained and tired, having worked hard all day. Except for the occasional baying of a German watch-dog, the sullen roar of the random gun, the 'wheep' of a bullet by the ear, there is an unnatural quiet. A slip of moon plunges suddenly out of the clouds and the sentry, peering anxiously over the parapet, sees the pale glimmer of the wire, the roof of a chateau and the opaque depth of wood. His scrutiny discloses nothing, but he teases the industrious Hun with a volley, as if he were personally malicious, slips another charger into his magazine and lowers his head behind the sheltering sandbags. But Fritz is still plodding bravely in his dug-out.'[83]

The Germans were digging the dugouts which would allow them to survive the week-long bombardment at the end of the following June, allowing them to emerge from their shelters on 1 July 1916 and inflict massive casualties on the British Army. While hindsight is a wonderful thing, it is a great shame that the offensive spirit and the munitions necessary to dominate No Man's Land were not available during the summer and autumn of 1915. They would become standard by the end of the war. Whether it would have been possible to halt the building programme is, of course, speculative. Given the scale and the industrious nature of the programme, it is unlikely. But, given that British artillery failed to destroy the dugouts, the only thing which might have disrupted the program would have been trench raids and satchel charges thrown down the excavations.

Conclusion

Before analysing how well, or not, the King's Regiment territorials performed in those desperate months of late 1914 and 1915, it is perhaps worthwhile looking first at how 'fighting strength' is assessed by the modern British Army. Fighting strength consists of three components: morale, physical and conceptual. Morale is the 'will to fight', and is stronger amongst volunteers (rather than conscripts), well led and well supplied, fighting for a cause they believe in. The territorials clearly met this criteria. Physical capability is not only individual strength, but also war fighting equipment. Physically, the territorials, especially those socially exclusive battalions, represented the cream of Edwardian society (shown most vividly by the presence of rugby internationals). However, in terms of equipment, they were seriously limited, both in pre-deployment training and in France by a failure to equip them to the same standard as the regulars, especially if they were then going to be asked to fulfil the same function as them. That brings us on to conceptual and, of course, the territorials were never intended to fight overseas, so their pre-war training and equipment were provided accordingly. Indeed, many of them deployed on operations within the six month mobilisation period that was laid down for their Home Defence role. Yet, despite this, the territorials volunteered in full knowledge that their equipment and training was below that of the regulars. Not that the Regular Army had any greater understanding of how to deal with trench warfare. Despite all of this, there is nothing to show that they failed to perform the tasks asked of them.

Throughout late 1914 and 1915 the territorial infantry battalions fought as individual units. Although there was a deliberate policy to brigade them with 1st King's or with fellow territorial battalions, this undermined the *esprit de corps* which Haldane had intended to create with the TF divisions. One should, however, not be overly protective about such matters – operational necessity must always come first. And, in any case, as will be seen in the next chapter, Major General Jeudwine very effectively created (or recreated) both *esprit de corps* and corporate identity when the West Lancashire Division was re-formed.

The six first line infantry battalions had differing experiences. The information does not survive to determine the combat effectiveness or the readiness states (to use modern terminology) of individual battalions. The only comparison that can be made is between the 1/5th and the 1/7th where, despite only arriving in theatre a fortnight apart, the 1/7th, which arrived second, seemed to get the 'post of honour' at Festubert.

Initially their tasks tended to be subordinate to the regular battalions; for example, in third line support positions to brigade attacks, or flank protection duties. Again, this should not necessarily be seen as an insult. The territorials were an unknown quantity. Command relationships were less well established. Each newly arrived battalion was an unknown quantity. They clearly did not match up to Regular Army ideas of discipline and drill. Despite this, 1/7th King's and the London Scottish in Green Force at Loos, or the Liverpool Irish with the Highland Division, the Liverpool Scottish at Hooge, or the 1/7th at Festubert all showed what they could do, despite the fact that their pre-war and post-mobilisation training had not prepared them for the realities of 1915.

1915 was not a great year for the BEF. Alan Clark's *The Donkeys* has been harshly derided for his critical portrayal of British generals of the First World War. While I do not entirely agree with his interpretation, it is important to note that *The Donkeys* was referring almost exclusively to the 1915 battles – a fact which is usually omitted by those criticising him. In his own words: 'This is the story of the destruction of an army - the old professional army of the United Kingdom that always won the last battle …

and were machine-gunned, gassed and finally buried in 1915'. He goes on to say that 'I was drawn to this subject almost by chance. While working in another field I came across the diary of an officer in the Leinsters and was overcome by the horror of the contents and the sense of resignation and duty that characterised the writing.'[84]

It was into this maelstrom that the territorials volunteered – and volunteered they had done. Twice, in many cases. The pre-war territorials had voluntarily given up their free time, often for small remuneration, and had then volunteered for overseas service. Only 7 per cent of its strength had signed up for Imperial Service. Now they were swept up in the fervour to answer the nation's call. The difference from the majority of volunteers was that the territorials, with their limited military training, were thrown into a conflict which even the pre-war regulars – arguably the best ever sent overseas by Britain – could not comprehend.

The problem in 1915 was that generals down to the private soldier were faced with a new style of warfare for which they were untrained. How, then, should the BEF respond? All conflicts are unique in character. It was certainly not by expecting it would all be over by Christmas. There were TF battalions waiting to deploy to France while Lord Kitchener was recruiting several tranches of 100,000 men. These would become the Service battalions, including the Pals, and they would not be deployed to France in large numbers until 1916.

1915 identified several of the key issues of the war, for example: anti-gas measures; cutting the wire; co-ordinating artillery support; and the timely commitment of reserves to plug a gap or exploit an opportunity. Some of these factors, like the ability to call up reserves or artillery support, were never really resolved in this war. Despite this, there were tactical innovations to overcome these difficulties, such as the night attack at Festubert.

This was also not the period of deep trenches offering protection against German fire, as contemporary photographs of the trenches show. There were opportunities to break the deadlock in 1915, unfortunately missed, in part due to an inability to call for and deploy reserves when and where required. The Germans had yet to develop their deep dugouts and reinforced concrete bunkers which would dictate the battlefields from 1916 – the Liverpool Irish heard them digging their dugouts but were powerless to intervene.[85]

Liverpool's territorial infantry was flung into this conflict despite their limited military ability and they performed the tasks asked of them. The information does not exist to analyse their military effectiveness other than on a purely numerical basis. It can, however, be safely assumed that it was below that of a regular battalion of comparable strength. Therefore it is no surprise that the territorial battalions were initially given subsidiary or supporting tasks: their military effectiveness was less or, at the very least, an unknown quantity. Yet for all this, there is no evidence that they performed any worse than the regulars. The territorials did not break and run, nor did they fail to advance when ordered. They did hold the line when there were simply not enough regulars left to do that. And they did this without the pre-war training to prepare them for a general war.

Chapter 3

55th (West Lancashire) Division, TF

On 3 January 1916, the old West Lancashire Division was re-formed, and numbered 55th, based on units that already held a considerable degree of combat experience.[1]

Although this book is not a study of the 55th Division, it is worth studying the only GOC, Major General Sir Hugh Jeudwine in some detail. Born in 1862, he was commissioned into the unfashionable Royal Garrison Artillery in 1882. In the decade before the outbreak of war, he held a series of staff, rather than command, posts, including Assistant Superintendent of Experiments at the School of Gunnery, Deputy Adjutant General of Aldershot Command and at the Staff College, Camberley. From 1914 he served as a brigade major, where he gained a reputation as a hard taskmaster, and then brigade commander before promotion to command of 55th Division. From 1923 he was Director General of the Territorial Army, which

Divisional Insignia. The Red Rose of Lancashire with two stems each of 5 leaves, symbolising 55.

may well reflect on his wartime experience, and was also Honorary Colonel of one of the West Lancashire artillery brigades.

'Juddy' set about creating a 'corporate identity' around the division's Lancashire recruiting ground. This included the use of the Red Rose as the divisional sign and, towards the end of the war, he initiated enamelled plaques for divisional graves, emulating French practice at the time, the Lancashire Rose surrounded by 'They win or die, who wear the Rose of Lancaster'. The unofficial motto was penned by Liverpool-born Lieutenant LC Wall:

When Princes fought for England's crown,
The house that won the most renown,
And struck the sullen Yorkist down,
Was Lancaster.

And blood red emblem stricken sore,
Yet steeped her pallid foe in gore,
Still stands for England evermore,
And Lancaster.

Now England's blood like water flows,
Full many a lusty German knows,
We win or die, who wear the Rose of Lancashire.

Leonard Comer Wall was killed on 9 June 1917 in the Ypres Salient. Aged 20 when he was killed, Wadsworth said he had been with the 1st (West Lancashire) Brigade since mobilisation, but it is uncertain whether he was a pre-war territorial: given his youth, it is unlikely. Already Mentioned in Dispatches, he was described as having 'all the courage and sprit of youth'. He was the son of Charles and Kate Wall of Hill Top, West Kirby, Cheshire. Killed at the time with Wall was another 20 year old lieutenant, W Smith, son of Thomas and Mary Smith of Astley, Manchester. Both men are buried in Lijssenthoek Military Cemetery.

There was also a divisional magazine was *Sub Rosa*, or Under the Rose and a divisional entertainment troupe, The Red Roses.[2]

Lieutenant LC Wall, who penned the poem which became the divisional motto. (*Wadsworth*)

Jeudwine was also politically astute. He exploited the patronage of the Earl of Derby, a pre-war member of the West Lancashire County Association, lead on the recruitment of the Liverpool Pals and the Secretary of State for War. At the Battle of Cambrai in December 1917 the Germans counter attacked and broke through the British lines; Jeudwine used his personal contact with Derby to deny rumours of panic in the division.[3]

He also knew what he wanted from his division. In a conference held on 24 January 1916, he ordered more horse riding for the officers because they were unable to keep up with the men walking; they were also poor at saluting. He also recognised talent from within and looked for between twelve and fifteen commissions from the ranks per month. It was not all about the officers. He wanted more ranges. Nor was this a single event. In his training notes of 11 September 1917 he wrote 'More fire control is required in action…. Don't forget that the rifle is still effective up to 2000 yards or more, if there is good fire discipline and control….'[4]

Nor was he a 'Donkey' or political appointee. Following the division's involvement in the Third Battle of Ypres, he ordered reports from the senior survivor of each platoon, which still survive as a fascinating insight into the battle at the lowest level. The German counter attack at Cambrai in December 1917 was the low point of the division's history, but the following spring, when faced by the same situation, the division did not cede any ground. Lessons had been identified, learnt and correctly implemented.

Cavalry

A Squadron North Irish Horse	} Departed to become Corps
1st West Lancashire Cyclist Company	} troops, May 1916

Artillery	Renamed in May 1916
1/1st (West Lancashire) Brigade, RFA	275th Bde, RFA
1/2nd (West Lancashire) Brigade, RFA	276th Bde, RFA
1/3rd (West Lancashire) Brigade, RFA	277th Bde, RFA
1/4th (West Lancashire) (Howitzer) Brigade, RFA	278th (Howitzer) Bde, RFA
Divisional Artillery Column	

Engineers	Renumbered in September 1917
1/1st (West Lancashire) Field Company	419 Coy, RE
2/1st (West Lancashire) Field Company	422 Coy, RE
2/2nd (West Lancashire) Field Company	423 Coy, RE
55th (West Lancashire) Divisional Signals Company	

164 Infantry Brigade	1918 Restructuring
1/4th King's Own	
1/8th King's Regiment	to 57th Division
2/5th Lancashire Fusiliers	
1/4th Loyals	

165 Infantry Brigade	
1/5th King's Regiment	
1/6th King's Regiment	
1/7th King's Regiment	
1/9th King's Regiment	to 57th Division

166 Infantry Brigade	
1/5th King's Own	
1/10th King's Regiment	to 2/10th, became 10th King's
1/5th South Lancashire Regiment	
1/5th Loyals	

Machine Gun Corps	From 7 January 1917
164th Company	A Company, 55th MG Bn
165th Company	B Company, 55th MG Bn

166th Company	C Company, 55th MG Bn
196th Company	D Company, 55th MG Bn

Pioneer
1/4th South Lancashire Regiment

Royal Army Medical Corps
1/3rd (West Lancashire) Field Ambulance
2/1st (West Lancashire) Field Ambulance
2/1st (Wessex) Field Ambulance
55th Divisional Sanitary Section   To Third Army March 1917

Army Veterinary Corps
1st (West Lancashire) Mobile Veterinary Section

On 29 January 1916 the division paraded and was inspected by Lieutenant General the Earl of Caven, commanding XIV Corps. The division then relieved the French in a sector of the front, the rear area lying between Wailly and Brétencourt, south west of Arras. By way of comparison, a French territorial division was a third line formation of aged reservists, suitable only for holding the line. Although the relief was generally uneventful, the Liverpool Scottish was unfortunate to have two killed by a shell on the morning of 12 February while at breakfast; Corporal Shimmin and Private Rae are buried at Couchy-les-Ayette Cemetery. Then, on the 29th a shell killed two more – 19 year old Private William Coy of Eastbourne Road, Aintree, and 30 year old Corporal William Roberts, son of Thomas and Catherine Roberts of Oswestry. Coy fits the territorial idea of a Liverpool man joining a Liverpool battalion, but at 19 he was only just old enough to deploy overseas. It would be interesting to speculate whether he had been a pre-war territorial, or as a 17 year old had been swept up in the patriotic fervour of eighteen months' earlier. Roberts followed a different military career path; he is recorded as being a member of 4th Battalion, the Extra Reserve battalion of the King's. Pre-war, he would have undertaken a period of full time service, either as a regular or in the Extra Reserve, and then maintained his skills with part time service. The 4th Battalion

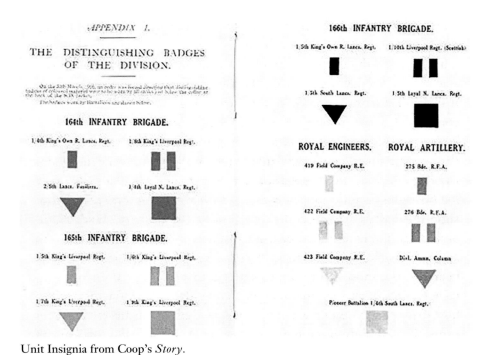

Unit Insignia from Coop's *Story*.

served in France with the Indian Corps for a while until 26 February 1916, when it transferred to the 33rd Division; but it would appear that Roberts was drafted into the Liverpool Scottish at some point to bring them up to strength. Although his parents were from Oswestry, at some stage he would have been a resident of Liverpool to join the 4th Battalion, and so fits in with the idea of another Liverpool-based reservist.

Another uncomfortable inconvenience heaped on the poor Tommy at this stage of the war was the general distribution of the steel helmet. Many men disliked the new headgear, saying it was heavy and gave them headaches but, as Wyrall put it, 'better a headache than a bullet'.

Wailly and Brétencourt Sector

The trenches now occupied had not been left in a good state of repair and the division spent much of February and March improving them, often in awful weather conditions. One problem raised by Lieutenant Colonel Shute, now commanding the 1/5th, was the lack of overall coordination:

The month has been spent principally in labouring work and digging, deepening and revetting contributing a great part of the work done. There are two things to be noted in connection with this part of trench warfare. One is that there is apt to be too much decentralisation and the result is that many communication trenches, etc., are started, and one comes back to the trenches days afterwards to find most of the previous labour has been rendered useless owing to falls, heavy rain, etc., and the opening up and deepening all (or nearly all) has to be begun again. In addition, it is most aggravating that trenches are made all ready for boarding, a gully dug in some and everything in order, then the supply of boards fails altogether. A couple of days' rain supervenes and once again hours and days of labour ruined and wasted. If those who are responsible in the original instance for the production of trench boards – the most useful improvements that have yet been made to trench conditions – could come up frequently and see for themselves how easily swallowed up are the 'doles' of boards sent up for use, it is probable that more attention would be paid to this item, and so the disheartening of the men (an important moral consideration) by their often having to laboriously re-dig once, twice, and sometimes oftener, the same work, would be avoided.[5]

After a month in the line, the Liverpool Irish conducted the division's first large-scale trench raid. The plan was carefully worked out and rehearsed but, despite that, the first attempt on 16/17 April was abandoned. First, the wire cutting party under Second Lieutenant Limerick encountered a German work party, which delayed the wire cutting by an hour; and then the wire proved to be deeper than expected. Meanwhile, the raiding parties moved into No Mans' Land, laying white tape and telephone lines behind them. Despite the assistance of a relief wire cutting party under Second Lieutenant Baxter, at 3.45 am the raid was postponed until the following night and the equipment recovered. Fortunately the Germans failed to notice that part of their wire had been cut.

The following night the wire cutting party moved forward under cover of a heavy machine gun barrage that disguised their noise. Then a box barrage was laid down around the target area, which isolated it.[6] The two raiding parties under Baxter with twenty three other ranks were brought forward. As they entered the German trenches the wiring party remained in No Man's Land to provide covering fire if needed. Eight Germans were killed and three dugouts were bombed; but an attempt to take back a German prisoner failed as the trenches were found to be twelve to fifteen feet deep and their ladders were only six feet long. On the order to retire, Baxter helped the last man up and out of the trench, but was not seen again. It was assumed that he re-entered the German trench for some purpose. The raiding party then safely withdrew. The only casualty was Second Lieutenant (Temporary Lieutenant) EF Baxter, who was posthumously awarded the Victoria Cross:

> For most conspicuous bravery. Prior to a raid on the hostile line, he was engaged during two nights in cutting wire close to the enemy's trenches. The enemy could be heard on the other side of the parapet. 2nd Lieut. Baxter, while assisting in the wire cutting, held a bomb in his hand with the pin withdrawn, ready to throw. On one occasion the bomb slipped and fell to the gound, but he instantly picked it up, unscrewed the base plug and took out the detonator, which he smothered in the ground, thereby preventing the alarm being given, and undoubtedly saving many casualties. Later, he led the left storming party with the greatest gallantry, and was the first man into the trench and assisted the last man over the parapet. After this he was not seen again, though search parties went out at once to look for him. There seems no doubt that he lost his life in his great devotion to duty.

Baxter's body was subsequently recovered and is buried at Fillièvres British Cemetary.

The DCM was awarded to Sergeant McClelland and Military Medals to Sergeant Burke and Privates Fussell and Crowe.

Their success drew compliments from Army, Corps, Divisional and Brigade commanders, for example:

> The Corps Commander congratulates the officers and men of the Liverpool Irish on last night's successful raid. He considers it was skilfully planned and that its execution reflects great credit on all

concerned, including the artillery, whose co-operation appears to have been admirable.

Trench raids continued throughout June but not all with the same level of success as that of the Liverpool Irish. 1/5th King's planned a raid for the night of 3/4 June, led by Second Lieutenants Taylor and Welsh with eighty seven other ranks. They left their trench just after midnight and signalled 'all correct' for the artillery barrage to commence. Unfortunately, some of the shells fell short, resulting in ten killed, eight missing and thirty nine wounded. The raid was abandoned. Later that day, a stretcher bearer, Private Proctor, noticed two wounded men in the open:

> Noticing some movement on the part of two wounded men who were lying in the open in full view of the enemy about seventy five yards in front of our trenches, he went out, on his own initiative, and, though heavily fired at, ran and crawled to the two men, got them under cover of a small bank, dressed their wounds, and after cheering them with the promise of rescue after dark, and leaving them with some of his clothing for warmth, regained our trenches again, being heavily fired at. At dusk both men were brought in alive.

In his IWM recording, William Marshall describes Proctor as a 'decent chap' who left the trenches in broad daylight with just two waterbottles and bandages to treat the casualties, for which he was placed under open arrest for disobeying orders. Proctor was, in Marshall's opinion, one of two or three who carried out similar acts of heroism; for his, Proctor was awarded the Victoria Cross.

A number of large raids were planned concurrently for 28 June along a two mile front by the 1/5th, 1/6th, 1/7th, 1/9th and 1/10th King's with RE support. The raids were again extensively planned, with smoke and gas to cover the troops in daylight. The raids had varying degrees of success and there were casualties. They can be seen as the division's contribution to the deception plan for the forthcoming Battle of the Somme. Amongst those killed in the raids was Lieutenant Arthur Stephenson, 1/7th, who

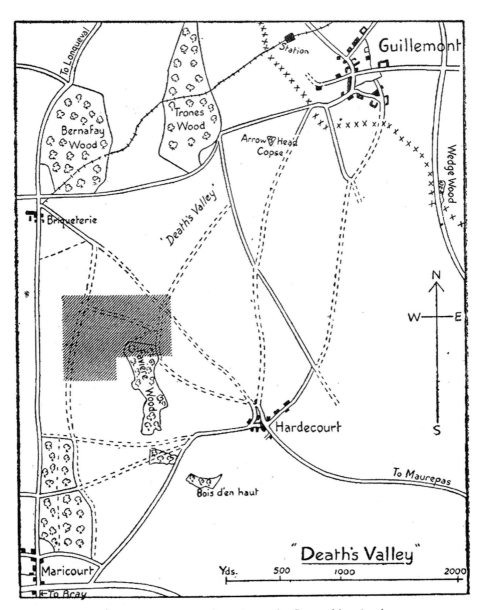

(Note—The shaded part indicates the Gun-position Area).

Death Valley, 1916. The area occupied by the guns of 1/4th Brigade in summer 1916 to support attacks from Trônes Wood to Guillemont. Gullemont Road CWGC is on the Trônes–Guillemont road, opposite Arrow Head Copse. Montauban is to the left of Briqueterie. (*History of the 359 Medium Regiment RA (4th West Lancashire) (TA) 1859–1959*) was commissioned in October 1914 and so would have been one of the more senior platoon commanders after nearly two years of war.[7]

The Reverend Coop wrote 'Nothing of further importance took place during our tenure of this front'. Although the front was considered 'quiet', the division had still lost sixty three officers and 1047 other ranks, killed, wounded or missing.[8]

Although the division was not involved in the 1 July attack, it launched an artillery bombardment as part of the deception plan. On 30 July the division moved south to prepare to attack Guillemont.[9]

The Battles for Guillemont

The fighting at Guillemont should be better known in Liverpool than is the case. After 30th Division's (including the Liverpool Pals battalions) successes on the First Day of the Somme, they were battered in the bloody Trônes Wood, which eventually fell on 14 July to 18th (Eastern) Division. There was another pause while Delville Wood to the north was attacked (it would not be finally cleared until 3 September), otherwise any attack on Guillemont risked creating a salient, exposed on three sides. 30th Division first tried to take Guillemont on 23 July, with 3rd Division (including 13th King's) in support. 55th Division tried three times, on the 8th, 9th and 12th August, with 2nd Division (including 1st King's) in support. 3rd Division tried again on the 16th and amongst their casualties in that attack was Lance Corporal (although the CWGC lists him as Private) Eric Peppiette, 1/10th King's attached 13th King's. Originally from Moseley, Birmingham, before the war he was an assistant librarian at the University of Liverpool, where a typescript of his diary resides today. His application for a commission had recently been accepted. Finally, on 3 September, 20th (Light) Division (supported by 16th (Irish) Division) captured the remains of the village. Serjeant David Jones, 12th King's, part of 20th Division, won another Liverpool Victoria Cross that day. Michael Stedman summed up the difficulty of the task. Guillemont was 'a very strongly defended location surrounded by an open glacis, utterly devoid of cover both to the west of the village and over the Maltz Horn knoll to the south-west of the village'.[10]

On 31 July, the Liverpool territorials relieved the Liverpool Pals. They used their time before the attack to dig trenches closer to their objective, frequently under heavy bombardment.

The plan was for 164 Brigade (left) and 165 Brigade (right) to attack with the French 39th Division on their right and the British 2nd Division on their left. 55th Division was to attack Guillemont, including Guillemont Station, while 2nd Division attacked slightly north, towards Ginchy. 2nd

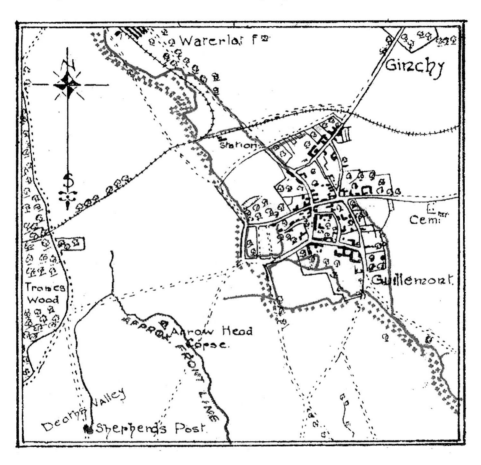

Guillemont. The area in detail from Trônes Wood to Guillemont and Ginchy, overwhich the Liverpool Territorials and Pals attacked, and which Ernst Jünger defended. (*Coop*)

Division's right hand battalion was 1st King's, so there was a significant Liverpool presence.

164 Brigade attacked the village 'two up' (Liverpool Irish left and 1/4th King's Own right). The inter-battalion boundary was the Guillemont Trônes Wood road. 165 Brigade would attack 'one up', with 1/5th King's leading and the Liverpool Rifles in support.

The attack was launched at 4.20 am on 8 August. A thick mist covered the battlefield. An hour later, the Liverpool Irish occupied Guillemont Station. Unfortunately they outstripped their flanking battalions: 1st King's were reported badly cut up while the King's Own were forced back. The Liverpool Irish were now exposed and suffered heavy casualties: fifteen killed, fifty-five wounded and 502 missing. The *Official History* described the 'great dash' as the Liverpool Irish 'fought its way into Guillemont', but then:

> As soon as [Liverpool Irish] got into the village, it appears that the enemy came up out of the ground below then and cut them off entirely by means of machine guns. This is practically what happened on the previous attack on Guillemont on the 30th July, and it is possible that the village is an underground warren of passages in which the garrison is immune from shell-fire, and from which they can emerge with their machine guns after the attacking infantry has passed over.[11]

On the right, 1/5th King's advanced and maintained contact with the French Army on their right. After 130 yards, A and B Companies on the right were forced to dig in. C and D Companies on the left advanced 350 yards before doing the same. This was the only ground to be gained that day. As was usual, the Royal Engineers provided direct support to the infantry, and were on hand to blow in a section of trench to form a stop that the 1/5th King's could defend.[12]

The division's fourth Victoria Cross was won that day, by Second Lieutenant Gabriel Coury, 3rd South Lancashire Regiment attached to 1/4th. Although no longer in a Liverpool unit, Coury had joined the Liverpool Rifles in August 1914. He was the son of Raphael and Marie, of Sefton Park, Liverpool, close to the Rifles' Prince's Park drill hall. Educated

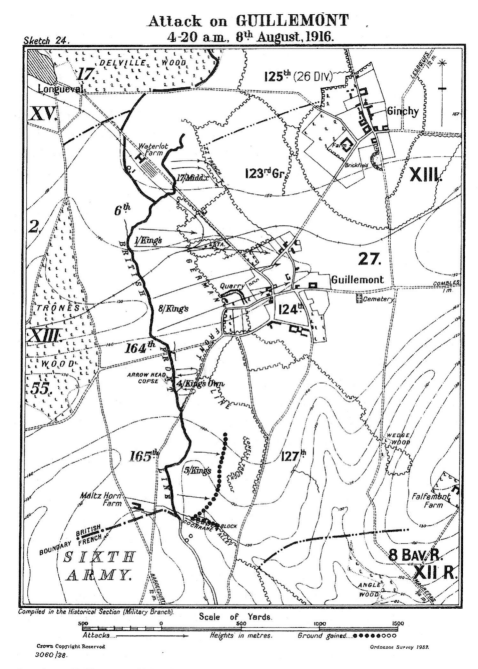

Attack on Guillemont. 55th Division's first action, with 1 King's fighting alongside in the Station. (*Official History*)

at Stoneyhurst College, he won sports prizes and was apprenticed to a cotton firm. His background was similar to Noel Chavasse and Arthur Twentyman. He was commissioned in April 1915 and later transferring to the RFC as a navigator and survived the war, as a captain. On 8 August, he commanded two platoons digging a communications trench to new positions, which he 'patrolled … under heavy fire, and by his coolness and utter disregard of personal safety, kept the spirits and confidence of his men [up]. Then, hearing that his CO had been wounded, and after Serjeant Roughly MM, of 423 Field Company had been killed, Coury successfully rescued his CO. Coury then rallied the troops and lead them into an attack.'[13]

Heavy German shelling of the British front line trenches disrupted all attempts to support the Liverpool Irish, survivors of which, together with members of 1st King's, would hold out at Guillemont Station until the evening of the 9th, when they ran out of water, ammunition and the means to treat the wounded.

Another loss that day was Lieutenant Walter Duncan, Liverpool Irish, who was captured when the battalion withdrew. Duncan was unusual in holding not only a degree in law, but also a master's degree (both from the University of Liverpool) and was a pre-war private in the Liverpool Rifles; he was commissioned into the Liverpool Irish in January 1915. Escape stories are more often associated with the Second World War, but there are many instances of them in the First. Duncan managed to a successful breakout from his PoW camp and made it to neutral Holland on 3 February 1918, and from there to Britain, where he was received by the King on the 22nd. Promoted to captain, and then married, he was posted to the intelligence staff in Britain. Unfortunately, he died of pleurisy and pneumonia in December 1918, one of the millions of victims of the Spanish influenza pandemic.

A planned attack at dusk on the 8th was postponed until dawn by Corps HQ, but even the extra time was not sufficient. Overnight the division tried to reorganise for an attack at 4.20 am. In the dark there was confusion, with engaged battalions exhausted from the battle and new units moving forward. The CO of the 1/5th King's reported soldiers still making their way to the front line at 3 am, and suggested that the attack should be postponed. His HQ was also visited by three other COs, each believing that this this was now their HQ. It was not until 10.30 am that the 1/5th was finally relieved

Guillemont Road Cemetery looking towards Guillemont. This illustrates the open terrain the Liverpool Pals and Liverpool Territorials had to cross 1916, and which Ernst Jünger defended.

by Liverpool Rifles. On the right, they (less one company) and the 1/7th relieved the 1/5th. 166 Brigade relieved 164 Brigade, with the Liverpool Scottish (right) and 1/5th Loyals (left).

The Liverpool Scottish arrived in their jumping off positions just twenty minutes before zero hour and set off behind a barrage at 4.20 am. Chavasse's biographer, Ann Clayton, called the affair 'a chapter of errors', which is to put it mildly. They found the wire uncut; after four assaults, the now wounded CO ordered a withdrawal back to the trenches. 1/7th King's and 1/5th Loyals were no more successful.

Amongst the casualties that day was Lance Corporal Slater Baines, Liverpool Rifles, in peace time a clerk at the Royal Insurance Company, who enlisted on 8 August 1914. He received gunshot wounds in the left thigh and arm and was evacuated eventually to England; but his wounds turned gangrenous and he died on the 21st. He is buried in Great Crosby, close to his home, unlike so many of his contemporaries.

The impression is that the second attack attempted to achieve too much and without adequate time to prepare, with units arriving at the last moment, unfamiliar with the terrain and their objectives. It was during the Liverpool Scottish's attack that their medical officer, Captain Chavasse, won his first VC, supplementing his MC:

> For most conspicuous bravery and devotion to duty. During an attack he tended the wounded in the open all day, under heavy fire, frequently in view of the enemy. During the night he searched for wounded on the ground in front of the enemy's lines for four hours. Next day he took one stretcher-bearer to the advanced trenches, and under heavy shell-fire carried an urgent case for 500 yards into safety, being wounded in the side by a shell splinter during the journey. The same night he took up a party of twenty volunteers, rescued three wounded men from a shell-hole twenty five yards from the enemy's trench, buried the bodies of two officers, and collected many identity disks, although fired on by bombs and machine guns. Altogether he saved the lives of some twenty badly wounded men, besides the ordinary cases which passed through his hands. His courage and self-sacrifice were beyond praise.

In a letter home, Chavasse was understated about his role:

> In the evening I took up a party of volunteers, and we pretty well cleared No Man's Land. We collected a lot of identification discs and so cut down the tragic missing list.
> We found and brought in 3 badly wounded men lying only about 25 yards from the Hun line, but 2 have died since I am sorry to say. Then we started off again, but this time we ran into the Hun trenches and got bombs thrown at us for our pains, but the whole party got in with only one scratch between the lot of us.

A third assault was planned for 12 August, with zero hour at 5.15 pm. 165 Brigade was ordered to clear the enemy from Cochrane Alley, in support of a French attack against Maltz Horn Ravine. A and B Companies of 1/9th King's attacked over 400 yards and reached their objectives amongst fierce hand-to-hand fighting, despite the loss of one company commander and six platoon commanders. Amongst those wounded at Guillemont was Richard Trafford, 1/9th King's. His orders were to get into the German trenches as quickly as possible, but was hit by shrapnel and medically evacuated back to the UK. On recovering he was posted to 1/2nd Monmouths, 29th Division; this illustrates that not all the casualties suffered were lost to the army, but there was no guarantee that a soldier would return to his original unit. Fortunately, unlike the territorials of 9th King's, Trafford would enter Germany with the Army of Occupation.[14] The French attach on the Ravine failed, leaving the 1/9th exposed and, despite being reinforced by C and D Companies, were forced back to their starting points by midnight. Meanwhile, the bombers cleared Cochrane Alley and formed a new block, which was the only gain that day. General Lord Caven was appreciative of their efforts:

> The Corps Commander wishes you to express to the companies engaged last night his admiration, and that of the French who saw them, for the gallant and strenuous fight they put up.

Zero Hour. Sketch from 1/4th Brigade, RFA. (*Wadsworth*)

Had the Ravine been captured by the French there is no doubt our objectives could have been realised.

13th August 1916

On the night of 14/15 August the division, less its artillery, was relieved and moved to an area west of Abbeville to rest and refit. While at Guillemont, the division had advanced the front line 500 yards on the left and 300 yards on the right, and dug 13,000 yards of new trenches, of which 3000 yards were forward of the original front line. However, this was a small gain for the casualties sustained: 219 officers and 3907 men.

To gain an understanding of the full horror of Guillemont, we can look not only at the British sources, but also a German one. In the summer of 1916, Ernst Jünger was a platoon commander in a Hanoverian regiment which had served in the Siege of Gibraltar during the American War of Independence when the Elector of Hanover was also King George III. His *Storm of Steel* sits alongside Erich Maria Remarque's *All Quiet on the Western Front* as German classics of the Western Front.

Jünger's regiment left the relatively quiet Arras sector on 23 August 1916. The only other date he gives was a reference to the British taking Guillemont. There are no identifications of British units, so it is impossible to identify his opponents. Jünger moved to Combles was they used as a base for troops in the Guillemont sector:

Ahead of us rumbled and thundered artillery fire of a volume we had never dreamed of; a thousand quivering lightnings bathed the western horizon in a sea of flame. A continual stream of wounded, with pale, sunken faces, made their way back, often barged aside by clattering guns or munitions columns heading the other way.

Their guide wore a steel helmet, the first Jünger had seen, which made him appear 'as the denizen of a new and far harsher world'; of course steel helmets were also relatively new to the British, although their comments focus on the weight and discomfort of wearing it. The horrors in front of Guillemont had destroyed any emotion from his voice, only apathy remained: 'If a man falls, he's left to lie. No one can help. No one knows if he'll return alive. Every day we're attacked, but they won't get through. Everyone knows this is about life and death.'

His first position appears to have been south of Guillemont. He describes it as 'a couple of hundred paces to the left of Guillemont, to a little less than that to the right of the Bois de Trônes' which may have placed him somewhere facing the Arrowhead Copse. But first they had to get there. Their guide became lost, they had to double back despite being in the middle of an artillery barrage – the smell 'told us that this passage had already taken a good many lives'; one group of dead served as a way marker for their guide.

Their positions were no more than a row of shellholes. Dawn revealed a cratered landscape full of uniforms, weapons and dead bodies:

> the country around, so far as the eye could see, had been completely ploughed by heavy shells. Not a single blade of grass showed itself. The churned-up field was gruesome. In among the living defenders lay the dead. When we dug foxholes, we realised that they were stacked in layers. One company after another, pressed together in the drumfire, had been mown down, then the bodies had been buried under showers of earth sent by the shells, and then the relief company had taken their predecessors' place.

Guillemont itself was 'just a whitish stain' and Delville Wood 'ripped to splinters'.

Despite the impression given in British sources that the Germans had all the advantages, Jünger did not see it that way. For one thing, the only aircraft he mentions were those of the 'RAF'. The RFC dominated the air war over the Somme and prevented German aircraft either supporting their troops or interfering with the British. There were also some thirty British balloons to not a single German one.

The next day it rained, every soldiers' nightmare, but for Jünger it brought relief from the dust and the dryness of their mouths. The swarms of flies which coated the bodies and basked in the sunshine – 'they were like velvet cushions to look at' – were dispersed. He spent the whole day sitting in front of his foxhole smoking and eating, despite the environment.

In the afternoon they watched a British attack towards Guillemont Station, hundreds of them 'little troubled by the weak gunfire we were able to direct at them'. If the attackers had been the Liverpool territorials, it would not have felt so weak, given the outcome of the attack.

A similar fate befell two lost British soldiers of a ration party – one with a container of food, the other with tea – both 'were shot down at point-blank range.... It was hardly possible to take prisoners in this inferno, and how could we have brought them back through the barrage in any case?'

Jünger and his platoon were relieved and marched back to bivouac in Hennois Woods – where it rained again – until three days later they moved back to Combles. There Jünger received the German equivalent of a Blighty wound. Afterwards, he pieced together the fate of his platoon which returned to Guillemont: 'With barely a handful of exceptions – those men who were hit during the march, and were fit enough to get back to Combles – the outfit disappeared without a trace in the fiery labyrinths of the battle.' The platoon returned to their positions, but now with growing gaps between units; Jünger likened the defence to a net whose meshes had become too wide to catch anything. Overnight, the British barrage had destroyed the defensive positions to their left. The survivors of the platoon took cover in a shelter. One survivor, Schmidt, the last in and therefore closest to the door, warned that the British were attacking – Jünger calls them storm troopers, paying them a compliment usually reserved for the German tactics of 1918. Schmidt was wounded by a hand grenade; after him there was a just a cluster of dead bodies around either entrance. The shelters which had protected the Germans during the pre-attack bombardments were becoming death-traps. Schmidt would be collected by British stretcher bearers and survived the war.[15]

In the words of the *Official History*, 'if [the division] had failed to capture Guillemont, [they] had at least pushed forward the British right to within close assaulting distance'. It also noted that 'the Germans never fought better than they did at Guillemont and Ginchy in 1916'. So, while the Somme campaign is seen as a bloody learning experience for the British, it also saw the gradual degrading of German fighting ability; as the British Army would become more experienced and proficient from late-1916, the Germans were losing their earlier superiority. By late September 1916, when the Liverpool

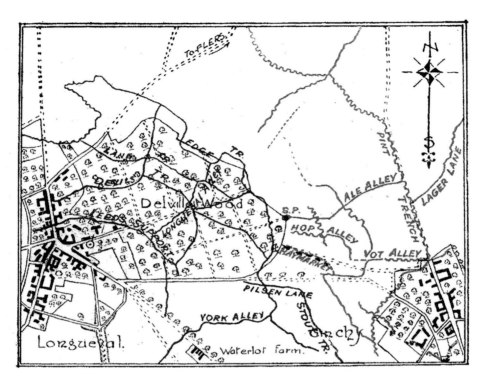

Delville Wood. Although not involved in the attacks on Delville Wood, this map shows the trenches approaching Ginchy. (*Coop*)

Irish attacked at Morval, the *Official History* wrote that the battalion 'took its objectives in splendid style with little loss: the enemy appeared to be demoralised'. But the process of degradation would take another two years to complete.[16]

The Battle of Ginchy (9 September 1916)

From 4 September the division started returning to the trenches, relieving 24th Division and part of 7th Division, and occupied trenches east of Delville Wood. As with Guillemont, the Germans had shown great tenacity on this section of the front, turning piles of rubble and brickdust into all but impregnable strongholds that would only fall to all but the most determined, bloody and protracted assaults.

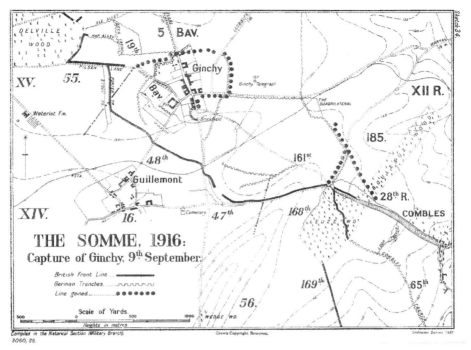

Capture of Ginchy, 9 September 1916. With 55th Division's positions in front of Delville Wood. (*Official History*)

The British attack resumed at 4.45 pm on 9 September. 55th Division had all three brigades in the front line but the centre brigade, 166, stayed in position and supported the other two attacks. On the right, 164 Brigade attacked in a south easterly direction with 16th (Irish) Division, while 165 Brigade on the left would attack in conjunction with 1st Division on its left. An artillery bombardment commenced at 7 am until zero hour (4.40 pm), when it switched to a creeping barrage. According to Wadworth, creeping barrages were not used at Guillemont and so were a new development. Wadworth also mentions a battle in early September, without specifying which, where white smoke was projected, covering the battlefield and greatly hindering German observation. The German artillery responded by bombarding the support trenches and using gas shells against the batteries.

16th Division captured Ginchy, but in 164 Brigade's assault the Liverpool Irish failed to eject the Germans from their maze of well prepared trenches.

Another attack on the 10th was similarly unsuccessful. The casualties for the two attacks were thirty killed, 114 wounded and five missing. Over the next two days, when there were no attacks, the battalion lost a further eighteen killed, seventy-eight wounded and thirteen missing while just holding the trenches.

165 Brigade, on the other hand, had more success when the 1/5th (supported by the Liverpool Rifles) and the 1/9th secured their objectives and pushed the Germans back to the north of Ginchy. The division was relieved over 10 and 11 September and, although they did not capture the village directly, at least they had supported the successful attack.[17]

The Battles of Flers and Morval

The third phase of the Battle of the Somme commenced on 15 September, the Battle of Flers – Courcelete, during which tanks were used for the first time. 55th Division were in reserve on that day, entering the trenches a few days later. However, Lieutenant JA Evans of the divisional artillery recorded the arrival of the tanks:

> We were comfortably housed 30 feet below the ground, discussing the 'push' that was to take place at dawn, when a very unusual drone was heard and with one accord we whispered 'Hush, Hush!' We trooped out to verify the suggestion. Not ten yards away from No. 1 gun was the first of seventeen tanks. In our wildest imaginings we never conjured up ideas of such strange inventions.
>
> Our eyes bulged as each tank crawled past. Hope ran high – the war was going to end with the aid of these seventeen monsters![18]

55th Division was allocated the objectives of Grid Trench and Grid Support to the north-west of Gueudecourt, with 21st Division on their right and the New Zealand Division on their left.

Between 15 and 22 September atrocious weather conditions prevented major operations. Zero hour was set at 12.35 pm on the 25th. 165 Brigade launched the attack with 1/7th King's on the right, the Liverpool Rifles in the centre and the 1/9th on the left. The 1/5th were in reserve.

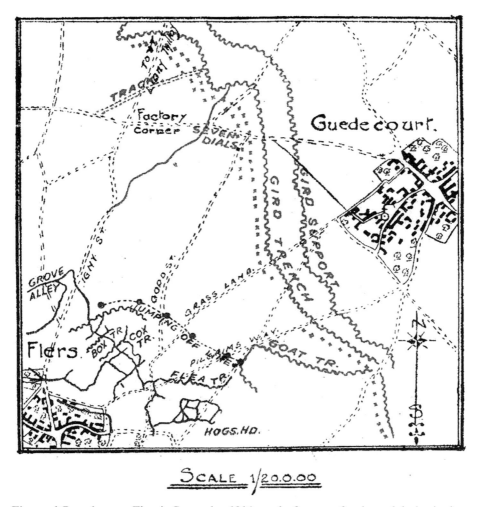

Flers and Gueudecourt. Flers in September 1916 saw the first use of tanks, and the beginning of a new style of warfare. Despite that, 55th Division's final advance was using 1914 troop types. Tanks had a way to go. (*Coop*)

The assault would be supported by a creeping barrage, with a standing barrage and a heavy barrage on German fixed positions: the latter would keep on the German side of the creeping barrage. The Reverend Coop noted that the men 'kept closer to the [creeping] barrage than ever before, preferring to suffer some casualties from possible short shells, … rather than to run the risk of allowing the barrage to get away from them and of being compelled to face the enemy's uninterrupted machine gun and rifle fire, as had on more than one occasion happened previously'. Wyrall also notes at this point that the war was becoming more 'scientific', with detailed Operational Orders, accurate maps and the ability to pinpoint German positions. The infantry in this battle attacked in four waves, soldiers in the first two carried two hand grenades and two sandbags each; the second two waves carried consolidating tools and stores. Company bombers acted to clear the positions (a lesson learnt at Guillemont) while the battalion bombers with the fourth wave acted as flank protection. The engineers would construct strong points with the support of the infantry. Lessons were being learnt and, more importantly, applied. Indeed, we have already seen Ernst Jünger describing British soldiers as Stormtroopers.

The tactics succeeded and Grid Trench was occupied. The barrage remained stationary while they consolidated Grid Trench and when it moved forward again the 1/7th and part of the Liverpool Rifles repeated the process and captured Gird Support. The situation with the flanking divisions was not so clear. Contact with 21st Division could not be established and it was unknown if they had taken Gueudecourt until 6.30 pm, when it was confirmed that they had failed. On the left flank the New Zealanders were known to have captured Factory Corner, although communications were not established until 8.30 pm. In the light of 21st Division's failure, 1/7th King's right flank was left in the air and exposed. 1/5th King's provided a company each to support the Liverpool Rifles and the 1/7th in consolidating their positions and building strong points for flank protection. They were completed by dawn on the 26th.[19]

To build on the success of the 25th, a joint attack by the 55th and New Zealand Divisions was planned for the 27th to capture the remainder of Grid Trench and Grid Support north of Factory Corner as far as the Factory Corner–Ligny Thilloy Road. 164 Brigade was given the task of taking the divisional objective, with 1/8th King's being the assaulting battalion. This attack was preceded by a seven hour bombardment and, at 2.20 pm, when the barrage started, the 1/8th were close up behind it, just as it had been two days previously. Ten minutes later they were in Grid Trench and at 3.15 pm had taken Grid Support, busy consolidating their gains. The retreating Germans were caught in the open by the artillery. When they tried to counter attack they were again caught by the artillery and failed to reach the trenches. The 1/8th's casualties were light – thirteen killed, 134 wounded, thirty four missing and eight cases of shellshock.

On the night of the 28th, the division was relieved by 41st Division but, on this occasion, would not be returning to the Somme front. Their next fighting would be in Ypres. However, its actions in August and September had established a fine reputation as a fighting division. Their efforts and sacrifices were appreciated:

55th Division
As the Division is now leaving the Fourth Army I desire to express to all ranks my gratitude for the good work that has been done, and my congratulations on the results achieved.

The hard fighting in which it took part about Guillemont and Delville Wood during August and September was a severe strain on all ranks, and the progress made in these areas reflects great credit on all concerned. When put into the line for the third time to carry out the attack near Gueudecourt on September 25th, the Division exhibited a spirit of gallantry and endurance which was wholly admirable and which resulted in the capture of all the objectives allotted.

The co-operation and support of the Divisional Artillery was all that could be desired.

I regret that the Division is leaving the Fourth Army, and trust that on some future occasion I may have the good fortune to find it again under my command.

H. Rawlinson
General
Commanding Fourth Army
Headquarters, Fourth Army
4th October 1916[20]

The Liverpool Territorials left the Somme for Flanders after three demanding months. Throughout 1915 the performance of individual battalions had been tested and not found wanting. Organising effective brigades and divisions was another matter. The progress from the rushed, failed second attack at Guillemont to the much more successful second attack at Morval is striking.

Paddy Griffiths goes further and sees the development of 'elite' divisions and commanders in the BEF; including the 55th and Jeudwine, so that by the end of September 1916 'we can.... start to glimpse some truly effective individual commanders within the BEF'.[21]

The Third Battle of Ypres

The 55th Division was transferred to Plumer's Second Army and would remain in the Ypres Salient until September 1917. In October 1916, they

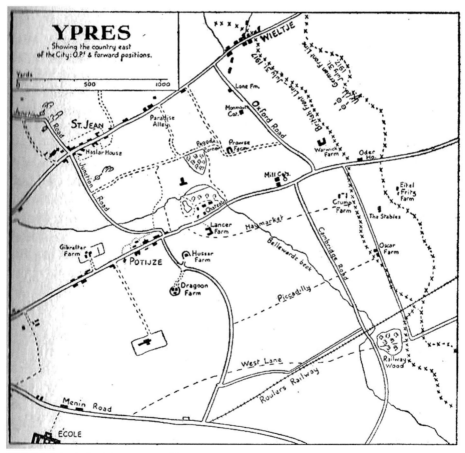

55th Division's Positions, Ypres 31 July 1917. Before the Third Battle of Ypres started. Just to the south east of Railway Wood is Bellewaarde Ridge, where the Liverpool Scottish first went into action. (*Wyrall*)

relieved the 29th Division and took over the section of the line from Wieltje to south of Railway Wood. Despite the Ypres Salient's reputation, in late 1916 this was a 'quiet sector' because so much of the German artillery had been moved to the Somme front. Quiet was, of course, a relative state of affairs and there was no shortage of raids on both sides. As the Reverend Coop wrote 'To give even a brief account of the constant raids and minor operations undertaken… would take more space than can be afforded'. Leave resumed. There was the opportunity to rest and rebuild after the strenuous summer, and to fully acquaint itself with the new sector of the front line. Only the divisional artillery was involved in the Messines Ridge attack of June 1917.[22]

31 July 1917: The Opening of the Battle of Third Ypres

Wadsworth, the gunner, considered that the battle was well planned, even over planned: 'all very definitely laid out – too definitely, we thought, in the light of what followed. Every detail was arranged weeks in advance.… It was certainly an improvement on some of the rather haphazard battles of earlier times, but perhaps erred a little in the other direction, since Brigade Commanders on the spot could not act freely to suit the circumstances of the day'.[23]

The objective of the attack was the capture of the enemy's Gheluvelt – Langemarck line. For this attack, the division was transferred to XIX Corps, part of Gough's Fifth Army. The Corps attacked with 15th (Scottish) Division, which would act on the right and 55th Division on the left, with 16th (Irish) and 36th (Ulster) Divisions in reserve.

55th Division would attack with 165 Brigade right, 166 Brigade left and 164 Brigade in reserve in three phases:

1. At Zero-Hour (3.50 am), the lead two battalions from each assaulting brigade would capture enemy trenches up to and including Blue Line.
2. At Zero-Hour plus 1 hour 15 minutes, the remaining two battalions from the assaulting brigade were to capture and consolidate enemy trenches (Stutzpunkt Line) up to and including Black Line
   a. At Zero-Hour plus 3 hours 33 minutes, 166 Brigade to advance its left to capture Canvas and Capitol Trenches up to Border House, if not already captured, in conjunction with 39th Division.

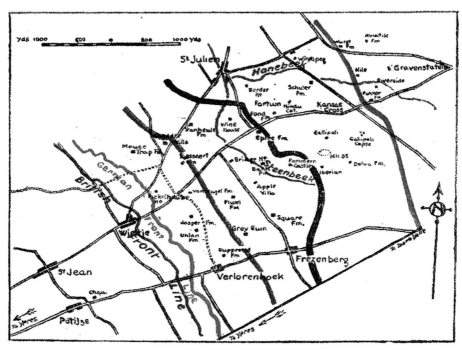

55th Division's Objectives, Ypres, 31 July 1917. Showing the key objectives, even if they were usually no more than German bunkers in an otherwise featureless landscape. (*Coop*)

3. At Zero-Hour plus 6 hours 20 minutes, 164 Brigade is to pass through 165 and 166 Brigades to capture the Gheluvelt-Langemarck Line up to the Green Line.

Up to 29 July the weather had been ideal for the coming battle; but on that day a thunderstorm filled the shell holes with rain and the roads were churned into mud. On the 31st itself, low clouds made aerial observation and support difficult, while the morning was particularly dark, which made keeping on the correct axis of advance difficult.

At zero hour, the 1/5th and the Liverpool Rifles advanced closely behind the barrage and occupied the Blue Line without difficulty. The main German machine gun position was at Plum Farm, beyond the Blue Line and, while it was under the British barrage, it was attacked and captured, complete with three machine guns. The Loyals and King's Own had similar success. Behind them, the Lancashire Fusiliers and Liverpool Irish acted to mop up German positions: the lessons of Guillemont had been learnt.

The capture of Plum Farm assisted the second phase's attack on the Black Line, which was executed by 1/7th, 1/9th and 1/10th King's and 1/5th South Lancashires. However, they still experienced far more opposition than the Blue Line attack. First of all, 1/7th King's were delayed by machine gun fire from Square Farm, located in 15th Division's area, but which had to be captured by the 1/7th. 1/9th King's were held up by fire from Bank Farm, but this was captured with assistance from a tank. 166 Brigade was also held up, by opposition from Capricorn Trench, Pond Farm

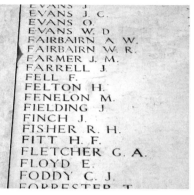

Private Fenelon. Remembered on the Menin Gate, but whose descendent, L/Cpl Fenelon was a Liverpool Territorial 80 years later.

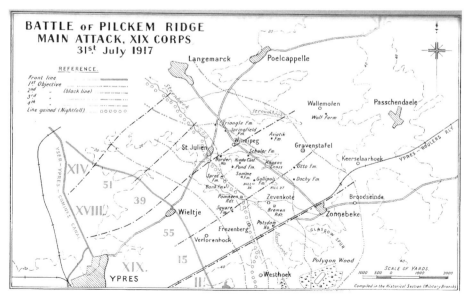

The Battle of Pilckem Ridge, Ypres 31 July 1917. Showing 55th Division in relation to the wider attack, and during which Private Fenelon was killed. (*Official History*)

and Spree Farm. 1/5th Loyals were despatched to assist. Capricorn Trench was taken but the farms would not be taken until 164 Brigade advanced.

Amongst those killed was 204232 Private Michael Fenelon of 1/9th King's, who is remembered on the Menin Gate; the CWGC incorrectly lists him as being the son of James and Winifred of 31A Bidder Street, Islington, London, which should read Liverpool. The significance of Private Fenelon is that eighty years after his death, his great-granddaughter, Leanne, served with the author in the Territorial Army's 55th Signal Squadron (V), the unit which bore the same number as the divisional signal company that supported the attack on his fateful day. In a very real sense, the territorials are still living and serving in Liverpool.

The King's Own and Loyals led the advance on Green Line. They took Square Farm while the Lancashire Fusiliers, in reserve, took Spree Farm. The advance kept close behind the barrage but, on this occasion, Reverend Coop wrote that it was 'insufficiently dense to prevent enemy machine guns from firing through it'. While the assaulting battalions took the Green Line, by the time the two supporting battalions reached them they had suffered serious casualties as well. On their left, 118 Brigade (39 Division) was forced to retire, so the Fusiliers and 1/8th King's were ordered to adjust the line backwards. The Germans then counter attacked and forced the brigade back on the Black Line, with heavy losses to both sides. That night the rain started, turning the battlefield in to the flooded moonscape for which the Passchendaele campaign is infamous. Tanks were called upon for assistance on two occasions and provided it by giving direct support to achieve their objectives.

The Black Line was held against counter attacks until 4 August, when the infantry was relieved by the 36th Division. The pioneers and artillery remained behind to be relieved at a later date.

Again, the division had taken all of the objectives required of it, but had been forced to abandon the Green Line largely due to the failure of the troops on their left flank. Sixty German officers and 600 other ranks had been captured together with a large amount of ordnance, including five batteries of 77mm guns. However, the division had suffered 168 officer and 3384 other ranks losses in just six days – the Liverpool Irish alone suffered eighteen officer and 304 other rank casualties. Also killed were the Reverend Greene, padre to the 1/9th, and Captain Chavasse, medical officer of the Liverpool Scottish.

The division returned to the same section of the line on 15 September; until then it rested and refitted, was visited by Haig and enjoyed an athletics program. In their absence from the line, two attempts had been made, and failed, to achieve the Green Line objectives. The division was ordered to make another attempt.[24]

20 September 1917

The division's return to the Ypres offensive was premature. A thousand reinforcements arrived, but they were still 2,500 men fewer than before the loss of the casualties suffered in July and August. Furthermore they had insufficient time to train the new arrivals so that they failed to clear the German positions adequately – a lesson painfully learnt at Guillemont and Ginchy and effectively implemented on 31 July – so that the assaulting troops were attacked from the rear, while the supporting troops were held up; it meant that they 'lost' the barrage, which was considered essential for success.[25]

In the rain and a very dark night, 164 (left) and 165 (right) Brigades occupied a line of shell holes, with a battalion each from 166 Brigade in support, forming up in the old German trenches, with the remaining two battalions, including the Liverpool Scottish, as divisional reserve. The initial deployments were successfully achieved through a combination of careful reconnaissance, tapes and placards to mark locations (German prisoners later said that the tapes had been seen and the attack anticipated) and rehearsal of night-time manoeuvres. Zero hour was 5.40 am but accurate German artillery fire disrupted the assaulting troops at the critical movement.

165 Brigade attacked and occupied German positions by 8 am but were unable to capture Hill 37. Both of the 166 Brigade supporting battalions were deployed to assist and at 9.45 am two companies from 1/5th Loyals supported the Liverpool Rifles in an attack. At 11 am they succeeded, but were driven off twenty minutes later. 1/9th King's conducted mopping-up actions against German positions around Hill 37 in preparation for another attack. When two companies from 1/5th South Lancashires arrived, they were ordered to attack Hill 37 from the west with the Liverpool Rifles and 1/9th King's

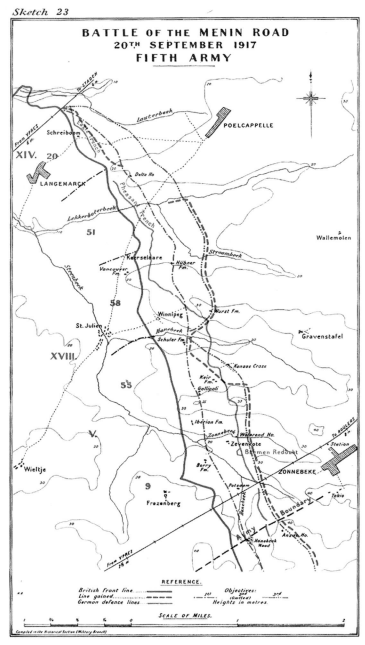

The Battle of Menin Road, 20 September 1917. The 55th Division's return to Ypres, during which Rifleman Hulm was killed. (*Official History*)

Rifleman Thomas Roberts Liverpool Rifles. Killed 20 September 1917 and buried in Tyne Cot. His parents were from Staffordshire and his children were listed as living in Yorkshire. Thomas illustrates the danger of assuming that every soldier originated in the regimental recruiting area.

while the 1/5th attacked from the south. At 5.10 pm, Hill 37 was occupied and consolidated. This including specially trained infantry turning captured German machine guns on their former owners. A German counter attack was driven off with support from the artillery and enfilade fire from machine guns. Two companies from the Liverpool Scottish were positioned near Hill 37 and ordered to put in an immediate counter attack if there was a threat that the hill would be lost.[26]

164 Brigade seem to have suffered disorganisation caused by flanking fire due to the two assaulting battalions inadequately clearing enemy positions before moving on. The Liverpool Irish and the Lancashire Fusiliers were first engaged in clearing the Schuler Galleries – 300 yards of dugouts, linked with concrete trenches and wired. The Fusiliers then moved on to the Green Line, but arrived with insufficient numbers to hold it. Meanwhile, the Liverpool Irish failed in their attack on Schuler Farm due to fire from flanking German positions and would not capture it until 4.30 pm the following day.

By the end of the 21st, the British gains had been consolidated and counter attacks against the Hill 37–Hill 35 ridge repulsed. Similar counter attacks against Kier Farm got into the British trenches but were quickly evicted. During the night of 22nd/23rd, the division was relieved by the 39th Division. The actions had cost another 127 officer and 2603 other ranks casualties but the Green Line objectives of 31 July were finally secured.[27]

Critically, Jeudwine was no donkey. Alan Clark's book focuses on 1915, when Jeudwine was serving on a brigade staff, so these 1917 battles are not applicable to his ideas. Nonetheless, the 'donkeys' view prevails, as indicated by General Melchet in *Blackadder Goes Forth*. Jeudwine was neither. Liverpool Record Office holds the 'Narratives' he collected, like that of Corporal Claire, of D Company, Liverpool Irish. His account recounts how Second Lieutenant Stone was shot in the head while rallying his platoon, having already fallen on a German bayonet. Captain Wilde (C Company, 1/9th King's) considered that the use of rifle grenades 'was fully proved' and the account of Second Lieutenant Lunnon (D Company, 1/9th King's) stated that rifle grenades had been used against an enemy position and then all parties had rushed in. However, Second Lieutenants Dodd (OC Number 2 Platoon, 1/5th King's), Raymond (C Company, 1/5th King's) and Cullern (OC 12 Platoon, C Company, 1/5th King's) all considered rifle grenades to be 'a wash out again', in Raymond's words.

Major Duckworth, commanding Liverpool Irish, noted four 'Lessons Identified':

1. Drills – battle formations should be practised continually.
2. Dress – officers should wear their own dress, because they lose half their power of command at anything more than a short distance.
3. Formations – small columns were more manageable than the present system because, when in line, men get into shell holes and are beyond the control of the officers.
4. Reorganisation – to reorganise when the enemy is active is impossible in daylight.

Second Lieutenant Clarkson, OC B Company, 1/5th King's, despite his youth and the lack of more senior officers, provided five lessons, including the importance of carrying extra ammunition to create a local ammunition dump (with

202768 Rifleman Hulm. 1/5th King's claimed Rifle status. Aged 30 from Bootle. The divisional motto must have had some impact on his family to be included. Buried at Tyne Cot, another 20th September 1917 fatality.

which Second Lieutenant Astley, OC 6 Platoon agreed). The most pertinent point was the need to increase the training for section commanders to lead their men during the advance. Clarkson thought that the men would 'follow the crowd', so that the platoon commanders had to push the men forward 'at great risk'. Second Lieutenant Thorpe (OC 12 Platoon, C Company, 1/7th King's) made the same point about the need for better trained section commanders. The impression from these reports is of junior officers needlessly exposing themselves in order to urge their men out of cover and forward. Under these circumstances, it is hardly surprising that Lewis-Stemple's history of junior officers is entitled *Six Weeks*.

Dodd, Raymond and Cullern also recommended more spades for quicker consolidation, carrying a second waterbottle, the need for more 'moppers up', and more runners for carrying messenges. Raymond also mentions sending a message by pigeon, so that means of communication was used in the battle.

Perhaps the most telling comment came from Private G W Chapman, (8 Platoon, D Company, 1/7th King's), which started: 'May I suggest another form of attack....' Where else could a private soldier suggest to his superior officers alternative tactics? It suggests both a high degree of awareness on behalf of the soldier, and confidence in the willingness of his senior commanders to listen, rather than rebuke, his impertinence.[28]

The Battle of Cambrai – 20 November–7 December 1917

55th Division was transferred to the Third Army and relieved the 35th Division. They occupied some 12,000 yards of front, four times the length held on the Ypres front, between Honnecourt Wood and Lempire-Ronssoy villages. They would later have to take over even more of the line. The construction of the front line was different. Instead of a strongly defended trench system, the new positions were dominated by strong points with interconnecting trenches. The *1st West Lancashire Brigade* recalls the six or seven weeks after occupying the line on 2 October as being 'peaceful', with leave parties and plenty of football, although not without some offensive actions. Towards the middle of November it became evident that the quiet time was about to end, with the arrival of fresh troops and more cavalry than they had ever seen before in France.

On 18 November, the Germans launched a raid in force with about 200 men attacking under the cover of an artillery and mortar barrage. They entered the trenches at three locations but in which they were contained; on seeing a support company attacking them across the open, the Germans retired. There were ninety four British losses, including some prisoners. Information obtained from them by the Germans may have led to disastrous consequences a few days later.[29]

As part of the general attack on the Hindenburg Line, on the 20th the division launched a subsidiary attack along a 2500 yard front on Gillemont Farm and the Knoll to fix the enemy. If possible, they were to take and hold the objectives, but the attack was not to be pressed home if enemy resistance was too strong, nor were the objectives to be held against determined enemy counter attack. Significantly, the Divisional Order stated that the assaulting battalions' counter attack companies were not to be used to reinforce or drive home the original attack, but may: 'only be used for the purpose of immediate counterattack against any hostile penetration of our front after the objectives have been gained'.

Due to the length of the division's front, only 164 Brigade was available for the attack. The Liverpool Irish (right) and 2/5th Lancashire Fusiliers (left) were to attack the Knoll, while 1/4th King's Own attacked Gillemont Farm. 1/5th King's were tasked as a 'Counter attack reserve'. 1/9th King's provided a diversion using dummy soldiers and a dummy tank, which was apparently very successful, as it 'attracted much hostile fire'.

One criticism of the Battle of the Somme and Third Ypres is that the attack fronts were overly long and against strong defences. Here, though, limited objectives were given but if resistance exceeded the value of the target, the attack was not to be pursued. Increasingly sophisticated plans were also emerging, like the use of dummy tanks for deception.

Zero hour was 6.20 am for Gillemont Farm and twenty minutes later for the Knoll, which was supported by a creeping barrage. The artillery also fired 1320 gas cylinders, 335 thermite bombs and 170 smoke bombs on the left flank. The smoke was highly successful, as 2/5th Lancashire Fusiliers suffered from very little enemy machine gun fire.

The Liverpool Irish and Lancashire Fusiliers reported being on the Knoll at 7.30 am, but the Liverpool Irish requested reinforcements at 7.50 am and twenty five minutes later reported that they were falling back. At 10 am both battalions left the Knoll and withdrew to their jumping off trenches.

The Reverend Coop considered that the attack had been a success, in that both objectives were held and then given up when the German counter attacks became too intense, which held German troops to that section of the line while the Third Army attacked at Cambrai was launched with great success. But it was achieved at a cost of another 600 officers and men. Coop speculated that the Germans were anticipating the attack, possibly from information obtained from prisoners taken on the raid of the 18th/19th. General Jeudwine's narrative of the operation goes into greater detail. The Germans had largely evacuated their front line trench, but the second line positions were strongly held with troops ready for a counter attack. Furthermore, as soon as the assaulting battalions entered the front line trenches they received a heavy and accurate rifle-grenade barrage, for which a new section of trenches appears to have been especially dug. Jeudwine went on:

> The operation depended very largely for its success on the gaining of the whole objective in a short time. The gap caused by the failure of [Liverpool Irish] to penetrate on their portion of the objective enabled the enemy to attack the right flank of the [2/5th Lancashire Fusiliers].

The significance of the 20 November attack was not its success or failure, but as an example of evolving tactics and effective staff work. The assaulting infantry were protected behind a creeping barrage which aided them crossing No Mans' Land into the German front line trenches; another artillery barrage effectively screened them from flanking fire, while a dummy assault attracted attention away from the real attack, all of which saved lives. What appears to have gone wrong on this occasion was a breach of operational security so that the Germans were waiting for them.[30]

In the last days of November German activity on the front was increased, most noticeably by low flying aircraft and artillery registering on Little Priel Farm. The farm had been used for registering artillery in the past, but the increase in activity indicated that new batteries were being brought into the line. Jeudwine ordered additional patrols at 4 am and artillery fire at 5 am each morning. The reserve battalions were brought closer to the front line and placed on thirty minutes notice to move. VII Corps was advised of the increased activity but a request for heavy artillery 'counter-preparation' fire was refused. Coop stated that the division was holding some 13,000 yards of line with only two brigades of field artillery in direct support. Each of the six battalions in the front line had 1¼ miles to defend. Consequently, as previously mentioned, the front line was held by platoon-sized strong points with communication trenches to connect them. 166 Brigade held the northern sector, with the Liverpool Scottish holding the southernmost post, Ossus. Then came 165 Brigade, with the Liverpool Rifles holding Ossus Wood to Heythrop Post, 1/5th King's from Grafton Post to Ego Post and 1/7th King's from Cat Post to New Post. 1/9th King's were in reserve, while 164 Brigade formed the divisional reserve.

At 7 am on the 30th the divisional front came under heavy bombardment. 35 Brigade, situated on the division's left, reported seeing an SOS flare from 1/5th South Lancashires' positions and communicated this to 166 Brigade HQ. Communications with the battalion were attempted; at 7.43 am a message was received: 'We know nothing yet; O.K.' Nothing more was heard from the battalion and not a single man returned from those positions. It was subsequently discovered that, surrounded, the battalion had fought on until its ammunition had run out. The divisional artillery also reported seeing SOS rockets but, with no further information, was unable to support the beleaguered infantry effectively.

By about 8 am it became clear that the Germans had attacked and broken through along a ten mile front, which included the left of the division's frontage. The Germans were west of Villers Guislain by 9.30 am. Before the telephone line was broken, 1/5th Loyals reported the Germans had broken through on their left, and the Liverpool Scottish reported Germans were in Pigeon Quarry, between them and the Loyals. The Germans also attacked at Ossus II, on the Liverpool Scottish's front, while further south, on the Liverpool Rifles' front, the Germans had entered The Birdcage and Eagle Quarry, occupying the trenches for some 800 yards northwards. Another attack was launched at Gleeceall Post in 1/5th King's sector.

The Loyals now found their position extremely vulnerable but, with the Liverpool Scottish, made stands at Adelphi and Gloucester Road, delaying

German Attacks at Cambrai, 30 November 1917. Showing the extent of losses following the German counter attack. 55th Division lost most ground in the north, where some sources state that the German's appeared through 12th Division's area. 1/5th South Lancashires were lost in their entirety here. (*Official History*)

the Germans but suffering losses in the process. Meath Post fell at 4.30 pm and Limerick Post, garrisoned by the King's Own, Liverpool Scottish and Loyals, held until 5 am the following day, when the survivors escaped to their own lines. 1/4th Loyals counter attacked and blunted the German advance, but at the cost of their CO, 'shot through the heart at the head of his Battalion'.

166 Brigade was ordered to dig in and hold Épehy at all costs. Labour Companies and all available troops were put into the defences, in a move reminiscent of the First Battle of Ypres of October and November 1914.

Meanwhile, reinforcements were on their way. The 4th and 5th Cavalry Divisions were despatched, while 13th Middlesex were placed at 55th Division's disposal. A second battalion was later made available.

The divisional right was holding the line. By 9.50 am, 1/5th King's reported that the attacks there had been driven back. The 1/7th also reported that attacks against them had been driven back, while the Liverpool Rifles had contained the penetrations into their line, with Cruciform Post and Heythrop Farm held and Little Priel Farm recovered.

The Fusiliers dug a new trench from Lempire to Malassise Farm. 1/9th King's occupied posts to the right of the Fusiliers, with a company sent to assist the Liverpool Rifles. By midday the front was stabilising, although heavy fighting would continue throughout the afternoon.[31]

A counter attack was planned for 6.30 am on 1 December with two groups of tanks and elements of the cavalry divisions attacking. 164 and 166 Brigades were to advance if the opportunity allowed it, but only in conjunction with the cavalry on their left. In the event the cavalry suffered heavily for only a few gains. That night, 21st Division relieved 164 and 166 Brigades; and on the night of the 6th/7th the whole division was relieved by 16th Division.[32]

The division's time on the Cambrai front had seen it battered during a diversionary attack, which it had executed with great enthusiasm and professionalism and had achieved the objectives asked of it. It had then been hit by a German attack across a front which it was clearly incapable of resisting – the front line it was holding was far too long for a single division, let alone one which had suffered considerable losses in action only a few days before. That the front was stabilised within a few hours and the German breakthrough blocked pays tribute to the determination of those engaged that day. There would be an inquiry into these events, but when the division was transferred (yet again, this time to First Army) VII Corps Commander had nothing but compliments for their actions:

> The Corps Commander cannot allow the 55th Division to leave his command without expressing to the Officers, non-commissioned officers and men, his satisfaction at the way they fought and worked during the recent operations.
>
> It is not at present quite clear what happened on the left of the Division, but, from the enquiries made by the Corps Commander, he knows that the 30th November, 1917, in spite of the heavy losses incurred, was a day which will always reflect credit on the 55th Division.
>
> The fact that not a man returned from the 1/5th South Lancs. Regiment, when that battalion was attacked by overwhelming numbers, tells its own tale.
>
> He wishes the Division, and his old friend the Commander, the best of luck.
>
> (Signed)   J. Burnett Stuart
Brigadier-General
>
> 8/12/17   General Staff, VII Corps.[33]

Jeudwine set out on a campaign to limit the damage to himself and the division. As mentioned above, he sent a private message to the Secretary of State, Lord Derby, which worked. He flatly refuted allegations of 'panic', and emphasised how the division was understrength following Ypres, while overstretched taking over more of the front line to relieve troops for the attack. Griffith's observed the 55th 'did well until it bolted on 30 November 1917 at Cambrai' while Gary Sheffield places the blame squarely on the shoulders of General Byng, GOC Third Army:

> The British had been badly surprised, not because there were no indications of a threat, but because, when presented with the pieces of the jigsaw, they had failed to put them together to make a coherent intelligence picture. 55th Division issued an 'Urgent Operations Priority' order on 28 November warning of an attack. GHQ intelligence

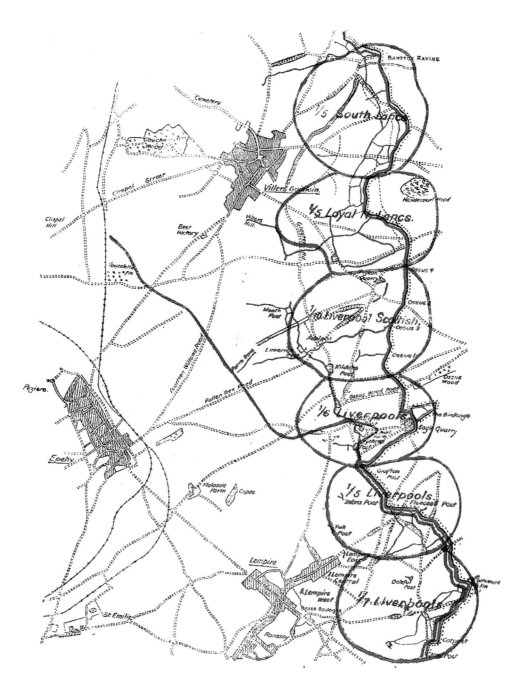

Battle of Épehy (Battle of Cambrai).

largely discounted the possibility of a major.... German assault. However, Byng and his staff were the worst culprits, paying little attention to the warnings from their subordinate formations.

Edmonds, the official historian, wrote that the division 'had no reason to reproach itself. Overwhelmed by numbers and by withering superior artillery, the troops had shown their quality by standing fast amid their broken defences.' In all likelihood, there probably was a panic: this was the first time the division had been attacked. The 1/5th South Lancashires were lost entirely, while the 1/5th Loyals and the Liverpool Scottish were isolated and had to fight their way out. The German gains pivoted on the Liverpool Rifles' defence so that, further south, the 1/5th and 1/7th King's did not lose any ground. They were not the only division to retreat in the face of the German counter attack.[34]

Ernst Jünger, again, fought at what he calls the Double Battle of Cambrai, more specifically in the counter attack, which he participated in from Vis-en-Artois, about 25 miles north west of the 55th Division and on the north side of Cambrai. He starts off by noting that a British observation balloon was brought down in flames, with the pilot circling round to shoot at the parachutists. How different the air superiority picture was to Guillemont. This fighting was in the trenches, rather than amongst anonymous shell holes. The British prisoners, he noted, were 'young, good-looking fellows in new uniforms'. 'With the waxing joy of the huntsman', Jünger watched the line of prisoners marching past, and counted 150. He met the company commander, wounded in the calf, whose opening words were "We were surrounded" to explain the quick surrender of so many men. Jünger then goes on to comment on all the weapons and equipment, food and drink which they liberated. The impression given is an initial collapse by demoralised troops, similar to the talk of 'panic' south of Cambrai, but this quickly stiffened. Jünger and his men took increasing numbers of casualties as they fought through each traverse to the village of Moeuvres, an advance of 11 miles towards Arras.[35]

First Army and Restructuring

The division, less the divisional artillery, which was retained on the Cambrai front, arrived at Bomy (near Fruges) on 14 December 1917. Training, especially musketry, was undertaken by the infantry. For the artillery and engineers, front line activity continued. 276 Brigade, RFA was ordered to Robecq on 8 January. 422 Company, RE was sent to the Givenchy-Festubert Line on New Year's Eve. On 20 January, 419 Company was sent to Hinges and on the 24th, 423 Company relieved 422 Company. The artillery rejoined the division on 4 January 1918.

In January 1918 came the news that the infantry brigades were to be restructured on a three battalion model. While the manning difficulties experienced by the army in general made these changes logical and necessary, it did not make it any easier when the 1/8th and 1/9th Kings, and 1/5th Loyals were transferred to 57th (Second West Lancashire) Division for amalgamation with their second line battalions. The duplication of territorial battalions in 1914 allowed the contraction to take place in the same lineage.

55th (West Lancashire) Division
Special Order of the Day
31st January 1918
On the departure from the Division of three battalions – the 1/8th The King's Liverpool Regt. (Liverpool Irish), 1/9th The King's Liverpool Regt., and 1/5th Loyal North Lancashire Regt. – I wish to assure all officers, warrant officers, non-commissioned officers and men belonging to them, how greatly I, and, I am sure, everyone in the Division, regrets their loss.

Some, I am glad to say, remain with us.

As to the Battalions themselves, I refuse to regard the separation as permanent, and I look forward confidently to the day when they will rejoin their old Division.

They have had their full share in all the hard fighting for the past two years, and have helped to make and maintain the reputation which the Division has gained – a reputation which, I am sure, makes every

member of it proud to belong to it. As for myself, to have commanded
it during these years is the highest privilege.

I hope that eventually the Liverpool Irish, the 9th King's, and the
5th Loyal North Lancs. may rejoin our ranks, and that the final blow
may be given shoulder to shoulder with them.

Till they come back again, I wish them, on the part of the Division
and myself, all good fortune and success, and can assure them that we
shall watch their career as keenly as if they were still with us.

H. S. Jeudwine
Major-General
Commanding 55th Division[36]

The 2/10th King's would merge with 1/10th King's to become 10th King's
once again.

On 4 February, the division was warned that it would relieve 42nd (East
Lancashire) Division, TF on the 15th. They occupied the left sector of 1
Corps' front, from the La Bassée – Cambrin Road to the Cailloux Road,
north east of Festubert; On 5 March the section south of the La Bassée
Canal was handed over to the 46th Division. On the left was 2nd Portuguese
Division. The length of the division's front fluctuated as flanking units came
and went, but on 9 April 1918 the right flank lay on the La Bassée Canal,
while the reserve brigade, 166, was located around Locon, preparing to
relieve a Portuguese brigade.

164 Brigade held the divisional right, with 1/4th King's Own right, 1/4th
Loyals left and 2/5th Lancashire Fusiliers in reserve. 165 Brigade on the
divisional left deployed 1/7th King's right, 1/5th King's left and the Liverpool
Rifles in support, with a company close behind the other two battalions.[37]

Operation GEORGETTE – 9 April 1918[38]

Operation GEORGETTE was the second of the German Spring offensives,
known collectively to the British as the *Kaiserschlacht*. The first, Operation
MICHAEL, was fought between 21 March and 5 April in the Somme area
where they broke through and forced back the British Army. Ernst Jünger
vividly recalled the March attacks in "The Great Battle" where he fought

against the 'flat helmets' in the trenches, and liberated the fine foods and drinks left behind in hurriedly abandoned dugouts, notably a whole crate of eggs. When it was halted, a second offensive was launched on the River Lys area, on the assumption that this area would be weakened now that the British had redeployed so many troops to the south to hold the Somme area. German losses in MICHAEL meant that the original German plan, GEORGE, had to be scaled back and renamed in the diminutive.[39]

The German plan was to punch through XI Corps (55th Division on the left from the German perspective, 2nd Portuguese on the right and 51st (Highland) Division TF in reserve) and XV Corps (40th and 34th Divisions with 50th (Northumbrian) Division TF in reserve), to capture Bailleul and then the communication hub at Hazebrouck, which would disrupt the supply lines to Ypres. Despite the reduction in the formations deployed, the German assault smashed a hole through the Allied lines several miles wide, through which four divisions poured and made gains of up to six miles on the first day. Dunkirk and the English Channel were only twenty six miles behind the British front line. According to Stevenson, the 'Principle weakness was the Portuguese, whom the Germans deliberately struck most heavily'.[40]

Martin Evans is complimentary about the state of the 55th Division. It was:

familiar with their complex of trenches, and were commanded by a man of skill who had mastered the new arts of defence. Major-General Hugh Jeudwine had brought this formation through two major episodes of the Third Battle of Ypres, the opening day and the Battle of the Menin Road, and the German counter-attack at Cambrai. In the seven weeks since taking position on this front, they had studied and extended their defences, establishing strongpoints and working out fields of fire for their guns. The terrain was cut through with a maze of trenches almost four years old, adding to the defensive opportunities and the confusion of the attackers.

The trenches around Givenchy were actually breastworks built up because the watertable was so high, making them vulnerable to repeated German shelling. Jeudwine himself placed great emphasis on tactical exercises, which meant that when the Germans did attack he was able to conduct the most effective defence possible. Units were given one of two tasks: either garrison, in which case they were to hold out until the last; or counter attack, to make immediate, local counter attacks. Even then, in his own words, 'practically every rifle in the Division had been thrown into the line to take their part as Infantry'. The artillery even registered on their own positions, with shots falling close enough to be 'uncomfortable'.[41]

A heavy German bombardment commenced at 4.15 am on 9 April along the divisional front, as well as targetting all roads, crossroads and bridges to and beyond Locon. Colonel Rettie, RFA, recorded that morning in his diary:

> Crash! – 4:20 a.m., 9th April – the hour had come. Hastily I drew on my best breeches, boots and jacket. (I always wear my best clothes when there is a prospect of a battle; one never knows what may happen, either to you or to your kit), and put my head out of the dug-out, only to withdraw it quickly. Mixed up with a thick mist was undoubtedly gas. Luckily our dug-out is fairly gas-proof when you have stuffed up all the visible cracks and the ventilator.

The code word 'Bustle' was given and units began to move into battle positions. The artillery responded with a counter-preparation bombardment but reported seeing no SOS rockets. This may have been because the infantry could not the enemy in the morning mist until it was too late, or perhaps an entry in 165 Brigade's account explains why: the Germans used phosgene gas rather than the usual mustard, which was a 'combat indicator' that an attack was imminent. The effects of phosgene were less persistent than mustard gas, which meant that it would clear sooner and be less of an impediment to their own attacking troops. The early morning mist reduced visibility to thirty yards or less, and there was no wind to move it. Three German divisions attacked with two more in reserve, against a single British division whose performance at Cambrai the pervious autumn, in the opinion of the Germans, had not been so impressive. When the German bombardment slackened at around 6.30 am, it was reported that it had covered a large

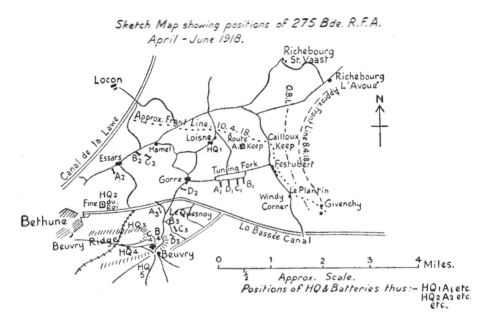

275 Bde RFA Positions, April–June 1918. Detail of artillery positions during and after the Defence of Givenchy, April 1918. In particular, note the way the front line bent around the north of the division and the importance of Route A Keep. (*Wadsworth*)

scale attack on the two Portuguese brigades on the division's left flank. 165 Brigade attempted to get in touch with the Portuguese to establish the situation. It later transpired that the Portuguese division had withdrawn which, by 9 am, left the 1/5th King's left flank exposed. There were some examples of spirited defence by the Portuguese – their 4 Brigade held out until 11 am – but this did not make any material difference to the defenders to the south. Abandoned Portuguese artillery would later be turned on the 55th Division, although individual Portuguese did fight alongside the 55th. William Marshall thought that the Germans they first saw through the morning mist were in fact Portuguese, which undoubtedly added further confusion to the defence. The Portuguese defence was not helped by a direct hit on its divisional headquarters early in the battle.[42]

At 9 am the Germans attacked 164 Brigade and, although their patrols penetrated some way through the British lines, the garrisons held, which effectively halted the German advance. Local commanders then conducted

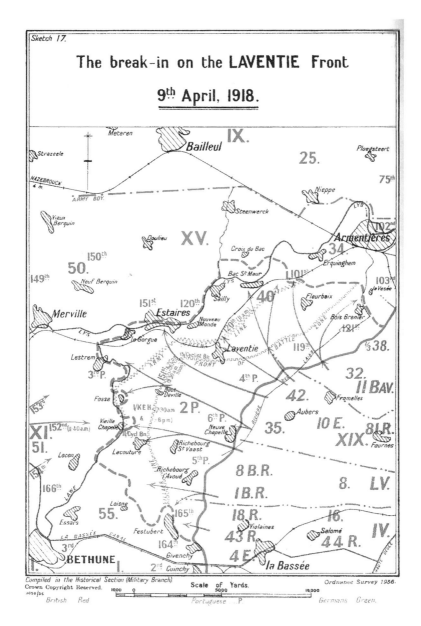

The break-in on the Laventie Front, 9 April 1918. The 55th Division was at the southern end of the attacked line, blocking the German advance on Béthune, in the south west, with its rail connections indicated. Had the Germans been as successful against 55th Division as they were further north, Béthune would have been imperilled. (*Official History*)

their counter attacks, so that by early afternoon the front had stabilised and by dusk all the original positions had been recovered. However, the fighting had been very intense. The Germans got into the rear areas. A bomb thrown into a battalion headquarters' signals dugout killed a signaller. Reinforcements brought with them much needed ammunition and bombs. In one counter attack, 2/5th Lancashire Fusiliers linked up with 1/7th King's at Windy Corner, cutting off and capturing 4–500 Germans and a number of machine guns, which were later turned against the Germans.

For 165 Brigade the situation was mixed. 1/5th King's, with a company of the Liverpool Rifles, held the left; while the 1/7th and another Liverpool Rifles' company were on the right. The remaining two Rifles companies were the brigade reserve and were deployed forward. On the right, the combination of garrisons and counter attacks had stabilised the situation. At 7 am, the Liverpool Scottish arrived from 166 Brigade. The soldiers in the transport lines were formed into another company to protect the rear

Second Lieutenant Albert Parkinson and colleagues. 2/Lt Parkinson, 1/5th King's, of Litherland, Liverpool and three others from 1/5th buried at Pont-du-Hem Cemetery, La Gorgue, killed during the Defence of Givenchy, 9 April 1918. There are also three unidentified 'Kingos'.

of Brigade HQ. An important post, Route A Keep, fell to the Germans at 11 am, as they were able to approach it from the rear under cover of thick fog. Shortly afterwards, Brigade HQ came under machine gun fire.

On the left, the withdrawal of the Portuguese allowed the Germans to get behind the garrisons. Two companies from 1/5th South Lancashires dug in to the north of Loisne to block that flank. Despite repeated attempts to break this line it held and the Germans never made any further headway there. 166 Brigade, meanwhile, had set off to its battle positions at 4.30 am but halted when reports were received that the bombardment had only been part of a strong raid against the Portuguese. When it became clear that this was an attack on 55th Division, the brigade deployed, with half its infantry supporting each of the other two brigades. 166 Brigade was then reinforced by the pioneer battalion, 1/4th South Lancashires, the three RE field companies, a detachment from 251st Tunnelling Company

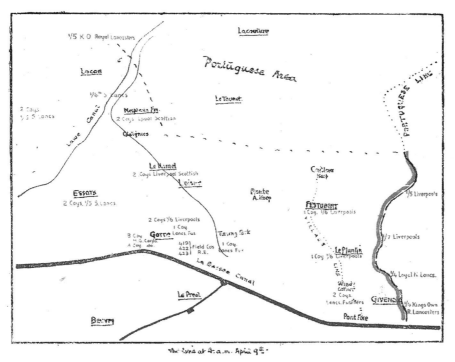

Givenchy, 9 April 1918. Showing the key units, positions and dispositions immediately before the division's most important action of the war. (*Coop*)

and 'miscellaneous Portuguese' who had been collected and returned to the front. Also in the area was 51st Division's 154 Brigade, which was placed under the command of 55th Division, with one battalion (1/4th Seaforth Highlanders) attached to 166 Brigade and the remainder deployed to cover Locon and Les Caudrons from the north. When the King's Own reported that the Germans were working their way around to the north and had occupied Le Touret, the Seaforth Highlanders were sent forward to block the gap between the King's Own and the pioneer battalion, 1/4th South Lancashires. This was accomplished by 5 pm.

By the end of the day, with the assistance of 154 Brigade the situation was stabilised along the divisional front and a considerable number of Germans had been taken prisoner. The division was holding some 11,000 yards of front line, with a 2,000 yards gap, between 164 Brigade, which still held its original front line, and 165 Brigade's positions.

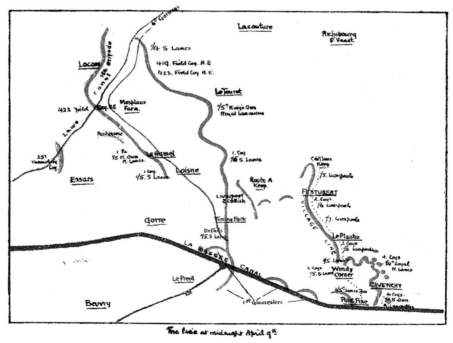

Givenchy midnight, 9 April 1918. The gaps in the line and the creation of new positions during the battle shows just how desperate the actin had been. (*Coop*)

The role of the supporting arms was vital to the defence. As the Germans approached as close as 200 yards, the guns were dragged out of the gunpits and fired over open sights, as in the 1914 battles. An anti-tank gun from A/276 Battery, commanded by Sergeant Parkinson, fired 150 shrapnel rounds with the enemy just 500 yards away until a round jammed in the breach. The detachment then manned the parapet as infantry. In Jeudwine's narrative he noted: 'The fire of this 18 pdr. gun at point blank range caused enormous casualties to the enemy & greatly helped in the successful defence of GIVENCHY HILL'. The remainder of the artillery was also closely engaged, and Jeudwine requested a summary of each battery's action. C/275 Battery, for example, had to retire 1000 yards when it came under machine-gun fire, and would move to three more locations during the battle. They came under artillery bombardment and suffered twelve killed, forty-eight wounded and three missing, including the battery commander, Major Eills, killed on the 9th. Eills was another soldier who represented middle-class Liverpool. The 31

year-old son of Alderman (Councillor) John and Florence, of Sefton Park, he left a wife, Agnes, and a young family.[43] The battery lost three guns but, critically, they could be replaced almost immediately. Several six-inch trench mortars had fired until the enemy were around them. Not one gun or mortar was lost to the Germans. The Lewis and Vickers gun teams similarly fought fiercely even when surrounded, with one Vickers gun team continuing to fire even as Germans were entering its bunker from the rear – the crew despatched them with their pistols.

The Signals Service was kept very busy. The cables to the forward brigades were generally operative where they were dug in six feet deep trenches, but for those to the reserve brigade and

Major Eills, 1/4th (West Lancashire) Brigade, RFA. Killed in action on 9th April 1918 during the Defence of Givenchy. Note the divisional insignia on his arm.

new positions established in response to the German attack, there had been no time to dig them in and were vulnerable and easily damaged. Over fifty miles of cable were laid during the Defence. The additional resilience of the buried cables saved lives. The Service lost three men wounded and one killed. Communications were not lost, although a wireless operator at 165 Brigade was unaware of overnight code changes, so his messages were not identified until 6.30 am. Visual communications were not used due to the early morning mist.

The medical services also put into effect their own plan, which included clearly signposted routes to a Walking Wounded Dressing Station at Le Hamel, from where a launch from the Inland Waterway Transport of the Royal Engineers took them to Béthune. This helped to clear the forward areas of non-urgent casualties and thus prevented congestion. Seventy two officers and 1,371 other ranks from 55th Division, and forty seven officers and 1,223 other ranks from non-divisional units were treated by the field ambulances during the Defence. These casualties were in addition to those killed in action or taken prisoner, including William Marshall.

The wider picture on the first day was not good. To the north of the Portuguese, 40th Division was outflanked and fell back, unlike the 55th who were still in place. By the 12th, the Germans were within four miles of Hazebrouck and, if Hazebrouck fell, Henry Wilson, Chief of the Imperial General Staff, feared that Dunkirk would fall too. The significance of Dunkirk falling is better known to the post 1940 reader; its loss in 1918 would have been just as critical. The German advance continued and threatened the Allies economically as well as militarily. The Bruay-Béthune coalfield supplied 70 per cent of France's requirements for ammunition production, and now came under German artillery. Production was reduced and had to be make up with imports, hardly ideal in the prevailing strategic conditions. The Germans were also able to shell the railway yards of Amiens, forcing resupplies and reinforcements to take the longer, coastal route.[44]

This was the Division's greatest moment and is the location of the divisional memorial. It held the German advance. The Germans offensive here continued and tried to break through at Givenchy again, without success; this meant that their plan had already suffered a major setback. In holding the German advance at Givenchy, the German second Spring

Unveiling the Divisional Memorial. Posted to Stan Taylor of Widnes on 25 July 1921: Hope you are in the pink. We go to Camp at Knott End on Sunday the 31st of July Lest we forget. Cheerio Dick. Officiating may well be the Reverend Coop, with General Jeudwine on the right.

Offensive, Operation GEORGETTE, was significantly disrupted. It went on to make major gains south of Ypres, but the failure at Givenchy was a crucial factor in halting the German tide. Yet, for all their success, the division's actions only warrants a single sentence in Stevenson's book ('In the south of the pocket the 55th Division of Lancashire territorials, occupying a more traditional trench line with machine guns, held the high ground around Givenchy against repeated attack.') Sheffield simply says that the 40th and 55th Divisions 'fought hard'. The limited references to Givenchy by Sheffield, Stevenson and Tomaselli speaks volumes of their success. The battle moved elsewhere precisely because they held the Germans back.[45]

Overnight, 3rd Division's 9 Brigade arrived to assist, with one battalion being kept back as the divisional reserve and one allocated to each of 164 and 165 Brigades. The 13th King's, sent to support 165 Brigade, must have been welcomed amongst the fellow Liverpudlians. 42 Brigade, RFA was also allocated to 55th Division and was ordered to support 166 Brigade.

Givenchy Memorial Hall. Donated by the City of Liverpool in 1924.

Throughout the 10th, the German main effort was to outflank the division's lines but the only success occurred when a second heavy attack at 1 pm against B Company 1/5th King's Own reduced its strength to forty men and forced it to withdraw 200 yards. A counter attack by the whole battalion at 2.20 pm restored the line and the arrival of 9 Brigade's 1st Northumberland Fusiliers secured the situation. A final, desperate attack at 9 pm gained some temporary footholds, but all of these were recovered and the Germans lost twenty one prisoners and two machine-guns for their efforts.[46]

Dawn on 11 April opened with another German bombardment that lasted until 11 am when an attack was launched on the left and centre of 166 Brigade, pressing them back and opening a potentially dangerous gap in the line. A counter attack by both 1/4th South Lancashire and 1st Northumberland Fusiliers prevented the gap widening and restored the situation. In the afternoon, Germans were observed forming up in the old British trenches; the artillery was directed on to them so that an attack against 165 Brigade failed to develop. In the evening a third attack was launched against two posts, Festubert East and Cailloux Keep, both of which fell after 4 pm. Counter attacks were launched and both were recovered by 7.30 pm.[47]

During the night of the 11th/12th there were some adjustments to the dispositions and a decision was made that Route A Keep should be attacked at midnight on the 12th, thus strengthening the division's left flank. 164 Brigade's attached artillery registered on the Keep and, throughout the 12th, trench mortars were set up and registered. A company each of the Liverpool Scottish and 13th King's attacked under cover of the artillery and mortar barrage and, after a stiff fight, took the Keep. A counter attack at dawn on the 13th was repulsed, as was another attack at 5.30 pm; desperate fighting but ultimately the King's prevailed and the Keep remained in the division's hands until the end of their time there.[48]

With the loss of the Keep, the Germans did not attempt any further serious attacks on the division's front, although they kept up their shelling. On the 14th, the relief of the division by 1st and 3rd Divisions commenced although, as usual, the artillery remained in the line afterwards. Coop likened the battle of Givenchy-Festubert to that the Cambrai 1917: the division had been forced to fight with a flank in the air, maintaining a thin defensive flank against an overwhelming and confident enemy. The failure of the division would have jeopardised the entire front, but the division held once more until relieved. This section of the line, held by the division from February to September 1918, was the only part of it which was held throughout. The division suffered 163 officers and 2956 other ranks killed, wounded or missing. German losses are unknown, but were heavy; there were almost 1000 prisoners, including a band, complete with all of its instruments, and seventy machine guns captured. Coop also quotes, but without a citation, an officer of the German General Staff who stated, publically, that the division's stand on and after 9 April 1918 marked the final ruination of the German effort in 1918.

The severity of the situation facing the British is summed up in Haig's Special Order of the Day:

To all ranks of the British Army in France and Flanders

Three weeks ago to-day the enemy began his terrific attacks against us on a fifty-mile front. His objects are to separate us from the French, to take the Channel Ports, and destroy the British Army.

In spite of already throwing 106 Divisions into the battle and enduring the most reckless sacrifice of human life, he has as yet made little progress towards his goals.

We owe this to the determined fighting and self-sacrifice of our troops. Words fail me to express the admiration which I feel for the splendid resistance offered by all ranks of our Army under the most trying circumstances.

Many amongst us now are tired. To those I would say that Victory will belong to the side which holds out the longest. The French Army is moving rapidly and in great force to our support.

There is no other course open to us but to fight it out. Every position must be held to the last man: there must be no retirement. With our backs to the wall and believing in the justice of our cause each one of us must fight on to the end. The safety of our homes and the Freedom of mankind alike depends upon the conduct of each one of us at this critical moment

D. Haig F.M.
Commander-in-Chief
British Armies in France

General Headquarters
Thursday, April 11th 1918

What the fighting man thought of this message is unclear, although Baker quotes an anonymous source asking 'What ******* wall?'. Along large sections of the front, there were no more prepared defences to fall back to other than the sea. This all sounds very much like another catastrophe in the making twenty two years later. But, if there was no wall behind the British Army, 55th Division did at least provide a solid pillar against which the army could anchor themselves.[49]

A few days later, another Special Order was received:

Special Order of the Day
To all ranks of
     The 55th (West Lancashire) Division
Now that the hard and anxious struggle of the last eight days has come to an end, I want to thank and congratulate the whole Division and tell you how proud I am of the magnificent fighting spirit you have shown. To have defended against determined and continuous attack the line originally entrusted to you, and to have held in addition against an incessant pressure an extended flank thrown back over several thousand yards when the enemy broke though on your left, is an achievement worthy of the best traditions of the British Army.

The result has been due to the foresight and dogged determination of Brigadiers and all Commanders, and of the troops under them, and to the resolution and self-sacrifice of all arms and all ranks.

The situation of the British Army is still critical, and must remain so until the enemy's strength has been worn down and broken. We have still much hard work and fighting in front of us before an honourable and satisfactory peace can be assured. Our present duty, as soon as all ranks are rested, is to fit ourselves in every possible way to meet the enemy again, and to prepare to teach him another lesson. If only this preparation is undertaken by the 55th Division in the same spirit of grim determination that is has shown in actions, I have no fear of the result.

H. S. Jeudwine
Major-General
Commanding 55th (West Lancashire) Division

17th April 1918[50]

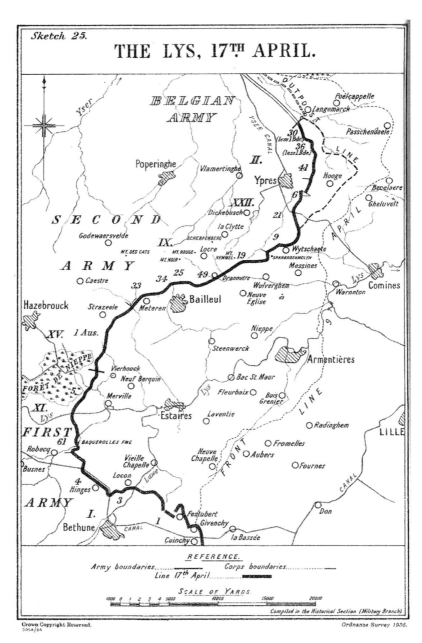

The Battle of the Lys, 17 April 1918, illustrating the full extent of the disaster that unfolded in the eight days after the Defence of Givenchy. German advances were made to the east of Ypres, recovering the losses from the previous autumn and threatening the city from the south. (*Official History*)

That the Germans were surprised at the extent of the resistance that they encountered is summed up by this passage from a copy of the orders given to the 4th Ersatz Division, dated 6 April 1918:

> In the attack our three regiments will be opposed by at most six companies in front and at most two reserve battalions in Festubert and Givenchy. One battalion in Divisional Reserve is south of the La Bassée Canal at Le Preol. It will be prevented by our powerful artillery fire from taking part in the fight for Festubert and Givenchy. Troops are elements of the English 55th Division, which, after being engaged on the Somme, has suffered heavy losses in Flanders and at Cambrai, and was described by prisoners in March, 1918, as a Division fit to hold a quiet sector, that is below the average quality.[51]

The impact of the division's defence was to force the German axis of advance northwards, away from Béthune and the vital lines of communications, but towards Ypres.

On 18 April, another German attack was launched, this time against 1st Division, which enjoyed artillery and trench mortar support from the 55th. The attack was repulsed, but not before the Germans occupied the British front line and the Givenchy Craters, which they would retain until the British advance of 24 August 1918.[52]

On 21 April, the division was back on the move. 166 Brigade moved forward and was placed under the temporary command of 1st Division. The same day, M. Clemenceau, French Prime Minister and Minister of War, visited the division. The 2/10th King's arrived from 57th Division for amalgamation with the 1/10th, which became 10th King's again. On 22 and 23 April, the division relieved 1st Division in the line. In their absence Keep A had been lost to the Germans, so the Liverpool Scottish were ordered to recapture it, which they did on the 24th. The also captured ten Germans, three light and one heavy machine guns. The Keep was handed over to 46th Division, although 55th Division kept a keen eye on 'their' Keep. Perhaps unsurprisingly, the Keep was lost to the Germans again, but 46th Division recovered it and from then on it remained in British hands; it had changed hands eight times.[53]

From Lieut.-General Sir A. Holland, K.C.B., M.V.O., D.S.O.
Commanding I Corps
21/4/18

The Corps Commander wishes to place on record his high appreciation of the work done by the Trench Artillery of the 55th Division during the attack on Givenchy on the 18th April. The detachments, by their heroic stand, assisted materially in the retention of the Givenchy position, and have added another page to the glorious history of the Royal Regiment of Artillery.[54]

Evans summarises the division's achievements:

Even when the men of the King's Liverpool Regiment were forced out of Route A Keep and the Germans occupied it, a counter-attack regained the strongpoint. The refusal of the 55th Division to give way prevented development of the German attack on this flank and left it exposed to enfilading fire from the artillery throughout the battle. It also prevented an attack on Béthune and the precious coal-fields nearby.[55]

From the beginning of May increased activity was noted, which indicated a renewed German offensive that intelligence indicated would be launched on 9 May. Harassment fire tasks by the artillery were increased. On the 8th a large ammunition dump was destroyed near Salomé while the following day Lacouture Church, which was being used by the Germans as an OP, was destroyed. Both of these missions were accomplished with aerial observation provided by the newly created RAF. The division placed the infantry on a higher state of readiness and maintained this posture until the 15th, when it was decided that the attack had been postponed. Whether the postponement was due to the damage inflicted by the artillery or, as German sources stated, due to a severe outbreak of influenza in the German ranks, is unclear. A similar attack was anticipated at the beginning of June; but again, nothing transpired.[56]

The Final Hundred Days

On 24 August 1918, the situation across the whole of the British front was favourable for 55th Division to take part in the final advance.

The division was deployed as follows:

	Left			Right	
	166 Brigade			164 Brigade	
Left		Right	Left		Right
1/5th South Lancs		1/5th King's Own	2/5th Lancs Fusiliers		1/4th King's Own
Reserve			Reserve		
10th King's					1/4th Loyals
Support			Support		
275th Brigade RFA			276th Brigade RFA		
D Coy, 55th Bn MGC			C Coy. 55th Bn MGC		

Reserve Brigade
165 Brigade
1/5th King's
1/6th King's
1/7th King's

German occupation of the Craters, to the east of Givenchy, had been a subject of concern for some time because it allowed them a commanding view of the British positions. 164 Brigade was chosen for the attack. In support, it had an impressive array of extra resources allocated to it: two batteries of artillery from 1st Division, 84th and 15th Army Brigades RFA, and part of 3rd Australian Tunnelling Company. 166 Brigade were to establish a post on Cheshire Road to support it.

Zero hour was set for 7.20 am. The morning was rainy and there was no barrage until five minutes before. The Germans were taken completely by surprise. By 8am the objectives had been taken and the front line pushed 200 yards beyond the Craters, at a cost of twenty killed and eighty three wounded. Two counter attacks were driven off and, although the division was shelled with HE and gas, there was no further attempt to recover the lost positions. Four days later Festubert East Keep was found to have been abandoned and that too was occupied.[57]

As was usual, Major General Jeudwine collected 'Narratives'. It was noted that Lewis gunners were still identifiable, despite carrying the gun in both hands like a rifle; it was recommended that the gunners should be placed at the rear of the section, reducing their exposure. Communications remained

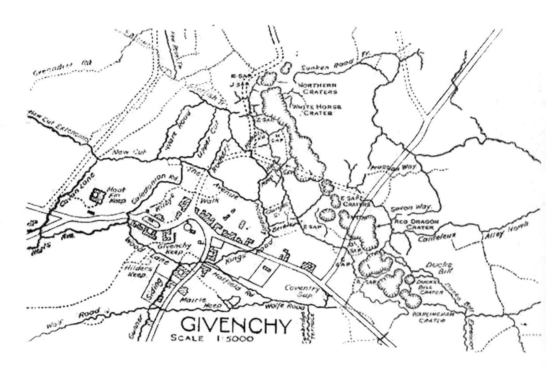

Givenchy Craters, summer 1918: the positions held by 55th Division during the summer of 1918 and from where they launched their final advance. (*Coop*)

a problem. After ten minutes of German bombardment, the artillery lines were damaged and only two messages were delivered. On this occasion pigeons were not used but it is implied that pigeons were still being carried. Visual lamps were used for a couple of messages.[58]

On 30th August 46th Division, on the division's left, reported that the enemy had withdrawn and prisoners indicated that they were falling back to a line running through Richebourg–St Vaast. 55th Division was ordered to advance rapidly if the German withdrawal extended across their front. When it advanced there was no attempt to maintain a continuous front line, instead fighting patrols were sent forward according to brigade plans. Both brigades occupied posts 500 yards east of the Craters on 2 September. There was some opposition, which was overcome, but it indicated that there was not yet a general retirement. The divisional artillery moved forward to cover each phase. The Army Service Corps resupplied food and ammunition along two roads that were repaired for horse transport: Estaminet Corner – Ration

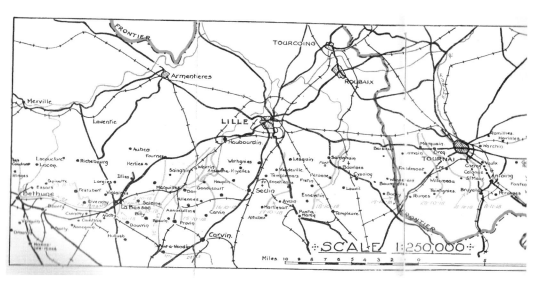

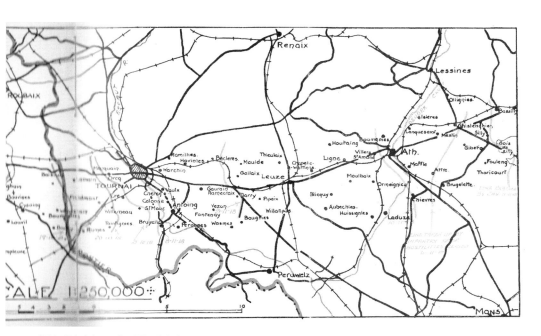

55th Division: the Final Advance. The relentless advance into Belgium in the last months of 1918 were what the war was all about. Unfortunately, in early 1940, the Territorials of the 42nd (East Lancashire) Division would find themselves in the same area against yet more German aggression. (*Coop*)

Corner – Festubert – Quinque Rue; and Westminster Bridge – Lone Farm – Windy Corner – Givenchy.

On the 3rd the advance continued, with 165 Brigade relieving 166; there were increasing levels of resistance until the 7th. On the 5th, 16th Division, on the division's right, met considerable resistance south of the La Bassée Canal which halted their advance. This in turn held up 164 Brigade's advance on the divisional right. On the division's left, 46th Division was relieved by 19th Division, who continued the advance.

An attack on the 7th by 164 Brigade against the southern part of Canteleux Trench and Aspe House was only partially successful and a strong counter attack forced the brigade back to its original positions. For now, at least, it appeared that the German retreat was over.

In the period to 17 September there were a series of attempts to break the German positions both by units of the 55th and in conjunction with the flanking divisions. On the 17th, 1/5th King's attacked Canteleux Trench with support from the divisional and corps heavy artillery. It was launched at 5.30 am and was a complete success, with only slight casualties. The southern section of Canteleux Trench and Aspe House was captured and posts were advanced to Towpath Alley and Aspe Road. On the right, 16th Division also attained their objectives. A German counter attack on the 18th recovered some of their lost trenches but these were quickly retaken.[59]

On 19 September I Corps was transferred from First to Fifth Army.[60]

The following day 166 Brigade, in support of 19th Division on the left, attacked and captured the Pumping Station at the junction of Serpent and Nora Trenches. A German counter attack against 19th Division on the 22nd recovered some of the lost trenches and 166 Brigade was obliged to abandon some of its gains as a result. 165 Brigade had also attacked on the 20th and captured Belt, Button and Braces Trenches, and pushed patrols close to the La Bassée – Aubers Line. Overnight, 164 Brigade relieved the 165th and also took over a battalion's frontage from 16 Division south of the La Bassée Canal.

Since the advance had commenced on 24 August the German tactic for creating defensive positions consisted of a deep zone of mutually supporting outposts east of the main line of resistance. But German resistance stiffened, they sent out hostile patrols and these even turned into counter attacks, launched from behind their La Bassée-Fromelles Line. The division began to construct a more substantial outpost line, coupled with more aggressive patrolling and redeployed the artillery to both cover the outposts and support any further advance.[61]

19th Division renewed its offensive on 25 September, with 165 Brigade, now holding the division's left, prepared to support it by an attack with objectives beyond those of the 19th, extending to the La Bassée -Estaires Road as far as Telephone Exchange. The Liverpool Rifles attacked at 8 pm, secured their objectives and drove off at weak counter attack at 10.30 am. They were, however, driven out of their new positions after a counter attack, supported this time by a heavy bombardment, at 6.30 pm, but regained their lost positions in a renewed attack at 3.30 am the following morning. As well as advancing the division's left flank, 105 German prisoners were taken, at a cost of fifty two British casualties.

The brigade line was now turned back, so an attack was planned for the 27th which would bring the two sections of the front line together. 1/5th King's attacked at 2.55 am and reached the La Bassée-Estaires Road between Telephone Exchange and Piano House. In a repeat of the Liverpool Rifles attack a few days earlier, the Germans counter attacked on the 29th with heavy artillery support. The 1/5th were forced back, but then counter attacked and, with support from 1/7th King's, restored their positions by the end of the day.[62]

I Corps advised all divisions that the enemy was expected to withdraw across the whole of Fifth Army's front, and so were to be prepared to push their posts forward south of the La Bassée Canal. This push was to commence on the morning of 30 September after a twenty four hour bombardment, thus a return to the old style longer bombardment. Two companies of 1/4th Loyals attacked and took their objectives but when 16th Division failed to achieve their objectives the Loyals were forced back across the canal. In a renewed attack on 1 October, the Loyals were again successful, as was 16th Division.[63]

In preparation for the anticipated German withdrawal, I Corps issued two objective lines:

1. Bois de Dix Huit – Hulluch – Cité St Elie – Haisnes – La Bassée – Illies.
2. Bois de Quatorze – Bénifontaine – Douvrin – Salomé – Petit Moisnil – Marquillies.

To support this advance, the brigades received the following additional troops:

1. One section of C Squadron, King Edward's Horse;
2. One section, RE.
3. One 18-pounder battery, one section 4.5" howitzers and one section medium trench mortars, the latter mounted on General Service limbered wagons;
4. One company from the machine gun battalion;
5. A detachment from the field ambulance;
6. An investigation party from the tunnelling companies to investigate any booby traps left behind by the retreating Germans.

This was, in effect, an independent brigade group with all of the assets which would be found at divisional level. Meanwhile the pioneers and engineers conducted extensive road repairing so that the advance would not be held up by logistical difficulties.

The division's codeword for the advance was 'Scurry'. It was never issued. The German withdrawal made it redundant; it was only discovered from a German officer on 2 October, who informed the British that a withdrawal to the Haute Deûle Canal had begun at 4 am that morning.

The preparations and the strengthening of the brigades turned out to be very effective in keeping the pressure on the German rear guard, so that the advance became dominated by actions at brigade, rather than divisional, level.

166 (left) and 164 (right) Brigades advanced at 1 pm and by 8 pm had captured the La Bassée-Fournes Road, with patrols in Salomé reporting that it was abandoned. The advance resumed on the 3rd and 4th, with each brigade only encountering resistance once; on each occasion, the resistance was overcome with the assistance of the integral artillery units. By the evening they had advanced to a line from just north of Berclau, within 500 yards of the Heute Deûle Canal, to a point opposite Don, and then along the west side of the La Bassée-Lille Railway. They had been held up by machine gun fire from both sides of the canal, indicating that the Germans' retreat had halted, again, and they had adopted strong defensive positions.

All the bridges over the canal were destroyed, although there were a number of temporary footbridges. The Germans added to the difficulties by flooding the ground to the west of the canal. The division had advanced five miles through damaged villages and found large quantities of abandoned material. Meanwhile, the engineers and pioneers were busy repairing some fourteen miles of roads. The roads west of Salomé were heavily cratered (to the east less so), in many cases, prepared with mines that had not blown, apparently due to the speed of the division's advance. Others had been set with delayed fuses.[64]

The nature of the German defences meant that any attack would have to be thoroughly prepared and that would take a week. The only infantry action during that time was an attack by the Liverpool Scottish on several bunkers and the railway embankment close to Don Station. The attack was initially successful, but the Germans were able to counter attack by approaching from behind a high embankment, get behind the positions and forced most of two platoons to surrender.

On 8 October 55th Division transferred to III Corps.

III Corps determined that to cross the canal required a corps attack. 165 Brigade would force a crossing at Don in conjunction with 74th Division, who were now on the division's left. While preparations went ahead, the 1/5th King's raided enemy posts on the railway sidings near Don Station. They brought in twenty prisoners, who reported that a withdrawal was expected daily. The same day 74th Division was able to cross the canal because the Germans withdrew; but on 55th Division's front they remained in place.

The following day patrols were met by strong opposition from German positions west of the canal. As a result, patrols from 1/5th King's (right) and 1/4th Loyals (left) forced the Germans from the west of the Canal.[54]

The Royal Engineers prepared to bridge various dykes and the canal. Each brigade had three light footbridges plus a number of more substantial 18-foot footbridges. Pontoon bridges for crossing larger obstacles were also available.

On the night of the 15th/16th, part of the Liverpool Rifles crossed the canal and occupied Don, assisted by 423 Field Company, who deployed a pontoon bridge. The following morning, the rest of the battalion crossed and forced the enemy out of Allennes, Annoeullin and Chateau du Bois. On the left flank, 164 Brigade also made successful crossings with the help of two light cork bridges from 422 Field Company. Resistance was light and, in the evening, 165 Brigade was ordered northwards from Herrin to cross the passage at Bac de Wavrin. 422 Field Company constructed another pontoon bridge. The advance continued during the 17th and 18th until a line was reached on the high ground west of Fretin-Fort d'Enchemont-Enchemont, where German resistance stiffened: an enemy patrol was dispersed in Fretin and there was further fighting in Péronne-en-Mélantois, with machine gun fire from woods east of Pont-à-Marcq.

By the evening the division had reached the west bank of the La Mercque river; bridges that had been prepared for demolition had been left intact. When the river was crossed the Germans were found to have withdrawn. The first attempt to do so by 164 Brigade, using ladders, ended in failure when they broke and the men drowned. The advance resumed on the 19th, 20th and 21st, which brought the division to the outskirts of Tournai, where they had their first check in their advance for several days.[66]

On the night of the 21st, 166 Brigade moved forward and attempted, but failed, to take Barges Chateau and its associated wood. It was clear that the Germans intended to make a stand here. Corps policy was not to attack such positions, especially where they corresponded to the Corps front. A line of resistance was to be established, with limited objectives to be taken and harassing fire from artillery, machine guns and mortars was to be maintained.

German artillery remained active but explosions were heard and fires were seen behind their lines; prisoners and civilians both indicated that the Germans were planning another withdrawal.

In preparation for the anticipated German withdrawal from Tournai, III Corps ordered the creation of a mobile force based on the division, under the command of Brigadier General Stockwell:

- HQ 164 Brigade
- C Squadron King Edward's Horse
- A Company VII Corps Cyclist Battalion
- A Battery 275th Brigade, RFA
- 2/5th Lancashire Fusiliers
- A Company 55th Battalion Machine Gun Corps
- 423rd Company RE (less bridging equipment)

- One section 2/1st West Lancs. Field Ambulance
- One Cable Detachment   }
- One Wireless Detachment   } Divisional Signal Company
- Detachment Divisional Artillery Column
- Detachment Divisional Train

A raid was planned for 2 November by 1/7th King's. In a pre-raid bombardment, harmless gas was fired, which was intended to make the Germans don their respirators, although this did not seem to have been a success. The idea of forcing the Germans into respirators while your own troops fought without them was ingenious and again shows an army constantly trying new and innovative ideas to gain an advantage. The raid was nevertheless a success, with fifteen enemy killed and eight captured. However, heavy enemy machine gun fire into both flanks of the wood meant that any attempt to capture it would be unsustainable unless the flank positions could be taken first. Intelligence obtained from the prisoners indicated that there was no intention to withdraw from Tournai.[67]

Information was also received of a withdrawal from the Escaut River on 5/6 November. Patrols found that the Germans were still in place on the 6th. Three raids by 1/5th King's were launched; the right and centre patrols were successful but the left patrol failed to reach its objective. The right patrol raided a position called the Factory and captured two prisoners, then moved along the railway, taking another seventeen prisoners. The centre patrol raided a cluster of houses north of the Factory, capturing one officer and thirty four other ranks. Both patrols held their positions until midday and then withdrew to their original lines.

Intelligence obtained now indicated that the German withdrawal had been delayed. On the basis of this, III Corps ordered the division and 16th Division on their right to force the Germans back and to establish bridgeheads across the River Escaut. 166 Brigade were to attack on the right and 165 Brigade on the left; but on the morning of the 8th it was established that the enemy were withdrawing from their posts west of Tournai. Patrols took two prisoners who confirmed a withdrawal across the Escaut.

Stockwell's Force was placed on one hour's notice to move, while the Liverpool Rifles lead 165 Brigade's advance to the west bank of the river almost unopposed. 1/5th South Lancashires attempted a similar feat for 166 Brigade, but the open ground was swept by machine gun fire and a platoon that made a desperate attempt to secure a bridge were almost all killed or wounded.

Crossings of the Escaut were carried out that night, with three companies of 1/5th South Lancashires crossing with the assistance of a footbridge deployed by 422 Field Company; while a company from the Liverpool Rifles crossed south of Tournai with a light bridge constructed by 419 Field Company. The initial objective had been secured by 8.30 am and they advanced further, until 2 pm, against a withdrawing enemy. Stockwell's Force crossed at 3 pm, followed by 9 Cavalry Brigade, which had been placed under command of the division. Stockwell's Force now came under the command of the cavalry (Brigadier General Legard), together known as Legard's Force. They were ordered to secure the crossing of the River Dendre at Ath.

Again, we see innovation away from static trench warfare. The division was led by a mixed brigade and a cavalry brigade to create a very mobile force, but there were no tanks. They were too slow. 1914 technology was proving itself useful in 1918 with the application of lessons learnt from four years' combat experience.

The infantry, meanwhile, was ordered to take positions just west of Leuze and then high ground west of Chapelle-à-Wattines. At 8 am, Legard's Force informed the infantry that Leuze was abandoned. They pushed through to Chapelle-à-Wattines, arriving by 1 pm. Legard's Force, meanwhile, had advanced towards Ath but had been checked by machine guns. The Lancashire Fusiliers deployed to neutralise them. By nightfall on the 10th, Legard's Force had reached the line of the Blaton Canal and the River Dendre, but again were halted by machine gun fire. The Fusiliers established outposts, with orders to make a crossing overnight; while the mounted force withdrew.

The division had advanced thirteen miles since the night of the 8th/9th along roads that had been mostly made impassable to wheeled transport. The engineers and pioneers gave invaluable service in repairing craters; 170 Tunnelling Company RE made safe some 500 mines. 422 Field Company built a bridge over the Dendre that was capable of carrying seventeen tons.[68]

The Attack on Ath

Orders were issued on 10 November for an attack on Ath the following day, the 11th. 165 Brigade was to attack south of the town while 166 Brigade attacked to the north. The Fusiliers were to hold their position and the mounted troops were to make a turning movement as far north as possible. A conference was to be held at Legard's HQ in Villers St Amand at 9 am, by which time all of the troops were to be in position. There were two intact bridges, one on the Leuze–Ath road and an iron bridge on the Irchonwelz–Ath road, but neither were to be used in the crossing. The Lancashire Fusiliers reported that the iron bridge was prepared for demolition and barricaded on the far side but, at 7 am, with support from a Lewis gun in a house near the river, they were able to rush the bridge and destroy the barricade before the Germans could blow it. They then advanced into the town and the mounted troops pushed though.[69]

The End

At 9.05 am, a message was received at divisional HQ that hostilities would cease at 11 am. This was telephoned through to the conference at Villers St Amand, with an order for all troops to stand fast. However, it would be 1.30 pm before the orders reached the cavalry, by which time they were seven miles east of Ath.

166 and 165 Brigades were ordered to establish an outpost line on the high ground Brugelette-Mévergnies-Ghislenghien, with the remainder going into billets behind the line. 164 Brigade concentrated at Villers St Amand. The artillery moved to Douaire. The pioneers and engineers found billets along the road between Leuze and Ath. Divisional headquarters were established at Chapelle-à-Wattines.

Since leaving the Givency-Festubert line, the furthest point reached by the division was the Bassilly-Thoricourt line, a distance of fifty miles. There is no evidence that the advance would have stopped had the Armistice not been signed.[70]

Popular images of the Armistice, like VE-Day twenty-seven years later, are of great celebrations in London and elsewhere at home. On both occasions the fighting troops were almost subdued. 1/5th King's entered Ath 'amidst most enthusiastic scenes' and the band played the National Anthem. The Liverpool Rifles had buglers blow 'Cease Fire', and resumed its march. The 1/7th announced the Armistice. Only the Liverpool Scottish showed any excitement. The pipers played up and down the street and the church bells rang out.[71]

Chapter 4

The Other Arms and Services of the West Lancashire Division

T he role of the other arms and services are fundamentally different from that of the infantry. Generally they provided a supporting function without exposure to high intensity battle. That is not to say that their routine did not increase in tempo in the build up to, during and, in some cases, after a battle; reading some of the War Diaries, one could be forgiven for missing that a battle had taken place. Most of the extra work was done well in advance, such as establishing communication networks or digging in and registering the guns. For the infantry, battle is a major event and was clearly recorded in the War Diary. On the other hand, the Signals Company War Diary for August 1916, during the tortuous Battle of the Somme, is empty of references to the battle. The first entry states that two of the subalterns from the 66th (Second East Lancashire) Division TF were sent to VI Corps Signals and the last records the opening of a Signals Office at the Advanced HQ, with divisional communications established.[1]

For this reason, the history of the other arms and services is thematic rather than chronological. There are changes over time, but these changes tend to be organisational or technological.

Field Companies, Royal Engineers

The pre-war establishment was for two field companies per division, but by 1915 it became clear that additional engineering capacity was required in what was now a type of siege warfare. On mobilisation there were the 1st and 2nd (West Lancashire) Field Companies, but when the 2nd was attached to the East Lancashire Division, TF in Gallipoli, the West Lancashire Division was left to raise two new field companies to bring itself up to the new, expanded establishment.

TF Title	Pre-War	Re-Numbered	Career	Career
1/1st	Yes	419	4 Division from February 1915	55 Division from March 1916
2/1st		422	57 Division until December 1915	Joined 55 Division January 1916
1/2nd	Yes	420	55 Division from mobilisation	42 Division August 1915–June 1916, then Salonika
2/2nd		423	57 Division until December 1915	Joined 55 Division January 1916
1/3rd		421	Joined 57 Division in December 1915	

Both the 55th and 57th Divisions were supplemented by field companies from the two Wessex Divisions, 43rd and 45th, which were broken up early in the war.

The OC of 1/1st Field Company was initially Major Campbell and for the 1/2nd Major Brown. Both were territorials, having been awarded the long service Territorial Decoration (TD). Each company had two further OCs, none of whom appear to have been territorials. The two, later three, field companies, plus the signal company and the pioneer battalion (1/4th South Lancashires), came under the Commander Royal Engineers (CRE); all three appear to have been regulars. Their adjutants, however, started off as regulars but it became a post held by territorials: Captain De'Ath was a regular, but the next two adjutants, Carr and then Hallas, were territorials. All three were awarded the Military Cross. The limited numbers of regulars in a pre-war Territorial Division were staff officers, such as the CRE and his adjutant, while the companies were commanded by territorials. The CRE remained a regular, whilst the command of the companies passed from territorials to either regulars or temporary officers, but the territorials did take over the adjutant's post, which was at least something.[2]

The field companies supported the infantry, maintaining trenches (including manufacturing parts for the trench) and providing advice on field fortifications. The actual trench digging was not done by the sappers. They also accompanied assaults where they could assist in consolidating captured ground or destroying wire with Bangalore torpedoes.

Out of the trenches, Field Companies were employed constructing dugout frames and machine gun frames, light Decauville railway tracks or Bangalore torpedoes to blow holes through barbed wire, or working on corrugated iron 'baby elephants', the semi-circular pre-fabricated trench shelters. Some of this work could be held up for the most trivial of reasons, like a shortage of trowels for brickwork.[3] One of the first tasks for 419 Company after it rejoined the division was for fifty men to clean up and drain a communications trench.[4]

The Field Companies in action

At the end of June 1916, 419 Field Company received the 165 Brigade Operation Order for a divisional attack on the 28th. There were three raids from the brigade, each supported by three sappers. Overnight, 150 yards of new jumping off trench was dug a hundred feet forward of the front line, by 150 men under the supervision of Lieutenant Skinner; and three saps were dug under the command of Lieutenant Gibbings. On the day before the attack, the OC 419 Company visited CO 1/7th King's, presumably to discuss engineer support to the coming raid. 423 Field Company appears to have provided sappers for the raids because the War Diary recorded that those attached to 1/4th Loyals returned safely; of the three attached to 2/5th Lancashire Fusiliers, one was wounded and two missing. The actual raids seem to have been a success and the result were noted as being 'excellent'.[5]

The engineers also provided close support in battle. At Guillemont on 8 August 1916, 423 Company supported the attacking brigade with three officers and fifty four other ranks. The attack failed and the following day the Company recorded one officer and fifty four other ranks as casualties. Despite this, the *Official History* was very complimentary about their deployment: 'The division adopted the sound principle of keeping its sappers in hand until consolidation was due to begin; sections then went forward to their appointed tasks'. This description and the high casualty rates show that the engineers were very closely involved in the attack.[6]

Another raid was practised and then conducted on 29 November 1916, under Second Lieutenant Dixon-Nuttall with twelve sappers. They raided, but found nothing to demolish and returned with one sapper wounded.[7]

A similarly unsuccessful raid was attempted on 16 June 1917, when two sappers were attached to 1/5th Loyals to demolish a German post with two 8lb charges. The raid encountered strong German working parties and returned.[8]

When the Third Battle of Ypres commenced on 31 July 1917, the OC 419 Field Company reported to HQ 166 Brigade. Most of the work that day seems to have been centred on road repairing and clearing of mines. The following day, 900 yards of Decauville (light railway) track was laid and the company was relieved on 4 August. In preparation for the division's return to the battle in November, 419 Field Company practised with dummy figures and tanks for deception and prepared to blow holes in the German wire with Bangalore torpedoes, so again they were right at the forefront of the fighting.[9]

In mid-September 1917, 422 Field Company were engaged in an 'offensive action', making and repairing a track north east of Ypres and a strong point. In the three days the work took, Second Lieutenant Scott died of wounds while, of the other ranks, both engineers and pioneers, seven were killed, twenty six wounded and two missing. 24 year old Noel Scott was the youngest son of Thomas and Elizabeth, of 6 Fortified Villas, Rothmines, Dublin: it is worth noting that the long connection between Liverpool and Ireland was not restricted to the Liverpool Irish battalions. At the same time, the horse lines were bombed and there were another twelve wounded. Clearly it was a demanding period for the men even though it was not a recognised attack.[10]

During the Third Battle of Ypres, the field companies were awarded the following honours and awards:[11]

Company	DSO	MC	MM	DCM	Croix de Guerre	MiD
419		4	11			4
422	1	2	5	1	1	1
423		2	6			1

Battles were not always offensive. On 30 November 1917, in response to the Battle of Cambrai Offensive, the Germans attacked 55th Division. 422 Field

Company reported that the whole of the front line was lost up to the Brown Line, where the Germans were held. 419 Field Company, under the CRE, moved forward to assist the pioneers but, in the absence of a clear picture, the OC and a subaltern went forward alone to find them. 422 Field Company's duties were either wiring or garrisoning the Brown Line. The crisis lasted until 3 December, 'work would probably continue again tonight': the 419 Company's War Diary does not give any indication of the crisis the division underwent.[12]

The next offensive mounted by the Germans, in March 1918, would nearly break the whole BEF. Tension was mounting throughout March, and the field companies were ordered not to disperse to work until after 9 am. Nerves relaxed after a few days, until the beginning of April. On the 9th, they moved to their Assembly Position with the pioneers. An artillery barrage stampeded the engineers' horses even before the codeword 'Bustle' was received. The Engineers and attached infantry formed a reserve at Gorre Wood composed of:

Unit	Officers	Men	Comments
419 Company	6	116	
Attached Infantry	3	35	
422 Company	2	81	
Attached Infantry	0	56	
423 Company	4	97	
Attached Infantry	2	68	
C Coy 1/4th S Lancs	NK	NK	Capt Frith MC commanding

From this position, the engineers were able to respond to the German attack, either with engineering support or as infantry to plug gaps in the line. The War Diaries are full of fragments of information coming back from the front line, like a request from the Liverpool Rifles for two officers and ninety other ranks to reinforce their positions; and later that the enemy were attacking the left of the Right Brigade. It was midday before definitive orders were received. 419 and 423 Field Companies were to report to pioneers at Mesplaux Wood. Throughout this action, the CO of 1/4th South Lancashires, Lieutenant

Colonel Fairclough, rather than the CRE, took control of tactical matters. When Colonel Fairclough was killed by artillery fire on the 11th, Major E Fairclough took command; but when he was wounded on the 12th, command passed to Major Russell, OC 419 Field Company. 422 Field Company remained in Gorre Wood, where it strengthened defensive positions. They also prepared bridges for demolition, some of which were blown. In contrast with the generally high level of praise heaped on the German stormtroopers during this battle, one of the War Diaries was less complimentary, saying that there must have been 'great slaughter' 'owing to his formations'. The British artillery was 'excellent and greatly helped to force the enemy to retire about 700 [yards]'. The relief of the division was completed in the early hours of the 14th, and the engineers went into rest for ten days, which included parades and an inspection by M. Clemenceau, the French Prime Minister.[13]

For their actions, the RE received the following awards:[14]

Company	Bar to DSO	Bar to MC	MC	DCM	MSM
419	1	1	2	2	1
422				1	
423					

At the end of August 1918, 55th Division went on the offensive, starting with the capture of the Givenchy Craters. When those objectives were achieved, the engineers supported the consolidation so that German counter attacks could be repulsed with light casualties.

The division advanced fifty miles in the Final Hundred Days. The field companies supported the infantry with footbridges and more substantial pontoon bridges. They were also busy with road building or repairing to ensure the rapid movement of wheeled vehicles of the supply columns, the artillery and ambulances. They were also involved in the removal of booby traps and cataloguing abandoned German stores.

419 and 423 Companies noted the Armistice, but 422 did not think it was worth mentioning.[15]

Mining was an aspect of engineering and usually undertaken by special companies of pre-war miners or tunnellers. 423 Field Company commenced a mine on 4 April 1916. That December, three sappers were buried when a tunnel collapsed following a trench mortar burst in the gallery. All three were safely rescued but suffering from shock. 422 Field Company formed a tunnelling section in August 1916; but there are no mentions of its actions except that in August 1918, Sapper Cobb was sent to England for commissioning into a Tunnelling Company. Counter mining was equally important. So when, on 17 July 1916, a sapper reported the noise of picks and falling chalk in the proximity of two saps, the report was rapidly sent up to brigade with a request for a trained listener. For several days all engineering works were suspended while the listeners worked, but nothing was heard. Meanwhile, for the infantry who had to live in those trenches, the tension must have been immense.[16]

Managing the Field Companies

Strange as it may seem, in March 1916 the enlistment of a number of sappers expired: Private Gates left 419 Field Company 'on being due for discharge', together with three more from 422 Field Company. This was a peculiarity of the territorial's four year enlistment, extended by one year under wartime conditions. How many territorials exercised this right is unclear. Alternatively, they could have accepted a month's leave, taken another bounty and reengaged for another four years or the duration. The move towards conscription throughout 1916 meant that those soldiers could have been back in uniform soon, and under those conditions there was no guarantee which unit or theatre they would be sent to.[17]

The end of July and beginning of August 1916 was a difficult time for the OC of 419 Field Company. First of all, Sapper Rogers was found 'unacceptably drunk' on 25 July and on the 31st sentenced to seven days Field Punishment Number 1. Then, on 8 August, Lieutenant Hallas negligently discharged his automatic pistol, wounding Sapper Bate in the wrist and stomach. Hallas was removed to a field hospital and a board convened, which found Hallas guilty. Despite this, Hallas was not imprisoned: he was back in the front line supporting the Liverpool Scottish on the 11th. On the 16th the case was passed to a higher formation and Hallas was tried by General Court Martial. Nothing is mentioned of the case in the War Diary until 26 December 1916, when Hallas rejoined the company from the

Divisional School and the following day was transferred to the 423 Field Company. He later returned to 419 Field Company. In May 1917, the OC handed command of the company to Captain Parkinson who, three days later, injured himself in a fall from his horse, and Hallas found himself as acting OC. No punishment was recorded. He became Adjutant to the CRE and would be awarded the Military Cross.[18]

The most senior engineer fatality occurred when the OC of 423 Field Company, Major McNeill, was mortally wounded on 7 January 1917 by a shell blast while visiting front line trenches. He had only joined the company from the New Zealand Division in December. He is buried at Lijssenthoek Military Cemetery.[19]

At the end of September 1918, a conference of CREs was held to discuss:

1. Education of the men;
2. Ongoing work;
3. Arrangements in the case of a 'gradual enemy retirement'.

The first point is interesting because it indicated that the end of the war was approaching. After the Armistice, the BEF was not immediately disbanded. The reconstruction of France and Belgium was a pressing task with which the engineers assisted, while the army provided educational classes in preparation for the demobilisation of the sappers and their return to the civilian workplace.

Divisional Signal Company, Royal Engineers Signal Service

The divisional signal company was responsible for communications from battalions to the brigade and divisional headquarters. Battalions had their own signallers for their internal communications, under the command of the Battalion Signals Officer.[20]

Before the war, the Signal Service was considered to be one of the more proficient parts of the TF, mostly because its members were all employed in similar jobs for the railways or the General Post Office. (The GPO was responsible for telegraphs and telephones until they were separated and privatised as British Telecom.)[21]

According to Coop, the Company suffered one officer killed and three wounded, plus nine other ranks killed, fifty eight wounded and one missing, in just under three years. However, the War Diary suggests that there were far more casualties than that. It lists the first casualty on 4 April 1916, when an unnamed sapper was evacuated to hospital with a head wound. The following month, Lieutenant Hayward and another unnamed sapper were also evacuated. We know that Hayward returned to the Company about two months later, so it may be that Coop was only counting those wounded and discharged as a result of their wounds, rather than those who were able to return to duty. The War Diary lists the awards for gallantry awarded to the Company. Three were awarded the Distinguished Conduct Medal. There were five Military Crosses awarded to the officers, nineteen Military Medals awarded to the non-commissioned men, and five Mentioned in Dispatches.[22]

In 1914 a Divisional Signal Company consisted of five officers and 170 men. By 1918, it had increased to fifteen offices and 400 men. Although it was still called a company, it was closer to the size of a modern Royal Signals regiment. This shows the growing importance of communications throughout the war. Effective communications remained the biggest weakness in all armies throughout the war and the problem was never effectively resolved. Time and time again, delays in getting messages from the front line to the appropriate headquarters, and for that headquarters not only to react, but to get the men, supplies or material into position, allowed success to slip away.

Communication types can be divided into three types: electronic, visual and physical.

Airline was a bare wire supported on lightweight poles, in a manner similar to telegraph or telephone lines, while cable was an insulated cable laid on the ground. The *Field Service Pocket Book* gives a daily working figures of five miles of airline or between one and six miles of cable (depending on the terrain and the length of time the cable was intended to be laid) per day. During the war cable became dominant, as it could be buried for extra protection, but the skills of airline would be needed if the cable needed to cross roads or in the rear areas where the line less vulnerable to artillery fire.[23]

Cable was the main means of communications. Number 1 Section was divided into two Cable Sections, A and B, which grew in strength from forty nine to sixty eight during the war. A section contained the cable laying wagons; a third of the strength were drivers, and there were also a farrier sergeant and/or a shoeing smith, just to look after the horseshoes. There was very little alternative to these wagons until the movement phase in late 1918. The War Diary records their use once, on 25 June 1917.[24] Throughout the war, most cable was laid by hand, which was a slow, dangerous and time consuming task. As the war progressed, cables would be 'armoured' and laid in trenches six feet deep to protect them from artillery fire. The task of digging these usually fell to infantry working parties from units at 'rest'. Duplicate lines would also be laid, to provide 'built in redundancy'. Another protective measure used around Givenchy was to lay cables along the bed of the La Bassée Canal, which ran through the divisional area. The canal included many coarse fish for which Sergeant Taylor RFA, and colleagues fished in their spare time; passing infantry assisted by throwing Mills bombs into the canal, which were effective but also broke the cables.[25]

Numbers 2, 3 and 4 Sections supported the three infantry brigades and remained fairly consistent in their size, increasing from twenty seven to thirty men by the end of the war.

Wireless communications grew in importance and extra soldiers were added to the establishment from 1917 to assist in their operations, although the War Diary shows that wireless was in use by at least August 1916. Initially there were eighteen men commanded by a sergeant; during the war the number grew to sixty two under the command of a subaltern. These were not particularly portable sets and their use in the front line trenches was limited.

Visual communications remained important throughout the war, dangerous as that may seem. Heliographs and semaphore flags do not appear to have been widely used, but the use of point–to–point lights, both in daylight and at night, remained. By using a narrowly focused beam of light, the chance of it being seen by the enemy was reduced. The receiving station closest to the enemy, the manual stated, should be blocked from enemy sight by a bank or a captured blockhouse. The *Field Service Pocket Book* gives the following planning ranges 'in suitable weather':

- Heliograph – in practice the limitation is the intervisibility of stations
- Flags – 3 to 7 miles
- Lamp:
    - Limelight 10 to 15 miles
    - Begbie Lamp 5 to 8 miles.[26]

All of these systems had suitable operating ranges for the Western Front battles but were not always suitable for conditions in Flanders. The heliograph required reliable sunlight and flags required visibility, neither of which could be guaranteed.

For the physical delivery of messages, pigeons are today closely associated with communications in the Great War. The War Diary reported that, on 2 March 1916, Pioneer Pinkstone and his team arrived from 'J' Carrier Pigeon Service, part of VII Corps Signals.

Motor cycle despatch riders, the Don-R, were another role. In 1914 the Company was established at twelve corporals commanded by a sergeant, but no sappers. This reflected that pre-war the ability to drive or ride any motor vehicle was a relatively rare skill. By 1918, the number of Don-Rs had only increased to twenty, but significantly the rank of fourteen motor cyclists had been reduced to sappers. It was clearly no longer such a specialist skill.

Runners were the final physical means of delivering messages. The men could be drawn from a number of units; staging posts would be set up so that individual runners did not have to travel too far, could rest and take shelter.

The Signal Services on the Western Front

The War Diary commenced when the company was ordered overseas from its base at Larkhill in the early days of January, 1916: Major Oppenheim TD RE commanding. On 11 November 1916, Captain C E Tebbitt RE arrived to take command of the Company.[27]

The Company sailed from Southampton on 7 January 1916, arriving at Le Havre the following day and then made its way through France to Hallencourt, where it took over a signals office from Third Army Signals Company on the 14th. Men were dispatched on courses and the Company was reinforced by two teams from the Carrier Pigeon Service and lorry-borne electric lighting plant equipment – the old and the new side by side.[28] The Company provided both training to other units, for example teaching 'buzzer' work to the gunners of the 1/3rd West Lancashire Brigade, RFA, and sent men on courses. The Company also received officers from other Lancashire TF divisions, like Captain Lamb of 57th Divisional Signal Company. On 22 May, a Lieutenant Paddock from '3/1st West Lancashire Signal Company RE' reported for duty. '3/1st' indicates a third line or training unit, it would appear that Paddock was from a training unit; as he was not a second lieutenant, he was not straight out of training himself. On the 22nd, three second lieutenants arrived from 66th (Second East Lancashire) Company for 'a Course of Instruction'.[29]

As with the field companies, on 30 March 1916 the War Diary records the expiry of the time of six men. As they did not wish to re-engage, they were sent to the Base Depot, en route to England. Exactly what happened to them for the remainder of the war is not recorded, but as conscription would be introduced later that year, they were surely back in khaki and in France before the year was out.[30]

The reality of war was brought home to the company on 4 April 1916, when an unnamed sapper was taken to hospital with a shrapnel wound. The first fatality in France was recorded in the War Diary on 27 February 1917, when an unnamed soldier died of pneumonia. The CWGC records the death of Second Corporal George Harper on the 1st of the month. He was 24 and the son of James and Mary, of 103 Boundary Road, St Helens. It would be April 1918 before the first battlefield fatality was recorded: Lieutenant Arthur Beer MC, the 23 year old son of the widowed Lina Beer, of 11 Livingston Drive, Liverpool. Strangely, Beer was commissioned into the RFA, 275th Brigade, not RE, so it is not clear why he should be listed in this War Diary, unless he was the RFA Brigade Signal Officer.[31]

The War Diary makes no mention of the division's first battle, at Guillemont, in August 1916: it was only interested in recording when and where the communications were established. On 7 August, there were cable communications established between Divisional HQ and Arrowhead Copse and a visual station was established just south of Arrowhead Copse to Divisional HQ. There were, therefore, two means of communication between Divisional HQ and Arrowhead Copse. A wireless station was established at the foot of Maltz Horn Farm. Presumably another set was at Divisional HQ: if that was standard procedure, then there would be no need to put it in the War Diary. The following morning, at 4.30 am, cable communications were established between Maltz Horn Farm and Divisional HQ, at the cost of one sapper wounded. There were two types of communications established between the locations. On the 9th, there was yet more cabling to be laid, this time between Divisional HQ and Dublin Trench, and Dublin Trench up to Maltz Horn Farm, so there was yet more redundancy built into the system. Six days later, on the 15th, the division was relieved by 3rd Division and the Signals Office closed.

On 31 August, the Company moved to Bellevue Farm and opened their Signals Office at 2 pm, with communications established with the Advance HQs of 7th and 24th Divisions and XV Corps HQ; and by 7 pm with 166 Brigade. On the morning of 5 September 164 Brigade entered the line, relieving 17 Brigade of the 24th Division and the War Diary confirmed that communications were established with the left and right divisional Report Centres and the Artillery of 7th and 14th Divisions. All this was in preparation for the forthcoming attack at Ginchy, but the Germans did not let the preparations proceed unopposed. Shelling around the Divisional HQ was reported between 8.30 pm and 9.40 pm, damaging numerous cable routes, but without seriously effecting the divisional communications plan. However, these cable routes had to be repaired.

Early in September the whole process was repeated again for another attack. The Divisional Communications Plan consisted of visual and wireless stations on the west side of Longueval and the north point of Trônes Wood, working to Pommiers Redoubt. Runner relay posts were established between 164 Brigade and 16th Division for their attack on Ginchy, and between 165 Brigade and 1st Division for their attack on the east corner of High Wood and Wood Lane. The only reported failing in the system was for an hour around midday on the 10th, when both of the Trônes Wood stations were put out of action by enemy artillery. However, the fact that communications were only lost for an hour shows that they were doing all they could to create a robust network. The following day, the Company was relieved by the New Zealanders and 4th Division and the Signals Office was closed down. Six days later, Military Medals were awarded to seven other ranks for their efforts during the battle.[32]

On 24 September 1916 165 Brigade relieved 166 Brigade in preparation for their attack on Grid Trenches the following day. Runner relay posts were established on the Flers – Longueval– Bernafay Wood Road. There were visual stations at Longueval, York Trench and Pommiers Redoubt, with wireless stations at York Trench and near the junction of Switch Trench and the Longueval – Flers Road. On the 27th, when 164 Brigade relieved 166, a forward brigade signals office was opened as well as more advanced visual points for working back to Longueval. As was normal, there is no mention of the battle. On 10 October 1916, Corporal Boyce was awarded the DCM.[33]

There is a common conception that the army willingly turned a blind eye to under age boys joining up: 19 was the minimum age to serve overseas. However, the War Diary recorded the discovery of an under age solider on 18 October 1916. He was removed and sent to base. On 5 November 1917, another under age soldier was discovered, so this was not a unique incident.

The first fortnight of December was spent burying the VIII Corps Cable System, which cannot have been a pleasant task. In practice, the digging would have been done by 'resting' infantry, but even supervising the more technical aspects would have been cold and dangerous. Even these buried cable systems were not immune to shell fire; on 25 March 1917 part of the system was cut. Fortunately the signallers were able to switch to an old buried route, so communications were only lost for ten minutes.

In January and February 1917, a divisional school of signals was held at Kiekenpot, which included instruction on methods of communications with the division in mobile warfare. At least they were planning ahead.[34]

From March 1917 the Company entered its busiest period, if the entries in the War Diary are a guide. The Company was constantly engaged in burying armoured cables, establishing redundancy through multiple cable systems and repairing the damage inflicted by German artillery fire. The buried cables were in addition to airlines, wireless and visuals communications, runner relay posts and dispatch riders. On 17 June a motorcycle was destroyed when it was buried under a collapsed building and, at the same time, dispatch riders were held up by the intensity of German shelling. There was also a steady flow of wounded soldiers; one on the 20th, another on the 22nd and, the following day, Lieutenant Gilbert was gassed and evacuated. Disaster struck on 21 July when all the lines went down, due to an explosion at a dump. The following day, two officers and four soldiers were wounded by shell fire, one soldier died of his wounds and the following day a second died in hospital of his wounds.[35] From May 1917, the War Diary starts to mention the burying of armoured quad (four cables sheathed together as a single unit) cables. All of this effort in digging in fixed communications was all very good while the front line remained relatively stable, but the static phase broke down following the German 1918 Spring Offensive. Throughout June and July 1917, the War Diary reported almost daily cuts to the cables, to such an extent that days when the cables were NOT cut received a special mention!

Gas is mentioned for the first time on 3 June 1917. The shelling appears to have been focused on the two brigades in the front line, but it was enough to force the signallers to don their gas hoods. No casualties were reported. Communications by telephone were lost between 10.30 pm and 4.30 am the following morning, but the telegraph systems remained working. The cause of the lost communications is not specified; it is most likely that wearing gas hoods meant that they could not use the telephone. Gas was used again on 3 July, during which the first gas casualties were sustained; and again on 17 and 18 July, which caused further delays and two more casualties.

An innovation was the use of the Fullerphone. The cables used for telephone and telegraphs were single line and used an earth return. The electronic signal leaked out of the cables. The close proximity of the Germans mean that from 1915 they were able to use the Moritz set to listen to British communications – a significant leap forward in electronic warfare. Captain, later Major General, AC Fuller, RE invented the Fullerphone. Once set up, it was almost impossible to intercept and made the transmission of sensitive information secure for the first time.[36]

September saw the division out of the line to conduct a divisional 'tactical' (exercise) which included establishing communications by telephone, sounder and visual means. Towards the end of the month, on the 20th, the division attacked again, during which five soldiers were injured. A month later, three Military Medals were awarded.[37]

In the 1918 New Year's Honours Gazette, the Military Cross was awarded to Major Tebbitt, Captain Mount and Lieutenants Hayward and Doig.

432001 Serjeant T Westwell Royal Engineer Signal Service. The Distinguished Conduct Medal, Mentioned in Dispatches and Discharge papers, a pre-war Territorial (and maybe a Volunteer) in the West Lancashire Divisional Signal Company.

Three soldiers were Mentioned in Dispatches. Also in January, two infantry officers were attached to the Company 'for duty'; Lieutenants Brown, Loyal North Lancashire Regiment and Bowling, 5th Essex. Exactly what those infanteers were doing with the signal company was not recorded but they were likely regimental signal officers.[38]

In April, the Germans launched Operation GEORGETTE against the division. Although it held its ground, the infiltration of the division's positions meant that headquarters units had to take up arms. On 10 April Serjeant Thomas Westwell was awarded the Distinguished Conduct Medal 'for great courage and initiative in action under heavy shell fire'. The War Diary for the same day recorded that all the 'line were continuously broken during day and repaired'. It is likely the DCM was for his work dealing with the events recorded in the War Diary. Lieutenant May was awarded the Military Cross and Lieutenant Bellamy and Sergeant Smith were Mentioned in Dispatches for their efforts.[39]

Throughout the movement phase of the final Hundred Days, the War Diary's style does not change; it records the establishment of communications with the various brigades and the towns and villages occupied. The changing nature of warfare is not evident without a map to plot the advance from one town to the next.

Even the entry for 11 November 1918 hides the magnitude of the day:

'Divisional Hqrs closed down at BARRY opened same hour at CHAPELLE–A–WATTINES.
Communications established to all Brigades'.[40]

The Royal Field Artillery

The West Lancashire gunners served in the UK with 57th Division until September 1915, when they were attached to 2nd Canadian Division until 55th Division was reformed in January 1916.

On 15 May 1916, the RFA brigades were renumbered 275 to 278. The howitzers brigade had received a third battery, formerly known as B/85th Battery, which became R Battery. With the restructuring it became C/278.[41]

Title	Number (15 May 1916)	Comments	Commanding Officers (January 1916)	Batteries	Renumbered Batteries	Disbanding of 278th Brigade (23 May 1916)	6 gun Batteries (4 Oct 16)
1/1st	275th		Lt Col Osborn VD	1st	A/275th		
				2nd	B/275th		
				3rd	C/275th		
				8th	D/275th		
1/2nd	276th		Lt Col Topping DSO	9th	A/276th		Left Section C/276 to A/276. Right section C/276 to B/276. 530th How Bty as new C/276th
				10th	B/276th		
				11th	C/276th		
				7th	D/276th		
1/3rd	277th	Left January 1917	Lt Col J. P. Reynolds	12th	A/277th		
				13th	B/277th		
				14th	C/277th		
				R	D/277th		
1/4th (Howitzer)	278th	Broken up Oct 1916		7th	A/278th	D/276th	
				8th	B/278th	D/275th	
				R	C/278th	D/277th	

The Howitzer Battery spent January 1916 bringing drafts from the 3/2nd (West Lancashire) Brigade up to the required standard. Despite having enlisted in May 1915, the drivers had not been on a horse a dozen times. The gunners had trained for an hour a day for three months on a single gun, and that was an old 13-pounder gun, not 18-pounder. They also knew no morse code. They were posted to the Ammunition Colum until they were at the required standard. Another draft of eight men arrived at the beginning of February, from the 3/4th and 3/3rd Brigades. Three were from 1/4th Brigade, who had remained behind when the brigade sailed. There does not appear to have been any problems with the quality of this draft.[42]

In February 1916 the division relieved the 36th Division. When the divisional artillery took over responsibility for the Wailly sector from the French 88th Territorial Division, Divisional Artillery Order No 2 stated that tactical control would change at midnight on 15/16 February. The three brigades equipped with 18-pounder guns were assigned to either the Left or Right Group; the howitzers of 1/4th Brigade was unassigned. Divisional

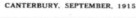

CANTERBURY, SEPTEMBER, 1915

Photo by]   Names (reading left to right)   [Moore, Canterbury

Seated—Capt. W. M. Cohan, Major G. B. Johnson, Major R. R. Heap, Lt.-Col. L. J. Osborn, Major G. L. Walker, Capt. Richards, R.A.M.C., Capt. J. T. Nesbitt, Capt A. F. Thomson.

Standing—Lieut. P. R. Playford, Lieut. E. R.B. Playford, Lieut. A. C. Forster, Lieut. W. Eills, Lieut. B. K. Ronald, Capt. Davey, A.V.C., Capt. W. W. Aikman, Lieut. J. R. Ritchie, Lieut. C. N. Cross, Lieut. C. M. S. Shore, Lieut. D. Brown, Lieut. W. W. Wadsworth, Lieut. L. C. Wall, Lieut. W. Beer.

The officers of 1/4th Brigade, RFA. (*Wadsworth*)

Artillery HQ was in Gouy-en-Artois. This arrangement into Groups was modified further in Artillery Order No. 4 of 23 February 1916. The three infantry brigades each occupied a sector with a supporting artillery brigade:[43]

	Right Sector	Centre Sector	Left Sector
Infantry Brigade	166th	164th	165th
Artillery Brigade	Right Group	Centre Group	Left Group
	1/1st WL RFA	1/2nd WL RFA	1/3rd WLRFA
	1/4th WL RFA (How) Less 7th Bty	7th Bty, 1/4th WL RFA (How)	4th N Midland (How)
	2nd Staffs Bty	3rd Staffs Bty	1st Staff Bty
May 1916[44]			
Infantry Brigade	None specified	None specified	None specified
Artillery Brigade	Right Group	Centre Group	Left Group
	A/275, B/275, C/275 Section A/278	B/278, C/276, B/276	A/125, A//277, C/278, C/277, B/277
	D/275 (How)	D/276 (How)	D/277 (How)
	Section A/278 Enfilade	Right Section A/276 Enfilade	Left Section A/276 Enfilade

March continued with the settling in process, including firing SOS rockets and testing the Begbie signalling lamps; but all was not going to plan. 1/1st Brigade reported an unsuccessful bombardment of a German blockhouse because the 8-inch howitzer did not fire and the 6-inch howitzers 'were all over the objective'. There was some way to go before the artillery would be able to provide the accurate support the infantry would need in the future.[45]

Not all of the artillery problems were the gunners' fault. In 1915 the so-called 'Shell Scandal' revealed that there were insufficient numbers of guns and shells; many of the latter were inadequate. It would be late in 1916 before the quality control of both guns and shells were adequately addressed.

On 3 September 1916, 277 Brigade reported that a premature explosion in a D Battery gun killed three men. The CWGC website only lists two killed around that date. Gunner Enstone, a 23 year old from West Hampstead,

London (a long way from West Lancashire) died on the 3rd, with Serjeant Brown dying two days later. There are no further biographical details of Brown. Part of the improvement was the arrival of the High Explosive No. 100 fuse, first used on 23 March 1916: They were reported most satisfactory, good detonation and pieces of shell blow back as much as 550 yards.[46]

Wire cutting was a critical function of the artillery. 3rd Battery conducted tests which were 'moderately satisfactory, shooting good'. Whether the infantry would agree was not, on this occasion, put to the test. The following month 1st Battery conducted further tests, including lashing the guns in place. It was found that the guns only shifted five minutes off target for the first two rounds and hardly any movement afterwards. Of the hundred rounds fired, only three or four were considered to explode 'high', which would have reduced the impact of the explosion on the wire. The results were considered satisfactory. The wire, which was twenty five yards deep, was reportedly cleared to a width of twenty five yards, although as the nearest Observation Post was 900 yards away how this conclusion was reached is unclear. However, the gunners were endeavouring to improve their skills.[47]

It was only natural that the Germans were not passive. On the same day that 3rd Battery tested its wire cutting abilities, fifty 5.9 inch shells were fired in retaliation but fortunately the British guns had already been moved. A week later another sixty shells also fell on 1st Battery's dummy positions, but the following day three bombs were dropped on the horse lines, killing or wounding thirteen of them. 277 Brigade reported a lucky 'blind' on 22 April 1916, when a German shell passed through the 14th Battery shell store, breaking the store open, and burying itself in the ground without exploding.[48]

An extra 575 shells were dumped in the 275 Battery gunlines on 15 June 1916, a sure sign of imminent operations, which commenced on 'U' Day, on the 24th. Fire missions continued until the 29th, with only 'slight' retaliation. The Divisional Artillery Order No. 34 (which was headed <u>NOT TO GO OUT OF THE POSSESSION OF AN OFFICER</u>), dated 23 June 1916, specified targets, timings, rates of fire and artillery to be used for the Battle of the Somme. 276 Brigade, for example, expended 1400 shrapnel rounds to cut fifty yards through the German wire.[49] Although the division's infantry were not involved in the First Day of the Somme, the artillery fired a diversionary bombardment.

The artillery played a key role in the division's attacks at Guillemont during August 1916. 275 Brigade's War Diary mentions the village for the first time on 3 August 1916, stating: 'All prominent points near Guillemont to be registered'. 275, 276 and 277 Brigades conducted fire missions, building up to the 7th, when a series of 'Chinese attacks' were fired. These consisted of a couple of minutes of fire, a pause of a minute or two to lure the Germans back into the trenches, and then further fire to catch the Germans in the open. Whether or not this tactic worked is unclear, but it certainly confused the Germans as to if and when an attack was to be launched. It also provoked a German response, with 277 Brigade being heavily shelled by German counter battery fire later that day. The divisional attack on Guillemont on 8 August is simply noted by 275 Brigade:

Operations commenced on GUILLEMONT
Result – very slight advance in a few odd places. 1/8th Irish advanced into GUILLEMONT but were cut off.

And the following day:

Operations. Result unsuccessful.

277 Battery did not mention the progress of the battle at all until an entry at 8 am on the 9th saying: 'All further operations cancelled. Personnel to rest.' The Diary was more concerned with the gallantry of Gunner AV Chennel from D Battery, for putting out a fire which had started amongst a hundred charges. On 5 August 1916, 277 Battery also recorded 'Capt. J. G. Brocklebank killed', which stands out amongst the otherwise largely technical entries.[50]

In October 1916, the three four-gun-battery structure was changed to two, six gun batteries. 277 Brigade disbanded A Battery into B and C Batteries. Two days later, a six gun battery from 278 Brigade arrived to re-form A/277. It also saw the disbandment of 278 (Howitzer) Brigade. The final entry in the War Dairy records how the personnel, equipment, horses and vehicles were transferred to 277 Brigade, with the exception of the CO, Lieutenant Colonel Morton, who took command of the Divisional Ammunition Column.[51]

September saw operations around Flers, which were 'successful'. 277 Brigade reported the use of 'Tanks' for the first time on 15 September ('proving a great success'). On the 16th, Martinpuich was taken and a line north of Flers established. Two SOS signals were received during the night of the 19/20 September. On the first occasion the 'Enemy did not reach our trenches', which defence was helped by a defensive barrage; but on the second occasion a small portion of the trench was lost.[52]

Aerial observation was another important tool in a war where direct observation of the enemy was impossible. The howitzers used this technique for the first time on 5 March 1916 but were hampered by unfavourable weather conditions: snow in the morning obscured ground signals, while cloud in the afternoon prevented target identification. A far more successful fire mission was conducted on 1 April 1916, when considerable damage was done to gun emplacements and two ammunition dumps were blown up, for which 8 Battery received a congratulatory telegram. 277 Brigade used aerial observation to register their guns around Guillemont in August 1916; and on 20 December 1916, D/275 bombarded a German battery with 'Several O.K's received' from the observing aeroplane correcting the fall of shot.[53]

Support of trench raids was another important task. On 15 October, 275 Brigade failed to cut the wire and the raid failed. In November, though, they supported two successful trench raids, one each by 166 and 165 Brigades. Artillery support cleared the way. The second November raid did not mention wire cutting, but recorded a successful barrage, which may have referred to a box barrage in which the artillery isolated the area to be raided by firing on three sides of a rectangle, while the infantry raided the fourth. Another raid by 1/9th King's on 4 March 1917 was similarly successful, but again only refers to a bombardment rather than a wire cutting pre-raid barrage.

In contrast, 276 Brigade's War Diary does not record the outcome of trench raids but does include the artillery orders. So, for example, on the night of 24th/25th June 1917, 1/9th King's prepared to 'rush' German working parties who were wiring a disused trench, to kill or capture the Germans, destroy the trenches and bring back unit identification. The signal for the raid would be three batteries opening fire (for twenty minutes) on the German wire, while a fourth battery fired on a depth position. 277 Brigade supported a raid by 200 men of the 1/4th King's Own on a front 200 yards wide during the night of 23 December 1916. The wire was cut over two days before the attack. For the raid itself, a box barrage isolated the German positions while the infantry advanced behind a creeping barrage. Creeping barrages had been experimented with since 1915, a procedure in which the artillery advanced at a set rate while the infantry followed close to the 'line' of shells, in theory, provided that the infantry could keep up. The problem was that the infantry could not communicate to the gun lines to slow down the rate of advance if they were held up. On this occasion, the artillery was pleased with its results: 'Both of these were very effective'.[54]

April 1917 saw a new term enter the artillery's lexicon, the hurricane barrage. 275 Brigade fired three of these that month. These were short, intense barrages, measured in hours or even minutes rather than days. The length of barrages had been steadily increasing from 1915 into 1916 following the failure of the 1915 battles, which were attributed to a lack of artillery support: insufficient guns, insufficient shells, high failure rates of the shells and difficulties in accurately targeting by indirect fire all reduced the 'weight' of fire which could be delivered. By 1917, more guns, more shells, better quality shells and improved target identification techniques meant that the required 'weight' of fire could be delivered in a more concentrated format It also meant that fewer shells had to be fired, which reduced wear and tear on the gun barrels and recoil systems, all of which were economically advantageous. On 5 April 1917 a hurricane barrage was fired that was only three minutes long.[55]

The Third Battle of Ypres was, in the words of Wadsworth, 'very definitely laid out', too much so in his own mind. Lieutenant Evans, attached to an Infantry Brigade HQ as a Forward Observation Officer (FOO), recalled:

The silence before the Zero Hour was intense; everybody lived in a peculiar atmosphere of expectation. Then Hell was let loose – it was a magnificent sight.

At this moment I fully realised the Infantryman's sense of security in the guns. Thousands of guns behind were doing their utmost, while their eggs were laid with beautiful precision beyond us.

The Infantry went over in magnificent style, glad to get on with the job. Details are too ghastly to record – even to recall.

The infantry gained their initial objectives, but thereafter the ability of the artillery to support the infantry was curtailed. Telephone cables were broken, so the opportunity to shell German infantry massing for a counter attack was lost. One fire mission (which was transmitted by Lucas lamps) was sent as some of the guns were moving forward; all the available guns fired a barrage but this was 'sadly too weak' to achieved the desired effect.[56]

From Ypres, 55th Division moved to the Cambrai sector to hold a part of the line during the battle which would be launched there on 20 November 1917. At the very end of November 1917, there was a marked increase in enemy artillery action against the division. This was incorrectly interpreted as the Germans registering new guns. However, following a preparatory barrage, the German infantry attacked through the morning mist on the 30th and infiltrated the division's rear areas. The guns were manned until the infantry retired past them; the guns were then stripped of their breachblocks and dial sights before they were abandoned. The 275 Brigade War Diary listed the guns lost, the dead, wounded and missing amongst the crews, all in a usual matter-of-fact style, which understates the severity of that day. 276 Brigade hardly mentioned the attack, just: 'Enemy attacked BIRDCAGE in conjunction with attack further North'. The reader would hardly know the extent of the disaster unfolding around the division. The following day the situation was gradually stabilised and on 3 December the infantry were relieved, although the artillery remained in post.[57]

During this desperate action, the Victoria Cross was won by Sergeant Cyril Gourley, D/276 Battery. Two 4.5 inch howitzers and the Liverpool Rifles held Little Priel Farm. About 7.30 am, with the Section Commander, Lieutenant Ridealgh seriously wounded, the howitzers were in danger of being overrun, so they started firing directly at the Germans over open sights. Eventually the guns had to be abandoned and the crews withdrew to the battery HQ. There Gourley was ordered to collect all available men, recover the guns and keep them firing. Despite the enemy being as close as 300 yards, he and the crew kept a gun firing throughout the day.

Sergeant Gourley was from Wavertree, Liverpool, a graduate of the University of Liverpool and before the war an employee of Liverpool shipping firm Alfred Holts and Co. He had won the MM in July 1917 for putting out a fire near to an ammunition dump. He was commissioned in 1918 and promoted to captain in 1919, just before the division was demobilised. Lieutenant Samuel Wallace, 63rd Brigade RFA, won a VC on 20 November 1917 in similar circumstances to Gourley's. Theirs were the first artillery VCs won on the Western Front since 1914, which shows the severity of the fighting amongst the gunlines.[58]

After Cambrai, new guns and equipment were received, along with fifty reinforcements. In the last days of January 1918 275 Brigade was able to conduct a Field Day. Training continued into February, including cooperation with aeroplanes. A hundred remounts arrived to make the brigade mobile again, in time to relieve other brigades in the front at Givenchy.[59]

A new technique learnt early in 1918 was that of anti-tank gunnery. 276 Brigade placed three 18-pounder guns in this role, which required them to be positioned in and amongst the infantry. Deployments like this had not been seen since 1914.[60] Significantly, there were lectures on counter battery work and on Defence of the Line at divisional and (infantry) brigade level. It was a sign of a raising expectation of a German offensive. There was an alarm on 10 March, so 1,200 rounds of 18lb and 240 rounds of 4.5 inch shells were fired to spoil the attack. This was the pattern for the month. Despite this, German artillery was observed concentrating in the front on the 20th. The situation quietened in early April, but on the 9th there was an intense bombardment followed by the German attack, opening what would become the Battle of the Lys. Casualties were considerably lighter than following Cambrai, and over the coming week 275 Brigade only reported three guns lost, all from B Battery and all on the 14th. The War Diary noted that they suffered heavy artillery fire, so it is likely that the guns were destroyed by that rather than overrun. The lessons from the previous November had been learnt. 276 Brigade took a heavier blow. The Germans nearly reached the forward gun of A Battery before being forced back. They were not out of trouble and by the end of the day all of the battery's guns were destroyed and the gunners were in the trenches with the infantry. They, and whatever material could be salvaged, were later ordered back to the wagon lines. D Battery was also required to bring back its forward gun to the main position.[61]

17 April was 'exceptionally quiet', but on the 18th there was another German attack across the whole divisional front – Wadsworth described this as 'The Worst of All'. Thirteen guns would be knocked out that day; but

B and C Batteries, 275 Brigade, were able to pull back to new positions. Again, no guns seem to have been overrun or lost to the Germans. The death of Major Eills on 9 April has already been described in Chapter 3. Two further majors were killed. According to *1st West Lancashire Brigade*, Major George Johnson DSO, of Stanhope House, Woolton, Liverpool (described as 'the greatest loss that the Brigade had suffered'), and the more recently arrived Major Victor Greenwood, son of John, of 'Iddesleigh', Park Road, Southport, and husband of Geraldine.

The Germans offensive was running out of momentum and the 19th was quiet again; on the 20th the division went onto the offensive. The division's sector had held while all about had given way and, unlike the previous autumn, the artillery had done so without abandoning guns to the advancing Germans. Between 9 and 18 April, 275 Brigade alone suffered losses of twenty out of twenty eight officers and 250 men.[62]

The summer months and on into September were dominated by War Diary entries starting: 'Situation Generally Quiet', interspaced with remarks about occasional raids or harassing fire. Then, on the last day of September, 164 Brigade attacked and that night A and D Batteries 275 Brigade moved forward. It was an indication that there was a return to manoeuvre warfare on the French Flanders front, with the Germans retiring. On 1 October, 275 Brigade's headquarters moved to Le Preol and the next day:

> Barrage put down in support of Infantry attack on LA BASSÉE – AUBERS – FROMELLES Line, all objectives gained, posts pushed forward to B13 b & d and along LA BASSÉE – HAUBOURDING Road. Btys moved forward to cover advance of Infantry.

276 Brigade reported that the enemy had withdrawn the following day. A Battery and a section of D Battery were put under direct control of the infantry advance guard. Under the 'Place' column in the diary, the Brigade was listed as being in 'France', then 'France and Belgium', then just 'The Field', as the movement phase gained pace again.[63]

There would be delays, such as on the approach to Tournai, when all the artillery had to be brought up to support the infantry advance, but the optimism can be shown by the creation of a flying column, Stockwell's Force, which included A/275 Battery. Despite this movement phase, registration and wire cutting still had to be carried out, whilst on occasion German artillery could be very active. Tournai was abandoned by the Germans on 8 November, and the following day the infantry were reported as having difficulties keeping up with their retreat.[64]

The Armistice came as a surprise. In 275 Brigade: 'Men cried with joy, drivers kissed their horses, all were overcome with a sense of relief. But our thoughts were with our comrades who could not share our joys.' They moved into billets in St Antoine, where they remained for the week. 276 Brigade concentrated in Maffles.[65]

Before ending this section, it should be noted that Wadsworth highlighted the role of the RFA Signallers several times throughout his work. One signaller specifically named was Gunner Shearman who, being underage, refused the chance to be sent home, and was killed a few weeks later. The CWGC gives his age as 19, so he must have been only just short of that age when he turned down the opportunity to return home. He is listed as the son of Edward and Jean, of 114 Beainerd Street, Tuebrook, Liverpool.

Royal Artillery Signallers, summer camp 1913. Not necessarily from West Lancashire, but they are showing the dress and equipment used.

In the Ypres Salient during late 1917, the signallers were 'among the first to be affected by all the shelling on the road. No one did more walking about in the open than the telephonists.' Gunner Cargill would be awarded the Military Medal for doing just this. Wadsworth described 18 April 1918 as 'the worst of all', and he named eleven signallers for their efforts that day.[66]

Divisional Ammunition Column[67]

On mobilisation, each of the four RFA brigades included an integral Brigade Ammunition Column, which were combined into the 55th Divisional Ammunition Column on 18 May 1916. These brigade columns do get the occasional mention in the War Diaries; but they are dominated by fire missions, targets and technical innovations, rather than routine matters like supply.

With the re-formation of the division, it received the former Lahore Divisional Ammunition Column. Obviously, those men were not Liverpool Territorials, although there is no indication that any of the soldiers were Indian. Mostly likely, the West Lancashire Division took over the vehicles which the Lahore Division had left behind when it sailed to Mesopotamia in 1915.

The first entry in the DAC's War Dairy, for 11 January 1916, describes the routine work it undertook:

Ordered to fill up with ammunition and hand grenades, bombs, etc.
Received 856 Rounds of 18 Pr Shrapnel 44 Rounds 18 Pr HE
160 Rounds 4.5″ Howitzer Lyddite 120000 Rounds SAA[68]

The delivery of ammunition was not the only role undertaken, as is shown by the circumstance behind the first fatality in 55th DAC. Driver T Burman died of wounds on 29 April 1916 at 19th Casualty Clearing Station in Doullens. The injuries were sustained while burying telephone cables for an artillery brigade.

In contrast with the RFA War Diaries, that of the DAC is dominated by the movement of personnel. The reader gets the impression that it was used as a holding unit for officers and men before they were posted on. There are relatively few entries about the loads carried. There was a vital requirement to move ammunitions forward to where it was needed, either at a front line trench or to the gun positions. In common with the 55th Divisional Supply Column, supply was routine business and did not warrant mention in the War Diary.

Wadsworth gives more colour to the work of the drivers (both the DAC and for moving the guns) and compliments them thus: 'The physical strain of keeping up the supply of ammunition was, if anything, greater than the strain of firing it off'. Half asleep drivers were able to rely on their horses returning to the horse lines on their own initiative (obviously something not possible with a motor vehicle) and, on one occasion at Ypres, when the drivers dismounted for coffee, the horses decided to continue home without them. During the Battle of Flers in mid-September 1916, the dry summer weather abruptly ended. The mud contributed to the congestion; one ammunition delivery set out at 11 pm, only to return at 8.30 am the following morning. July 1917 in the Ypres Salient was apparently the worst, and Wadsworth thought 'it was a wonder that any transport managed to get through at all'. One fatality was Lieutenant Patrick Playford, a 25-year-old from Bognor in Sussex, described by Wadsworth as one of the 'old officers'. Realising one of his men was missing after delivering their load of ammunition, Playford returned to the front to find the missing man, but was killed by a German shell. In August 1917, in the second phase of the Third Battle of Ypres, pack-saddles were issued for the first time, which were more useful in the muddy conditions.[69]

Royal Army Medical Corps[70]

Three Field Ambulances (FAs) supported the division, two of which were from West Lancashire, the 1/3rd and the 2/1st (West Lancashire). The third was from Wessex and so sits outside this study.

'Ambulance' referred not merely to the vehicles but to a mixed organisation of stretcher bearers and tents, where medical procedures could be conducted. Each field ambulance consisted of about ten officers and 224 men in three sections (A, B and C), each section with a bearer and tented sub section.

The Field Ambulance was the second RAMC facility that a casualty would likely pass through, and the third stage of medical care if you include 'self-

Four medics from 1/3rd (West Lancashire) Field Ambulance. At least three of them are wearing Imperial Service broaches, indicating they are Territorials who volunteered for overseas operations. None appear to wear T-titles.

help' basic first aid by the individual or by nearby soldiers. Triage, the process of prioritising casualties for treatment, would be conducted at first by stretcher bearers, either regimental or from a bearer section of the field ambulance. They would assesses whether or not the casualty would make it back to the Regimental Aid Post (RAP) and the care of the Regimental Medical Officer (RMO). From there, casualties were evacuated back to a tented sub section of the field ambulance, then to a Main Dressing Station (although there could be an intermediate Advanced Dressing Station). Casualty Clearing Stations would be the first permanent hospital they encountered, where more complicated procedures could be conducted. From there, the casualty moved to Base Hospitals on the French coast and then to a General Hospital in the UK. How far down the evacuation chain a casualty went would depend on their injury, the stage of the war and the prevailing operational conditions: in August 1914, hospital ships were sailing directly into Liverpool.[71] It was realised that more lives could be saved by conducting more procedures closer to the front line. This was only possible when the techniques and trained staff were available, and had to be off-set by the risk of losing expensively trained personnel to enemy action. A FA was established to handle 150 casualties. During a quiet period, the casualty could expect a good level of care and attention by the RAP and at the FA, but during an offensive the FA would rapidly become overloaded, so there was an increased emphasis on evacuating the casualty as quickly as possible after a minimal amount of stabilising care.

Private, West Lancashire RAMC. A respectable member of the RAMC, as shown by his shoulder title.

The Field Ambulance was responsible for the evacuation chain from the Regimental Aid Post to the Main Dressing Station. This could mean stretcher bearers (including establishing bearer relay posts where they could rest and exchange casualties) to the field ambulance and establishing an exchange point on to ambulances (motor or horse) for the rearward journey. The field ambulance could also establish walking wounded collection stations for those who did not need a stretcher, and a 'moribund' ward for those to whom all that could be done had been done as the casualty would not survive the next stage of the rearward journey.

Both field ambulances left Larkhill for France on 14 January 1916. As was common with many territorial units, the pre-deployment OC, Major (Temporary Lieutenant Colonel) WT Blackledge, handed over command of the 2/1st to Major Wood, also a territorial. Wood was promoted to lieutenant colonel on 23 June.[72]

The 1/3rd Field Ambulance was commanded by Lieutenant Colonel A Gordon Gullan. There is no evidence as to whether he was a territorial or regular. He commanded the field ambulance until probably 14 July 1916, when he was evacuated to 37 CCS with an unspecified condition. The Senior Major, R Coffey TD, took command; this appointment became permanent in October, when he was promoted to lieutenant colonel.[73]

The 2/1st Field Ambulance establishment was given as ten officers and 219 men, RAMC and ASC, with fifty three horses and seventeen wagons. The three sections were commanded by a captain (Stott, Walker and Reed respectively) and assisted by two lieutenants. By the end of January, the 2/1st had established a hospital in Merelessart under the charge of C Section. They did not stay there long, and from the middle of February an

Three long-serving RAMC territoritals. Taken during what appears to be a pre-war summer camp, in both Home Service and Service Dress uniforms.

Advanced Dressing Station (ADS) under C Section was established at Beaumetz, while the remainder of the field ambulance was located at Couturelle. The ADS took over a large house next to the town hall and set about making alterations. A 'large opening' was made and sandbagged, and steps built down into the cellar where the ADS operated.

Lieutenant Shields was attached to 1/5th King's to relieve their RMO from 24 January 1916. The field ambulances acted as a reserve of medical officers who could stand in for a RMO during their leave, for example. On 20 and 21 February, three further officers were detached to 1/7th King's, 1/4th King's Own and 2nd (North Midlands) Brigade RFA (then part of the division). This reduced the available medical officers from ten to six, which must have impacted on the quality and quantity of medical care that could be provided; but it illustrates the emphasis on providing medical care as far forward as possible. MOs were not just attached temporarily. Lieutenant Levene joined the 2/1st on 21 February 1916 but on 7 March was permanently posted to 2/5th Lancashire Fusiliers as their RMO. It was not only the officers treated thus: on 11 March 1916, Private AT Bagnall was promoted to corporal and permanently posted to 1/5th King's on 'Water Duties'.

Expiration of service during the war has been noted in Royal Engineer field and signal companies. QMS Yorke and Sergeant Andrews were both granted one month's leave at their expiration of service on the 23 and 24 March 1916 respectively. Both returned in April. At the end of April 1917, Driver G Large ASC and Private T Bromilow RAMC were both 'retained in the Service under Military Service Act (1916). These were pre-war territorials whose term of service had expired but, with conscription now in force, could hardly be released from the service. There were three similar entries at the end of May.

Field ambulances had to deal with the full range of medical conditions, not just battlefield casualties. In April 1916, a trooper of the North Irish Horse was brought into the 2/1st from 1/3rd Field Ambulance with 'delirious tremors'. After being observed for three days, his condition worsened and he was despatched to the CCS where Cerebro Spinal Meningitis (CSM) was diagnosed.[74] At the same time, a private from 1/8th King's was admitted with acute rheumatism, which was also subsequently diagnosed as CSM. A third case, this time a driver from 1/4th Brigade RFA, was admitted with a history of epileptic fits, but on this occasion it was determined not to be CSM. After the first case, the building, personnel and patients were put out of bounds; but following the second case full quarantine procedures were introduced. A special isolation hut was used, but when the number of contacts reached fifty, tents were erected in an isolated area. Throat swabs of the nursing orderlies were taken, all of which proved negative, whilst all fifty were ordered to gargle 'insufflations of saline' three times a day. The outbreak was contained. What this incident shows is not just the importance of non-battlefield medical procedures in an environment where the images of battlefield casualties dominate, but also the potential degradation of capability from disease: for two confirmed cases, fifty personnel were 'out of action' and if the contagion had spread further the degradation would have increased significantly.

A monthly return for April 1916 lists, by day, the number of officers and men who remained injured in the Divisional Rest Station (not the number admitted). There were between six and eleven sick officers and one or two injured officers. For the other ranks, there were between 130 and 180 sick and between one and fourteen wounded at any one time. There were special columns for scabies and trench foot. Throughout the month there were no cases of trenchfoot or scabies amongst the officers, but amongst the other ranks there were between seventeen and sixty-four scabies cases. 2/1st Field Ambulance also held between one and fifteen sick other ranks. It also dealt with what was probably one wounded other rank on two consecutive days, and two cases of scabies over two and three consecutive days. The complete absence of trench foot is noticeable and goes against the popular image of an army constantly suffering from that debilitating condition. This could be as a result of the spring weather, but it also reflects improvements in treating the condition – Captain Noel Chavasse, RMO with 1/10th King's, suggests that after the winter of 1914/15 trench foot was no longer a major problem. A rare exception occurred when the 3/1st recorded five cases for January 1918 'due to the bad weather…. none of them severe'. May's monthly return did not even bother with a column for trench foot. Scabies, which does not appear in the popular image, was a far greater concern, and the Divisional Sanitation Section (discussed below) was charged with disinfecting hundreds of scabies–infected blankets. 1/3rd Field Ambulance reported its patients in a different format. At the end of January 1916 it had 157 cases, of which eight four were scabies. Fifty scabies cases had been discharged, together with seven to either a CCS or a Stationary Hospital, two gonorrhoea and nephritis cases, and one each of 'paraphismosis with suppurations', myalgia and influenza. Again, scabies, not trench foot, is the dominant problem, although by 12 February it was influenza which was causing most concern.

Disease was also a constant threat to the field ambulance personnel. Twenty one year old Private Norman Laycock of St Helens was admitted to hospital on 9 June 1917 and was evacuated the same day to a CSS. He died on the 11th in Number 2 Canadian General Hospital of septicaemia, although his death was not recorded in the War Diary until the 19th.[75]

In late June 1916, 2/1st Field Ambulance moved to Gouy and were unaffected by the first day of the Somme. There the tented sub sections were established, while the bearer sections were co-located with their infantry brigades in Happy Valley. Five days later, these Bearer Sections were reinforced with twenty five men and were distributed throughout the reserve position, Dublin Trench, to the RMOs or to one of three Collecting Posts. This was a sure sign that an offensive was due. The battle itself is not directly referred to in the War Diary, but 2/1st Field Ambulance reported two killed and nine wounded 'whilst bearing from Reg. Aid Posts to RAMC Collecting Posts in advance of DUBLIN TRENCH'. Privates Harold Cooke and Thomas Smith are both commemorated on the Thiepval Memorial.[76]

Late September 1916 saw the 1/3rd Field Ambulance supporting operations from The Quarry and The Shrine as the Evacuating Field Ambulance, with the stretcher bearers from the other two field ambulances under their command. An officer and forty men were placed in support of the Ambulance Wagon Rendezvous at Longueval and the most advanced bearer post on the Flers road. The rendezvous posts were instructed to be as far forward as possible, thereby reducing the distance a casualty had to be carried. Each RAP received another four stretcher bearers, but with orders that they were only to be used forward of the RAP in an emergency. The Advanced Dressing Station at The Shrine was reinforced with an officer and seventy one men from a tented sub section, while 38 CCS at The Quarry was reinforced with three officers and twenty three men. There were nine horse drawn ambulances, which worked in three eight hour shifts. The stretcher bearers worked twelve hours shifts, six in the forward areas and a further six back at The Shrine, where the work was, presumably, less onerous.

Even these provisions were inadequate. A report was received that large numbers of casualties from 41st Division needed recovering. Additional stretcher bearers were requested: an officer, one sergeant and 135 men arrived from the other two field ambulances. About seventy casualties were recovered. A further hundred stretcher bearers were requested, which came from 1/10th King's. The horse and motor ambulances were supplemented with two Ford cars between The Shrine and the Ambulance Wagon Rendezvous, but when the rain fell the road became slippery and a Ford had to be dragged up the hill between The Shrine and Montauban by a caterpillar tractor. There was also insufficient accommodation in the dugouts at The Shrine. A tunnelling company arrived to increase capacity by means of six shelters, each accommodating four lying cases. After ten days of working under these extreme conditions, the field ambulances were relieved. No casualties were reported.

October saw the field ambulances in Poperinghe, where they took over from 29th Division and may well have met fellow West Lancashire Territorials in 87th Field Ambulance (formerly the 1/1st). An Advanced Dressing Station was located in the town's prison and Casualty Collecting Posts were at Potijze and on the Menin Road; the latter included an Advance Post close to the Regimental Aid Posts. A Main Dressing Station was located at Red Farm. Initially there was a scabies hospital at L' Ebbe Farm, but this was closed, cleaned and re-opened as a hospital for all skin conditions other than scabies.

On 13 November, Captain Chavasse VC MC was posted to 2/1st Field Ambulance, while Captain Rusby took over his duties as RMO with 1/10th King's. At the end of the month, Chavasse took over the L' Ebbe Farm skin hospital for a month, after which Chavasse returned to the Liverpool Scottish and Rusby returned to the 2/1st. Chavasse did not find this an enjoyable experience and he missed being with his men. He had been critical of the inability of the field ambulances to remove casualties from the RAPs fast enough. He wrote to his superiors expressing his concerns and suggesting improvements. This was not well received and as a result he and the other RMOs had to spend time in the field ambulances: Chavasse arrived under a cloud. He thought the field ambulances no place for young men of action, but suitable for older, married men with families.

2/1st's War Diary makes a lot more reference to soldiers than is commonly found in such documents. In early June 1917, for example, it recorded that leave to England was granted to other ranks, eight men were granted their first Good Conduct Badge, five were appointed First Class Nursing Orderlies and granted Third Rate Corps pay, one was promoted to lance corporal (unpaid) and another was detached to work with 1/4th King's Own. All were individually named, with their rank and number.

By the end of July 1917 there were preparations for the division's next offensive, at Ypres: three officers and ninety-eight men from the RAMC; three horse transport from the ASC plus two horse ambulances; eleven motor transport from the ASC plus seven motor ambulances from the 2/1st, concentrated with parties from the other two field ambulance. These were then divided between Wieltje, St Jean and Potijze Chateau bearer relay posts. From there, casualties were conveyed to the Main Dressing Station at Red Farm by motor ambulance. The 1/3rd concentrated three bearer officers and ninety other ranks, and four tented sub section officers and eighteen other ranks. There were also three horse and four motor ambulances, one water cart and a motorcycle. Almost as soon as the offensive began, it started to rain, making the ground soft and muddy; the stretcher bearers' operating conditions thus made even more difficult than normal. According to the 1/3rd, they 'had a rough time [due to the rain] and a big percentage of the Bearers lost their equipment during the time they were in action. I suggest that in future engagements they be sent forward with rations water bottles and anti-gas appliances and belts and haversacks.' According to the 2/1st, the rain turned the land into a 'veritable quagmire of mud + water' until they were relieved by stretcher bearers from 36th Division's Field Ambulances.

2/1st Field Ambulance suffered one killed and three wounded, the fatality being 26 year old Private George Earl of 1 Tunstall Street, Earle Road, Liverpool. The Field Ambulance also sent Captain Morrison RAMC to 1/10th King's, where their RMO, Captain Chavasse RAMC, was 'severely wounded'. Chavasse would, unfortunately, never recover. He was awarded a Bar to his VC, making him the second of only three to achieve this in the history of the award. On this occasion it was for his 'conspicuous gallantry and undaunted devotion' between 31 July and 2 August 1917, during which time he refused to leave his post after receiving a head injury early in the battle. On 2 August a German shell exploded in the doorway of the bunker which he was using as his RAP, mortally wounding him. He was treated initially by the 46th Field Ambulance, which was commanded by Lieutenant Colonel Martin-Leake, the first recipient of the VC and Bar. Chavasse died on 4th August and is buried in Brandhoek New Military Cemetery, not far from that of his soldier-servant, 20 year old 356629 Private Rudd.[77]

Mid September saw the three field ambulances returning to Ypres, where they relieved the ambulances based around Wieltje and the Advanced Dressing Station at St Jean. Four evacuation routes were established between Pond Farm, Bank Farm, Pommern Redoubt and Plum Farm back to Wieltje, where there was also a walking wounded collection post. By the 19th there were ten officers and 472 stretcher bearers from the field ambulances, plus bearers from 1/10th King's and 1/5th South Lancashires. The fighting was 'fierce and casualties came with great regularity', although they were mostly German. Private Woodard was killed and four more wounded. On the 23rd, the field ambulances were relieved and re-joined the division near Watou for training.

While in Belgium, 2/1st Field Ambulance had brought land under cultivation by digging, manuring (probably from their own stables), watering

Chavasse and Rudd. Although Chavasse's exploits are well recorded, less well recorded is the actions of officers' soldier servants, like Rudd, who experienced many of the same dangers.

and planting seeds. What happened to the gardens when they left Belgium us not recorded.

On 20 November 1917 the Germans launched their counter-attack to the offensive at Cambrai. 1/3rd Field Ambulance's War Diary entry commences with 'The Battle began early this morning'. The motor ambulances were able to get right up to the RAPs to evacuate the casualties and ensured that there was no congestion there. A Walking Wounded Dressing Station was served by ten lorries, with ten more in reserve but not needed. The severity of the fighting in those desperate days, which is common in most accounts, is absent in the field ambulances' accounts.

Major General Wright of the United States Army visited the division on 17 October 1917 and he inspected the 2/1st Field Ambulance and the divisional rest station. Four days later he returned. This visit appears to have paved the way for American medical officers to be attached to the field ambulances, starting with First Lieutenant ML Allen, who arrived on 11 January 1918. He was replaced on the 19th by First Lieutenant HF

Bailey until the 24th. A third officer, Lieutenant Goldman arrived on 18 March. The 3/1st Field Ambulance also received Americans on attachment, commencing with Lieutenant EE Thomas, who arrived from 1/7th King's on 21 February, departing on 6 March to 55th Battalion Machine Gun Corps. The following day, 1st Lieutenant DF Mathias left the 3/1st (his arrival was not noted) for 1/7th King's.

March and April 1918 saw pressure increasing on the division. On 2 April the field ambulances received secret instructions on where to concentrate should there be a general withdrawal. This is the first time such instructions were recorded that indicate that it was a possibility. On the night of the 8th and 9th April, the 2/1st Field Ambulance reported heavy bombardments and the following day large numbers of gassed and injured casualties reported to the Main Dressing Station at Locon. In the afternoon the MDS had to be moved to a safer location at Hingette. Casualties continued during the morning of the 10th, but the 2/1st's War Diary noted increased activity of the British guns and a subsequent reduction in the flow of the casualties. The 1/3rd Field Ambulance's first reference to the attack was that ten of its stretcher bearers had been wounded on the night of the 9th/10th April. But, thereafter, the offensive petered out, from the medical perspective. The next mention of casualties came from the 3/1st Field Ambulance, which was shelled on 22 April, with shrapnel damaging most huts and wounding one patient in the head.

164 Brigade planned a daylight attack for 27 April, which was supported by the 1/3rd Field Ambulance. More stretcher bearers were sent forward and a forward motor ambulance car post was established for four vehicles. An ambulance exchange post was also establish. It was 7000 yards between the forward motor ambulance car post and the field ambulance, and then another 5000 yards back to the Advanced Dressing Station. The horse drawn ambulances were allocated to a walking wounded dressing station, where the injuries were less severe and so the speed of evacuation was less critical. Between 4 pm on the 27th and 10 am the following morning, ninety two cases and twelve prisoners of war were passed through the Advanced Dressing Station. The arrangements for stretcher bearers and ambulances kept the flow of casualties moving through and which prevented the medical facilities becoming congested. The German artillery shelled the Advanced

Dressing Station, during which Private Foster was killed and one of the ambulances damaged.

Late June 1918 saw an outbreak of 'Three Day Fever'. The 3/1st Field Ambulance recorded the following cases across the division:

Date	25 June	26 June	27 June	28 June	29 June	30 June
Cases	246	142	99	104	72	69

Although all the patients made a full recovery within a week, the removal of over 700 soldiers from the effective strength of the division at a time of manning crisis (the infantry brigades had lost a battalion each early in 1918) would have given cause for concern.

The summer of 1918 passed almost like a summer camp. On 28 July, 2/1st Field Ambuance held an 'annual' (there was not reference to one in 1917) sports day with twenty races, the first six being specifically for the patients. The Matron of Number 1 CCS awarded the prizes. The War Diary for August recorded the weather: generally hot but occasionally heavy rain. On 4th August there was a special service for the anniversary of the outbreak of the war, and two days later the divisional horse show. In September, just as the division prepared for warfare in the open, the weather turned for the worse.

Mustard gas became a medical concern from August 1918, after its initial use by the Germans the previous month. This was a persistent agent, which could remain active in the soil days and weeks after it was used; its effect on the victim was as a blistering agent effecting the skin and eyes. On the 5th, 3/1st Field Ambulance received a degassing chamber for contaminated clothing; eleven days later 150 mustard gas cases were received. None of the cases were severe but gas had affected all their eyes, which made the condition all the more traumatic. All cases entered a decontamination tent, where they removed their clothing and were given a hot bath, 'soap being used', before entering a second tent, where clean clothing was issued. They then passed into the evacuation ward.

In late 1918, the war returned to one of movement and although it was approaching its end, army business continued regardless and the shortage of manpower remained. Private J S Lloyd and Lance Corporal Bethell were interviewed by Major General Jeudwine on 17 September 1918 about a commission in the infantry. Private Lloyd was successful and was attached to the Liverpool Scottish. He was killed in action on 4 October and is buried at Houchin Cemetery. The CWGC records him as a corporal, from Llandysilio, Montgomeryshire, who had previously served at 'Gallipoli 1914–15'. Setting aside the obvious error that Gallipoli was 1915–16, it would appear that Lloyd was a '1914 man'. The West Lancashire Division did not serve there, although there was a West Lancashire Field Ambulance with 29th Division and 53rd (Welsh) Division served at Gallipoli. It is possible Lloyd served previously with one of those Field Ambulances.[78]

The only indication that there was a change from trench to open warfare were the entries in the 'Place' column of the War Diary. Even 11 November 1918 passed unmentioned by either field ambulance. The 2/1st opened its hospital at 5 pm and the following day were receiving and despatching large numbers of patients. The 1/3rd arrived at a civilian hospital at midday and established a Main Dressing Station. It was business as usual.[79]

55th Divisional Sanitation Section

Sanitation was possibly not one of the most exciting roles in the army and very probably the least glamorous, but one which was essential if you consider that prior to the Great War more British soldiers died from disease than from enemy action. The section came under the control of the medical services, but their role was preventative.

In common with the other units of the 55th Division, the Sanitation Section deployed to France from Larkhill via Southampton to Le Havre in January 1916. It was the smallest unit recorded in this book, typically consisting of a subaltern, two sergeants, two NCOs, twenty privates and one batman; they were supported in their work by temporarily unfit soldiers.

Within days of arriving in France, the Section was put to work when, on 20 January, they were:

employed in cleaning sheets and surrounding of billets. Improving imperfectly constructed latrines. In compliance with order that men temporarily unfit are to be attached to the Sanitary Section 7 men from the 1/8 Liverpool Irish have been attached. Most have flat foot or other foot trouble, varicose veins – one is deaf. Drew money from Field Cashier and paid NCOs and men of unit.

On 24 January 1916 a further twenty one unfit men from 1/4th Loyals were attached, who were in an even worse state than the Liverpool Irish – fourteen were too unwell for even light work – with influenza, septic sores, rheumatism and scabies, some being found to be 'verminous'. Once those with sore throats had been separated, the remainder were disinfected.

Other duties included salvaging (reclaiming items for reuse), collecting and burning discarded clothing and kit, cleaning unoccupied houses and advising on the disposal of manure. On 29 February 1916 water samples were taken from the well of a chateau used by French civilians and was found to be heavily contaminated. More water-based work was carried out on 30 September at the baths in Poperinghe and Ypres.

The diseases that the section dealt with were the more mundane. Testing for mumps was one duty. 24 January 1916 saw the Section disinfecting blankets with scabies. This would be a major task for the Section, and the number of blankets involved were significant: 200 from 1/1st Field Ambulance and 362 from two other units on the 28th, the next day another 400 from 1/9th King's and 297 from 1/7th King's. The War Diary gives an insight into the world of the other units who did not record such details mundane, as the nine cases of Enteric Fever reported in 278 Brigade RFA on 8 September, or cases of potentially fatal para-typhoid in 1/9th King's and 278 Brigade on the 16th and 17th.

At the end of March 1917 the Section was transferred out of 55th Division into Third Army. The requirement to disinfect clothing and blankets at divisional level remained and, in April 1918, 1/3rd Field Ambulance received a 'Hoden Steam Disinfector' to prevent infection of patients by lice; and later a chamber for de-gassing mustard gas contaminated clothing.[80]

55th Divisional Train, Army Service Corps

The Train comprised an HQ and three Supply Companies:

West Lancashire Division		27th Division (Jan 15)	55th Division (Jan 16)
West Lancashire Divisional Transport and Supply Column	West Lancashire Divisional Transport and Supply Train (Oct 14)	27th Divisional Transport and Supply Train (Jan 15)	55th (West Lancashire) Divisional Transport and Supply Train (Jan 16)
West Lancashire Divisional HQ Coy	1/1st West Lancashire Divisional HQ Coy	No 1 (HQ) Coy	95th (HQ) Coy (before Jan 15)
Liverpool Brigade Coy	1/1st Liverpool Brigade Coy	No 2 Coy	96th Coy
North Lancashire Brigade Coy	1/1st North Lancashire Brigade Coy	No 3 Coy	97th Coy
South Lancashire Brigade Coy	1/1st South Lancashire Brigade Coy	No 4 Coy	98th Coy

The wartime career of the West Lancashire Transport and Supply Column is convoluted. The companies which joined 55th Division in January 1916 (95–98 Companies) were raised in November 1914 and supported 27th Division throughout 1915. Four new companies (505–508) were formed on 1 September 1915, but Young describes them as serving 'Home Front, 55th (West Lancashire) Division, Western Front 57th (West Lancashire) Division'. The wartime role is given as 'Train No 1 (HQ) Company (HT)', and on to No 4 Company. It is most likely that the pre-war Transport and Supply Train became 505 to 508 Companies and served with 57th (Second West Lancashire) Division.[81]

In October 1914, the War Office decided that the Territorial Force Army Service Corps should be incorporated into the Regular Army's Order of Battle; and so the Transport and Supply Column became a 'Train'. The geographical titles became numbers on 1 April 1915, although 55th Division was not concentrated until the following January. From the War Diary it is clear that the companies were part of 27th Divisional Train until January 1916 when they joined 55th Division. By August 1915, the strength of a territorial Motor Transport Company (MT, rather than Horse Transport [HT]) was 351 men, up from 101 in the pre-war establishment. A final change occurred in September 1916 when the territorial structure was finally brought in line with the regulars, and the establishment of the Train increased from about 500 men to almost 740 men. This change also simplified the posting of officers and men to different units but, of course, would dilute the regional character of the Train: that was the reality of total war in 1916.[82]

When the 55th Division was reformed, it received the Lahore Division's Train when the latter division left the Western Front for Mesopotamia. This would explain why, on 15 January 1916, the Train was ordered to paint the Lancashire Rose on the wagons. This is also the earliest reference to the use of this divisional emblem in the War Diaries. But the Lahore Division was an Indian Army formation, so you would expect to find Indian names in the War Diary, but there are none. Furthermore, as we will see, there are at least a few soldiers with a territorial connection. It may have been that when the Lahore Division left the Western Front it sailed for Basra with just its manpower and there it would have been re-equipped with vehicles suitable for a Middle Eastern campaign.

Where does this leave the 55th, and for that matter the 57th, Divisional Trains? The War Diaries of neither explain their origins and formation. There is one entry in the 57th's War Diary for February 1917, where the signature block stamp said 'Major O.C. Head-Qtr Co. West Lan. Divl. Train', which may indicate that at least part of the 57th Divisional Train was linked to the old West Lancashire Transport and Supply Column. If the ASC followed the same expansion experiences as the infantry, it is likely that the old West Lancashire TF expanded into Home Service and Foreign Service units, one going overseas and the other staying at home with the 57th Division. With the 55th Division Train overseas, the 57th Division Train may well have supplied Foreign Service volunteers to the 55th. Unfortunately, the 57th's War Diary is one of the most unhelpful consulted in the research for this book. It is full of entries like 'ITF [In The Field] Trench Warfare Routine' for the whole of April 1917.

The territorial connection remained and was recognised. On 24 October 1916, Farrier Staff Sergeant W Pullen of 95 Company was awarded the

Meritorious Service Medal and in November 1917 he was awarded the Territorial Efficiency Medal.[83]

The Train was inspected by a staff officer from Third Army on 16 May, and passed:

> The horses are in splendid condition, and compare favourably with any unit I have inspected in the 3rd Army.
>
> The 55th Division has never given any cause for anxiety as regards Supplies.

A fortnight later, on the 30th, both the Army Commander and General Jeudwine also inspected the Train and agreed with the previous inspection.

The BEF's supply chain on the continent started at one of several Channel ports; these were divided into a Northern Sector (Calais and Boulogne) and Southern Sector (Dieppe, Le Havre and Rouen), whence supplies were moved by rail to Regulating Stations. Here the bulk loads were broken down into loads for individual divisions for forward movement by rail to a railhead. The Divisional Train collected the supplies from the railhead and moved them forward to one of four refilling points (one per brigade and another for the Divisional troops), from where the supplies were issued to individual units. The distribution of supplies within a unit was the responsibility of the quartermaster rather than the ASC Company, although the QM might well have his own ASC men for that role.[84]

The two types of wagons referred to are either baggage or supply; the most common thing to be supplied were rations, so, for example, on 1 October 1916, two days' rations were supplied to the division less the artillery. The main entries referring to the movement of supplies relate to the railheads and refilling points. The routine delivery of rations to the units does not warrant a mention in the War Dairy, presumably because it was a regular occurrence. It is filled with the postings, leave and promotions of the officers, who are named and, to a lesser extent, the soldiers, who are generally unnamed.

Although the ASC were not generally considered as combat troops, from 7 April 1916, they started to provide one officer and nine men for a twenty four hour tour of duty in the trenches. The first detail all safely completed their tour, which was to be repeated ''til further notice'. Whether they spent their tour in an infantry or supply role is, unfortunately, not recorded. The first fatality in the Train was Driver AJ Gorham on 14 February 1916. Unfortunately, that month's War Diary is missing and so the circumstances are unknown, but as he was buried in Ste. Marie Cemetery, Le Havre, it would suggest that he was injured or wounded and evacuated to one of the base hospitals on the coast and died there. A year later, on 6 February (the CWGC says the 5th), a German aircraft dropped a bomb on the Proven refilling point, wounding three, of whom two died later: 25 year old Corporal Baker from Warrington and 41 year old Private Harry Hull of Blackpool. Three more casualties, two of them fatal, were suffered on the 14th: 29 year old Serjeant J Smith from Brighton and 28 year old Lance Corporal William French of Huntingdon. Of the four fatalities that month, two fit the make-up of a West Lancashire Division, two do not.

The German counter offensive at Cambrai on 30 November 1917 is mentioned in the War Diary but, as is common with the other arms, the reader would only know this if they were aware of the significance of the date. On this occasion it simply recorded:

> In consequence of orders received, 55th Divisional Train stood to from 10 am until 6 pm. All duties were carried out as usual.
>
> The day's reserve of rations were loaded at STORE VILLERS FAUCON on returning supply wagons and dumped at MARQUAIX.

In other words, it was business as usual.

The reduction of the size of a brigade from four to three infantry battalions in the spring of 1918 meant a reduction in the number of wagons required to supply them, so on 22 April 1918 the surplus wagons were sent back down the line.

The outbreak of 'Three Day Fever', which is mentioned by the RAMC, also afflicted the Train at the end of June 1918, with 146 NCOs and other ranks placed on the sick list. Half these men were hospitalised, while the other half were isolated in a camp. There is no record of any impact on the supply of rations to units in the division, probably because there would have been several days stockpiled, but it would not have taken much longer before those supplies started to run low.

The return to movement in the war, which gathered pace in October 1918, was potentially a major problem after so many years of near static warfare. As the division advanced over old battlefields, roads had to be repaired and trenches bridged. Horses could not cross barbed wire even if it had been flattened by tanks, unlike marching troops in boots. Finally, as the division moved further away from the railheads, delivery times to the units increased until more track could be laid which, even if it were, was unlikely to be laid as quickly as the advancing troops.

Despite this, the Train appears to have taken the challenge in its stride. Advanced Supply Sections moved forward and the War Diary (plus a separate list of 'Refilling Points for October 1918') shows how the railheads and supply delivery points moved forward. This continued into November, with an Appendix listing that month's railheads and refilling points. 11 November came and went without a mention but then, despite the peace, the rations still had to be moved forward and the soldiers fed. At least the demand for munitions would decrease. For the Train, peace would be almost as busy as wartime.[85]

1st (West Lancashire) Mobile Veterinary Section

The Army Veterinary Corps was another one of the smaller corps, one which was not part of the pre-war establishment, but whose role within the division adds another dimension that does not appear in the Divisional history. Not only were they involved in the care and welfare of animals, but they also ran breeding programs and oversaw the disposal of animals after the Armistice.

Captain Finch, OC Section, left Canterbury for Southampton and France on 14 January 1916 to join the division. He commanded the Section until March 1918, when Captain Laine was appointed. Laine commanded the Section until the end of the war and beyond. He handed over command to Captain Andrews on 14 February 1919 and the following day proceeded home for demobilisation. Most of the War Diary entries note 'Routine Work', occasionally with some elaboration, as on 21 January 1916: '5 horses + 4 mules received from Div Amm Col. 16 horses received from 4th W Lancs How Bgd RFA.' The inspection of saddles, harnesses, standings and stables,

Army Veterinary Corps. A fine portrait of George Hewitt, of Steelwood Farm, Halton, Runcorn.

with oversight of improvements recommended, are also common entries.[86]

In August 1917, eighteen mares were selected for the divisional breeding programme. The following March a divisional horse nursery was opened, so the breeding had evidently been successful. The demand for horses and for economising was constant; in March 1917, six 'surplus' mounts of Lewis gun officers were disposed of. Presumably the work undertaken by these officers made a riding horse unnecessary.[87]

It was not only horses that were in demand. In January 1918, one sergeant and ten other ranks attended a musketry course and the following March, during the manning crisis which nearly broke the British Army, eight other ranks were sent for a medical and, if found fit, transferred to the infantry. Their examination took place at Number 2 Veterinary Hospital, where one assumes there was a Medical Officer, rather than a Veterinary Officer to conduct the assessment. The fate of these unnamed eight is not recorded and, if they transferred to the infantry, this would be listed under the new regiment. The divisional history lists one killed and five wounded in the whole war. The War Diary only has one incident when casualties were sustained, on 3 September 1917. A German bomb wounded six, two seriously. On 12 September 1917 Private H Larder died and is buried at Longuenesse Souvenir Cemetery. The only other death in the Section, Private Adams, was recorded in the War Diary on 1 February 1919, but a search of the CWGC database does not record a commemoration for him.[88]

It was not only the men who were at risk. For four days at the end of July 1917 bomb proof trenches were constructed, and in September 1918 days were spent on constructing bomb proof screens for the animals. However, from the middle of October 1918, the advance of the Final Hundred Days caught up with the veterinaries and they went mobile again. Initially, this meant a different town or village each day; at the end of October they were in Cysoing, then to Cherq, Leuze for the Armistice (which went unrecorded in the War Diary) and then to Ath.[89]

Serjeant Lane, West Lancashire RAVC, attached RFA. Clarence William Lane's address is given as Chorley, but he was a native of Warrington.

From the beginning of January 1919, 'Classifying Animals' of the various divisional units became a regular entry and from the middle of the month their disposal commenced: on the 13th, seven animals were evacuated and two were destroyed and sold for 800 Francs. By the end of the month, as well as disposing of animals, animal hides at the local abattoir were being inspected. The veterinaries were moving into public health. This work continued until the end of April 1919, when the War Diary ended.[90]

It should also be remembered that Army Veterinary Corps officers and men were attached to other units. Captains Davey and Stuart MC, for example, served with 1/1st Brigade RFA throughout the war.[91]

Chapter 5

57th (2nd West Lancashire) Division, TF

As has been explained earlier, the role of the Liverpool Territorials and what became 55th Division was for Home Defence, although individuals could volunteer for Imperial Service. When the territorials volunteered to fight overseas, who would take up the Home Defence role? Kitchener's New Armies were also earmarked for overseas service (and some of them were sent to Gallipoli or France in 1915), but by and large they were untrained, without uniforms or equipment, and were inexperienced. The answer were those territorials who could not, or would not, volunteer in 1914. These formed the nucleus of a duplicate Territorial Force, the Second Line. Unlike the Service battalions of the New Armies which were numbered after the Territorial battalions, these new Territorial battalions were not considered separate to, but an extension of, the original battalion. They also served as a holding and training unit for the First Line battalion, especially in the early days of enthusiastic recruitment; they would provide a vital role in replenishing the battlefield casualties sustained in France while the New Armies were still in training.

Despite performing vital roles, in *Liverpool Scottish*, McGilchrist is critical of the way in which the 2/10th was trained, held in a Home Defence role for two years, and was not given the opportunity to prove itself in battle but had its numbers 'frittered away' until disbanded and merged into the 1/10th. Unlike the First West Lancashire Division, the Second had little time to prove itself. The new division only fought at Passchendaele and then again during the Advance to Victory.[1]

In the chaos of 1914, it is not clear when the Reserve, Home Service or Second Line battalions (various names were used) were formed. Wurtzburg gives the date of 10 September 1914 for the Liverpool Rifles and we have already seen that the Liverpool Scottish in Edinburgh created two new companies for the Home Service soldiers, to separate them from those going overseas.[2]

As a result of this dual function, the Second Line battalions would contain both Home Service and Foreign Service soldiers, with the latter undergoing training and awaiting to be called to France. Eventually, a Third Line unit would be formed for training. This combination of recruiting, training and providing drafts to France, especially after the Battle of Somme, meant that the 57th Division was insufficiently strong until it received drafts of 'Derby Men' (a precursor to conscription).[3]

As with all divisions during the war, the organisation was constantly being reviewed:

Divisional Troops[4]	
2/5th Loyals (Pioneers)	From 170 Bde February 1918.
173rd MG Coy	To 57 Bn MGC March 1918
57th Bn MGC	Formed March 1918
57th Div Train ASC	Originally 55th Div Train, transferred to 57th Div when 55th went to France
57th Mobile Vet Section	
248th Div Employment Company	Formed June 1917
170th (2/1st North Lancashire) Brigade	
2/4th King's Own	Left 20 Oct 1915
2/5th King's Own	
2/4th Loyals	
2/5th Loyals	Left to become divisional pioneers, February 1918
4/5th Loyals	Absorbed into 1/5th Loyals February 1918.
1/5th Loyals	From 55th Division February 1918; absorbed 4/5th Loyals
170th MG Coy	To 57th Bn MGC 1 March 1918
170th TM Coy	

171st (2/1st Liverpool) Brigade	
2/5th King's	Disbanded February 1918
2/6th King's	
2/7th King's	
2/8th King's	Absorbed into 1/8th King's January 1918, formed 8th King's
1/8th King's	From 55th Division January 1918
171st MG Coy	To 57th Bn MGC 1 March 1918
171st TM Coy	
172nd (2/1st South Lancashire) Brigade	
2/9th King's	Absorbed into 1/9th King's January 1918
2/10th King's	Left April 18 to 1/0th King's, formed 10th King's
2/4th South Lancs	
2/5th South Lancs	
1/9th King's	Joined from 55th Division January 1918
1st Royal Munsters	Joined April 1918
172nd MG Coy	To 57th Bn MGC 1 March 1918
172 TM Coy	
Divisional Artillery	Included First West Lancashire Divisional Artillery April to September 1915
285 Brigade (2/1 West Lancs)	
286 Brigade (2/2 West Lancs)	
287 Brigade (2/3 West Lancs)	Broken up 20 February 1917
57th Div Art Column	
W.57 Heavy Trench Mortar Battery	
X.57, Y.57 AND Z.57 Med TM Batteries	

Royal Engineers	Included 2/1st and 2/2nd (West Lancs) Field Companies until December 1915
421st (1/3rd West Lancs)	
502nd (1/3rd Wessex)	
505th (2/3rd Wessex)	
57th Div Sigs Coy	
Royal Army Medical Corps	Included 2/1st, 1/2nd and 1/3rd (West Lancs) until October or December 1915
2/2nd (Wessex)	
3/2nd (West Lancs)	
2/3rd (Wessex)	
57th Sanitation Section	

There is no divisional history or for that matter a divisional monument to remember their exploits. There are only the (usually) dry entries in the War Diaries. Captain Wurztburg's history of the Second Sixth is, therefore, an invaluable source for both the formation of the Second Line and the division's exploits in France. McGilchrist's history of the Liverpool Scottish also covers their second line battalion. This means that this chapter is skewed towards the 2/6th and 2/10th King's.

The Early Days

The Second Sixth was raised and trained by officers and Senior NCOs seconded from the First Sixth; but all was initially ad hoc, with companies being formed as numbers permitted.

> Those early days were amusing to look back upon. We came daily to the drill-shed for training in every form of costume that can be imagined – some men in everyday clothes of a clerk, some in shooting coats and grey trousers, others in khaki bought at their own expense, and so on.

Bowler hats were early discouraged, but except for that there were no restrictions as to dress.[5]

The middle class nature of the battalion is clear from this passage, and it should be remembered that these recruits would have paid to join the battalion, unlike those who chose to join a less socially exclusive battalion, or one of the New Army battalions. As has already been mentioned, the duplication involved in both doubling the territorials and raising the New Armies diverted recruits and equipment away from the territorials already (or soon to be) fighting in France. Despite the photographs of New Army recruits without uniforms, the territorials felt that whatever was available went to the New Army first. Even worse, the New Army soldiers considered themselves to be regulars. Despite this, on 4 November 1914 a draft of 240 men were sent from the 2/6th to the 1/6th and in return received back those underage, unfit or unwilling to deploy. Another 210 men were drafted

Looking more like a Clerk than a warrior, this Rifleman of the 'Second Sixth' is equipped with 1914 Leather Pattern equipment and the obsolete Magazine Lee Enfield. Not also his black puttees. (*P. Threlfall*)

in January 1915, including many senior NCOs who surrendered their rank to get into the war: 'That was ever the spirt', according to Wurzburg. The 2/6th also received officers. Some were keen, young aspirational officers, with some experience at a school Officer Training Corps,[6] while others had previous experience: four captains had previously served in the Boer War and one, Fletcher, who became the first Adjutant and later CO, had won the DSO there. There was also officer material from within their own ranks but, as has already been noted for the 1/6th, enlisted men tended to be commissioned into other battalions. For example, John Steward enlisted in the 2/6th but was commissioned into the 1/5th on 25 October 1916 – presumably as the quickest way to see active service. He was killed on 9 April 1917 in the Ypres Salient. The first CO was Lieutenant Colonel GA Wilson VD, an experienced territorial who had served in the pre-1908 Volunteers. By early 1915, the battalion was over establishment for officers, a situation about which few COs would complain. Clearly there was some fine material for the new battalion to work with.[7]

Pre-war territorial (and IWM Interviewee) William Marshall, was unable to lie successfully about his age and, with 1/5th King's 200 men over establishment, he was sent to Blackpool to the 2/5th. He would survive the war with 5th King's (when the two battalions were merged in February 1918), eventually being captured at Givenchy in April 1918. Another IWM Interviewee, Richard Trafford, enlisted in the 9th King's at Ormskirk. He was posted to the 2/9th, who drilled at Goodison Park with Japanese rifles and leather 1914 pattern equipment. He transferred to the 1/9th in March 1915.[8]

The 2/10th had a similar experience, with three officers and two permanent staff instructors to raise the battalion. At first the recruits also lived at home, with training conducted daily at Newsham Park, Lieutenant Colonel Nicholl commanding, formerly CO of the 1/10th. He was assisted by Donald Farmer VC. As a sergeant in the Cameron Highlanders during the Boer War, he was the first of his regiment to win that award. He was serving with the Liverpool Scottish as an instructor in 1914, but took the battalion to France as the RSM. He then received a Quartermaster's Commission in the 2/10th before becoming Adjutant and rose to become a lieutenant colonel. He died in 1956, still living in Liverpool, and is buried in Anfield Cemetery.[9]

Corporal McLEavy recalled drilling with the 2/10th in Childwall wearing his civilian clothes with a tartan armband and would not receive his uniform until the battalion was billeted in Blackpool. He was under age and so, despite volunteering for the draft to replace the 1/10th's casualties after Hooge, he was held back. He would not get to France until 1917 and fought at Givenchy. Oddly, he says he ended the war with the 3/10th in Kinsale,

Ireland, where he caught Spanish Flu but recovered and returned just in time for 'The Business', presumable the Irish Civil War.[10]

For the 2/6th, training took place in Sefton Park, Allerton or Arrowe Hall on the Wirral. This was short lived and, in November 1914, the Second Liverpool Brigade concentrated in Blackpool under the command of Colonel SH Harrison, a former King's officer, and 'a most courteous and kindly Irishman.... very keen and enthusiastic'. The divisional commander was Brigadier General FA Adam, formerly a brigade commander in Malta, who had been intended to command a division for more immediate service in France but, having accidentally fallen from his horse, was given command of the Second West Lancashire Division.[11]

Training proceeded on Blackpool's North and South Shores, musketry at Fleetwood and route marches. In January 1915 they marched to Garstang and back, 33¾ miles, and then, on 1 February, to Liverpool and back, via Preston and Ormskirk (the home of part of 9th King's, where patriotic fervour mitigated the rain), arriving at Exchange Flags, Liverpool. A few days later, the 2/6th moved to Canterbury to replace the 1/6th, who had just

2/6th King's in Margate. A jolly group photograph of 2/6th King's in Margate on anti-invasion duties. Note that their puttees are darker than their trouser material, indicating old Volunteer black puttees.

departed from there for France. There they found the band and 170 men from the 1/6th. The remainder of the brigade would follow them to Canterbury and the 2/6th then moved to Margate, were they were both popular and enjoyed the seaside facilities. The 2/10th also moved to Blackpool as part of Second South Lancashire Brigade and then on to Tunbridge Wells. If the 'English' infantry battalions were suffering from a lack of kit, the special attire required for the Liverpool Scottish took even longer to arrive and so their lack of uniformity continued.[12]

Although not in France, the division was no longer in training camps but in a military zone, where invasion remained a possibility. This was, after all, the purpose of the territorials. The First Line infantry, plus a RE Field Company and a Field Ambulance, were abroad; the divisional staff, plus the supporting arms and divisional troops completed 57th Division, with Major General JB Forster commanding, as part of General Sir Ian Hamilton's Central Force to repulse an invasion. It was just as well, for the division received Japanese rifles, not SMLEs – the fighting First Line battalions were still managing with Magazine Lee Enfield rifles – but the impact was important, and Wurtzburg writes that the 2/6th no longer felt like an 'ornamental' battalion. A real Vickers machine gun was received, which allowed more realistic training than on a wooden mock-up. It would be February 1916 before the first Lewis guns arrived, and another year before the 2/6th received its full complement of twenty eight weapons. About the same time as the Lewis guns arrived, the formation of the Machine Gun Corps meant that twenty two men were discharged and then re-enlisted in the MGC.[13]

April, May and June 1915 saw more changes. Those who had only enlisted for Home Service were posted to the 43rd Provisional Battalion; but Wurtzburg notes that many of them proceeded overseas sooner than the territorials as a result of the 1916 Military Service Act. The 2/10th conducted a route march on 1 June 1915 for two days, with one night in bivouacs. Those who were not fit enough, about 300, were also sent to the 43rd Provisional Battalion. Third Line Battalions was also raised, at Weeton Camp, near Blackpool. Officers and NCOs from the Second Lines were posted there. This left the 2/6th and the 2/10th each about 700 strong. Lieutenant Colonel Wilson resigned his command of the 2/6th, citing the pressures of his business. Strange as it may seem, officers of Wilson's experience were able to resign. However, many of the older, ex-Volunteer, commanding officers were not considered fit enough to take their battalions to France, and this may have been a polite way of letting Wilson resign with dignity. Similarly, Lieutenant Colonel Nicholl took command of 43rd Battalion, and was replaced as CO by Major Fairrie who, as a captain, had been sent from Edinburgh back to Liverpool to raise the 2/10th. He would lead the battalion to France in 1917. Another group would leave the battalion in August 1916. Five were under age and transferred from the 2/6th to the King's 5th TF Reserve Battalion in Oswestry; and nine more machine gunners departed. Finally, brigade trench mortar batteries were formed and more men were drawn from the battalions.[14]

In July, the 2/6th left Margate for Upstreet Camp, in the Thanet Marshes: pleasant in the summer; a quagmire in the autumn. August saw another draft of ninety six despatched to the 1/6th and a draft of 112 from the 3/6th was received. Captain, now Major, Fletcher, was promoted lieutenant colonel and took command of the battalion. The stay at Upstreet Camp ended in October when, 'wellnigh drowned and frozen', they returned to Canterbury.[15]

Meanwhile, the 2/10th moved to Randridge Park, Oxted, Surrey, where they worked on the London Defence Scheme until the end of October, when they returned to Maidstone for the winter. They spent almost seven months in Maidstone, during which time drafts of recruits arrived from the 3/10th. Curiously, just before leaving Maidstone, the 2/10th sent a draft to the 3/10th to complete their training before being sent to the 1/10th. This would be the last time the 2/10th acted as a drafting unit for the 1/10th, as the 2/10th's training stepped up a gear. About this time, the 3/10th were used as a training and drafting battalion for more than just the Liverpool Scottish – a kilted draft even arrived at 13th King's in Salonika. The special characteristics of the territorials were disappearing under the pressure of war.[16]

In September 1915 the Divisional Artillery departed for France and 2nd Canadian Division, whose own artillery were still in training. They moved to billets near Canterbury to be re-equipped and then sailed on the 28th. This would have meant that 57th Division now needed to raise its own second line artillery.[17]

Gunners in training. Although not necessarily a West Lancashire RFA unit, the design of the instructor's shoulder title is that of a Territorial. The recruits appear to be training on a wooden mock-up field gun, illustrating the difficulties faced by 57th Division.

Early 1916 saw the first Derby men arrived at the 2/6th. These men were enlisted under a system that preceded conscription.[18]

By July 1916 the old Japanese rifles had gone but their replacements were condemned too, so it would appear that SMLEs and other modern equipment were not yet being issued. Despite this, they were summoned to Aldershot and Salisbury Plain – the 'universities of the military student' – from where

> he was launched into the vortex of war, complete with all the necessary knowledge. That we had now at last been admitted must mean that our days in England were strictly numbered. Alas for our hopes![19]

A musketry course was fired in the first few days, at the end of which 2/6th King's came top in their brigade and second in the division: the divisional best shot was not recorded. Then there were a series of tactical exercises, during which the battalions combined in attacks against fellow battalions. Conditions varied between choking dust and deep mud, but all would be good practice for the future. After the exercises came leave back in Liverpool and a parade on St George's Plateau, where today the city's war memorial stands. The city was enthusiastic about their return. Ominously, this should have been their last leave before deploying overseas. September saw more exercises, culminating in a divisional attack under the eye of Sir John French – who had determined that two divisions, chosen by himself, should be retained in the UK for Home Defence. He chose the 57th. The division had already paraded for a final inspection by Major General Forster, after which he would hand over command. On the 23rd, the division was inspected by HM the King, which was completed to their great credit.[20] Units had been training for two years but had still not seen action: Wurtzburg wrote that the news was 'a terrible disappointment' and that the men were 'almost ashamed to go on leave and face the heartless gibes of those who did not know the facts'. When they received three days' Christmas leave, they realised that this was, at last, the final leave.[21]

Preparations continued in the New Year. Several officers from the 1/6th joined the 2/6th. More tellingly, the 2/6th paraded for the first time in khaki puttees instead of their old black ones. This was a regimental peculiarity, as the Liverpool Rifles had retained black puttees from the Volunteer days. Finally, in February, they were off.[22]

To France

The division was allocated to II ANZAC Corps, under Lieutenant General Sir AJ Godley, and would occupy a line Laventie, Fleurbaix to Chapelle d'Armentières, about seven miles. As usual, the incoming units underwent a period of introduction to the trenches under the guidance of an experienced unit: for 2/6th King's it was the 2nd Battalion, Wellington Regiment; the 2/9th trained with 1st Canterbury Rifles and for the 2/10th it was the 2nd Canterburys. The 2/6th had nothing but good words for their Kiwi hosts. Then they were into the trenches on their own. The 2/6th took over the line at La Boutillerie. Officers with experience from the 1/6th continued to provide guidance for the nervous men, for example putting an end to whispering in the trenches when the Germans were 400 yards away. The Germans were fortunately quiet, which helped. After four days, they

A rifleman, 2/6th King's. On his left shoulder is worn a diamond as a battalion indicator over a company bar. 57th Division adopted a shape to indicate the seniority of the battalion in the regiment (square, diamond, triangle, circle), with a different colour for each brigade. The company bars were also different colours.

He does not wear a black rifles buttons or shoulder titles. These latter could have been a blackened T/6/KINGS, KINGS or, later in the war, a red on green embroidered LIVERPOOL RIFLES over 2.

marched out of the trenches but not before suffering their first casualties when a 'minnie' shell fell on a post, killing three and wounding two. For the survivors, though, having finally served in France, they now felt 'twice the men they were but a few days before'.[23]

Out of the line in Fleurbaix, the 2/6th set about continuing the improvements to the billets which the 2/7th had started, the latter having replaced the 2/6th in the trenches. Across the road the 2/8th and the 2/5th had the same arrangement. Brigade HQ was nearby, as were a couple of 60 lb guns.[24]

Wurtzburg provides an incomplete list of code words to the battalions in the brigade: 2/6th used Gipsy, the 2/7th had Giddy and the 2/8th, Gilt. He did not give the code word for the 2/9th.[25]

In late April, the 2/6th took over a section of line from the Australians, at Houplines, near Armentières. The sector was 'most unfavourable':

The principle of gaps and localities was maintained here, and constant shell fire, combined with lack of any means of repair, gave the sector a most dilapidated and depressing appearance, which was intensified by a great superfluity of water and a number of useless and derelict trenches running in all directions. Lateral communications, too, as so often happens in a combined sector, were extremely bad.

And that was just the right sector. The left sector:

> Was notoriously the weak point, the left being bounded by the River Lys, which in winter rendered an area of several hundred yards along the bank quite impassable, though in the summer.... passable, and to a large extend undefended.... The sector, we found, was full of notices warning you that the spot you stood on was under direct observation from the Germans, which caused you to move round the traverses with alacrity. Most of these notices, we found, were obsolete but, on the left company's fronts, parts of the front line were certainly exposed, and till these spots were blinded casualties occurred from snipers.

The whole of the Houplines sector was 'a maze of useless and ruined trenches', lacking in lateral communication without a single dugout which would have withstood a direct hit from a 5.9 inch shell.[26]

Once relieved by 2/7th King's, the 2/6th were able to relax in reserve, where there were estaminets; Au Boeuf was 'ordinary', or Lucienne's for the more fastidious, and Madam Burberry's, where clothing and field kit was on sale. There was also the opportunity for the Battalion Orchestra to entertain the troops, which included, on first violin, a particularly fine musician, Rifleman Garrod, formerly of the Liverpool Philharmonic Orchestra. Rest was, as always, limited, and a platoon was detailed to undertake special training in new offensive tactics. The platoon was restructured into four sections, one each of Lewis gunners, grenadiers, bombers and riflemen, plus a platoon headquarters of an officer, sergeant, runner and signaller. These new structures and tactics, which were being implemented in May 1917, show that the Army was far from incapable of implementing new ideas to address the prevailing conditions. Lewis machine guns were integrated into the infantry platoon during the attack so that suppressing fire could be applied to a German position while other members of the platoon could close and kill the defenders under (relatively) safe conditions. This basic idea of a section providing fire support while another section assaults the enemy is recognisable by a British soldier even today. Less than twelve months on from the first day of the Somme, these innovations can been seen as major leaps forward in tactical thinking.[27]

The 2/6th were back in the trenches on 1 June. A few days later, the divisional artillery started fire missions against Messines Ridge. The division was not involved in the assault; perhaps because of this, Wutzburg starts an account of the opening battle with:

> the most tremendous mine explosions and the most magnificent barrage that can be imagined. It was a lovely morning, and there was not a cloud in the sky. With a stupendous roar and upheaval that baffles description the mines exploded. Simultaneously the whole weight of the artillery gathered together for the occasion, and hidden away in every conceivable place, opened on the enemy. From their trenches lights of many colours shot into the air, mutely appealing for assistance from their gunners.[28]

In support of the attack, the 2/6th planned a trench raid in great detail, including mock-up German trenches for rehearsals. The raid was conducted on 22 June, but was not a success, in part because a party led by Captain Parker got too close to the supporting barrage and several were wounded by shrapnel. Parker was wearing an other rank's jacket and so, when evacuated to the CCS, was placed in the other ranks ward, to the amusement of his fellow officers. Rifleman P G Jones, a battalion scout, described as 'one of our best and keenest' was killed during the raid. He had enlisted on 5 October 1914, so may well have been one of those recruits described by Wurtzburg in the early days of the battalion.[29]

Gas was a persistent threat, although not necessarily debilitating or fatal. 2/9th King's were heavily shelled with gas on the morning of 27 May and were complimented for their efficient and effective drills: 'The Divisional Commander congratulates the 2/9th King's Liverpool Reg on the very few casualties they had during the early morning of the 27 May from the enemy gas shell attack. The attack was one of some severity, and the promptitude with which Box respirators were put on and the local alarm given reflects great credit to all concerned'. The division's first experience of mustard gas was in July 1917 and was particularly distressing. Shells also fell in Armentières, where the civilian population's protection was limited to one or two PH hoods per family. Mustard Gas was a blistering agent attacking the skin and in particular the eyes. The gas had contaminated the food too, so all that was available was tea, but fortunately that evening a thunderstorm washed away most of the residual contaminants. The significance of mustard gas over the conventional asphyxiating gases should not be underestimated. The effects on the battalion were more critical. By the end of the month, one officer and at least twelve men were killed, sixteen officers and 428 men were wounded, not all of whom would be able to return to service. B and C Companies of 2/6th were particularly hard hit. 2/5th King's were reduced to about 50 per cent effectiveness.

Wutzburg is critical that the men were not made aware of the new threat earlier. They were familiar with the effects of conventional gas and understood that after the initial concentration the effects quickly dissipated. With mustard gas, the slightest breath 'was like inhaling red-hot air and choked you immediately', and the gas was 'insidious and of silent evaporation, practically free from smell, caused no one inconvenience, and in some places was so slight as to be barely perceptible. It was that it affected the eyes, an entirely new phenomenon to us.'[30]

The Small Box Respirator in use at the time was admired for its protection, but not for its design. After two hours' use while being gassed, it was 'apt to provoke considerable resentment on the part of the wearer'.[31]

The process of rebuilding began in earnest, while the remainder of the brigade had to undertake the duties of the two King's battalions. Two drafts of 192 and 131 men arrived for the 2/6th in mid August 1917; and by the end of the month its strength was 756 men, the strongest since February that year. In early September they relieved the 2/7th King's in the line: they were back in business. However, it was a relatively short tour in the trenches, and the division was relieved by 15th (Scottish) Division. The 57th Division had been in the trenches for seven months and suffered significant casualties from just holding the line, in addition to this there was the disaster of the mustard gas attack. It moved into 'Rest'.[32]

Rest was actually additional training but this was undertaken at a more leisurely pace, despite the anticipation that the division would participate in the Third Battle of Ypres. This generated a great deal of debate about how to proceed in an attack: two companies up, two behind; or three up and one behind; whether in 'blobs' or 'worms' or 'leap-frogging'. When taken together with the adoption of Lewis guns, this represented a major change to the platoon structure. They also received a deluge of instructions, which left the officers bewildered as to the best tactics to adopt. The 2/6th received another draft, 130 men from the East Surreys, which made the battalion stronger than ever, but actions such as these diluted the regional identities that was supposedly the strength behind the British infantry. Training continued into October, with larger and more realistic training, complete with live trench mortar bombardments and the use of contact aircraft, all under the seemingly never ending rain. On 19 October the division began the move back into the line.[33]

It moved into reserve trenches on 27 October. They vacated camps in the endless yellow mud, surrounded by the constant movement of guns, men and transport, and dotted with the supply depots necessary for the forthcoming battle. Battalions marched in single file with their colonels at the head, gas shells dropping around and shells targeting crossroads. Congestion delayed the advance still further. Once in the trenches, reconnaissance patrols were sent out. That of 2/6th King's (Lieutenant Clarke, Sergeant Powell, Corporal Stubbs and three riflemen) successfully reached the German lines and examined their objective. Unfortunately, on their return they were observed and fired upon, with Clark and Powell being seriously wounded. The casualties and the information made it back to the British lines and for their actions they were all awarded the Military Cross (Clarke) or Military Medal.[34]

The division's first offensive action occurred by mistake. OC B Company 2/6th King's realised that the positions they had taken over from the previous company was not the ones they were told they had. Memling Farm and Rubens Farm had long since disappeared, to be replaced by bunkers. B Company was ordered to reconnoitre and occupy both positions. No 7 and 8 Platoons were ordered to do this job. No 7 Platoon, under Lieutenant Vaughan, attempted to take Rubens Farm, but suffered heavy casualties. Then, at dawn, in support of a 58th Division attack on their right, 57th Divisional Artillery fired a supporting barrage. Expecting a coordinated attack by 57th Division, German artillery fired a spoiling barrage. Caught in the open, No 7 Platoon was practically wiped out. Neither bunker was taken.[35]

170 Brigade entered the 'line' of shell holes on 30 October and their experience was similar to that of the 2/6th – 'the work it did proved the value of the Division as a fighting and not merely a trench-holding unit, after taking and holding ground; but thereafter the weather conditions made further advances impossible.[36]

17 December saw a return to the front line. By now it was very wet, and snowing, so the prospects were not good. Soldiers drew 'Tommy cookers', extra socks and two days' rations. The route to the front line was the same as in October. The front line, when they reached it, consisted of unimproved shell holes for six or seven men each, creating the vaguest sense of a line. No improvement was permitted so as to prevent the positions being given away, and no movement was allowed in day time for the same reason (the same applied to captured German bunkers, because their doors faced the new German front line and so were vulnerable to enemy fire). Tommy cookers could be lit in the daytime only, and just one man was allowed to smoke at a time. German bunkers were occupied by the HQ, with the Commanding Officer, Adjutant, Intelligent Officers, RSM, a cook and servant, six signallers, three artillery signallers, two wireless operators and some runners: and they had just two bunkbeds. It is worth noting the large number involved in communications: nine signallers who would operate visual communications or telephones, and two wireless (radio) operators, plus runners if the other systems failed or where no line had been laid.

Overnight the temperature dropped and the mud froze, which at least made movement easier but made the entrenching of telephone cables, the digging in of 'baby elephant' overhead shelters and the collection of salvage all but impossible, despite thousands of pounds worth of discarded equipment being scattered all around. Tea and stew was brought up nightly in dixies packed with hay and stuffed in haversacks. Mules carried the loads for four hours each way to battalion headquarters. Night time also allowed exercise to be taken and to get the blood circulating. The bunkers did not warm up either, despite all the people in them, and two sandbags had to be worn over each foot for insulation. Dawn, although cold, was accompanied by a thick mist, which meant that inspections of the front line could be carried out in daylight, covered from German observation. The downside to the freeze was that whereas previously German shells had largely buried themselves into the deep mud and mostly threw up clumps of mud, now they exploded on the surface, making a far more deadly blast. A problem with gas masks became evident when the small box respirator outlet valves froze. These were trying times. The 2/6th endured four days of this until relieved by the 2/7th.[37]

In the last days of December 1917 the division redeployed from Ypres to Armentières. They were due to depart in pleasant, frozen, wintery conditions, but a thaw immediately before departure made marching considerably more difficult.[38] However, they had proved themselves to be more than just a 'trench holding' division in one of the worst battles of the war.

1918

The division re-occupied their old lines near Houplines; the comments in Wutzburg show that 2/6th King's were again unimpressed with the conditions, including an undefended section between the River Lys and No. 7 Post, frozen solid and therefore crossable by an enemy patrol. The 2/10th referred to the period as 'uncomfortable' and which 'could scarcely have been more miserable'.[39]

The link between the First and Second Line battalions continued, as in January 1918 Lieutenant Adam returned to the 1/6th in exchange for Captain Eccles.[40]

13 January saw the 2/10th King's relieving the 2/6th but, as usual, 'rest' was anything but. The 2/6th spent the next three nights engaged on badly planned wiring activities in very heavy rain, with one and a half hours march each way. They then had just three days in which to dry out before more heavy rain meant that the Lys flooded the trenches. The 2/10th had a very bad time there, so much so that they were relieved early. The support line and most of the front line were knee deep or more in water. Many of the duckboards were not nailed down and shifted, so soldiers went thigh deep, with water over the top of their gum boots. Despite this, the 2/6th only suffered two cases of trench foot.[41]

February 1918 saw the disbanding of 2/5th King's. The bulk of the men were posted to 13th King's, a Service battalion in 3rd Division. The 2/6th and the 2/7th also received drafts. The 1/9th arrived at 57th Division at the same time but, as the 2/9th were in the trenches, the merger did not occur until the 4th and 5th. The War Diary recorded that this process went well, with everyone settling into the new conditions and working well together.[42] The two Liverpool Scottish battalions merged in April, with the 2/10th transferred to 55th Division, together becoming 10th King's once more.[43]

Early in the morning of 10 March 1918, 171 Brigade was warned that it would be leaving at 8 am. Wutzburg paints a picture of chaos as the brigade moved from 'rest', with everything unpacked and the battalion transport all painted undercoat red, in anticipation of a forthcoming GOC's inspection. They debussed at Arrewage, a hamlet to the west of Merville, where the GOC inspected them and complimented them on their efforts: the transport's wet red paint was now coated with a thick layer of dust. The brigade's task was to strengthen the 2nd Portuguese Division holding Laventie. They set about reconnoitring and digging. However, by the 26th the brigade was back in the Houplines sector again and their support to the Portuguese over. At this time the two West Lancashire territorial divisions were separated in the line by the Portuguese.[44]

The division was not directly involved in the Battle of the Lys, in which the 55th Division played such a critical role. They were relieved on 2 April by 40th Division, and entrained for Doullens as part of the reserve. At this point, the 57th was the only uncommitted reserve division available to Haig and the BEF. The next fortnight was spent largely marching and counter-marching (they would pass through Doullens three times). And digging. 40th Division was heavily involved in the Battle of the Lys, and was supported for a time by 57th Divisional Artillery, which was relieved, as normal, later than the infantry.[45]

While on the march, the battalions received a further four Lewis guns, making twenty-four each, but the demands for Lewis gunners were starting to get difficult to meet from the companies. The companies were restructured too, into three rifle platoons and one Lewis gun platoon, the latter under a Company Lewis Gun Officer, with a Battalion Lewis Gun Officer to supervise. Tests were conducted on the effectiveness of a Lewis against eight rifles, during which it was found that unless the Lewis gunner was good, the rifles scored more hits; if the Lewis gunner was good, then the Lewis would win, but not by much.[46]

At this critical moment, influenza spread through the division. The 2/6th reported over a hundred cases. Many were hospitalized, never to return to their old unit, meaning that skilled and experienced NCOs were lost. Rest camps were established for the less serious cases because the Field Ambulances, anticipating battlefield casualties, could not afford to be full of influenza cases. Lice, bad living conditions and a poor diet were blamed for making the men more susceptible to the disease.[47]

Then, on 6 May, orders were received to leave their bivouacs and march towards Gommecourt, through the 1916 battlefields. Captain Oliphant, US Army, and two NCOs were attached to the 2/6th for two days' instruction. One problem experienced was that although it was possible to occupy the old trenches, the new front line was no longer aligned to the old trenches. Consequently, old communication trenches had to be re-designed as firing trenches, while firing trenches became communication trenches. May and July were largely quiet months, but June was relatively busy, with various battalions conducting trench raids, with differing degrees of success. On 2 July, the New Zealand Division relieved the 57th and, following a period of sports competitions, the division moved south to Fampoux, south of Arras – for Wutzburg, it was the most "cushy" sector the 2/6th occupied.[48]

From 18 August, the division was on the move to positions north west of Arras, participating in what would become known as the Battles of Baupaume and Second Cambrai and the Breaking of the Hindenburg Line. Between the moves there was time for lectures and demonstrations on tanks. They eventually reaching Barly on 24 August and then Mercatel. The countryside here was, unlike Passchendaele the previous winter, notable for its ripe corn and birds singing, although the villages themselves were overgrown ruins. At the end of August the division entered the front line to provide flank protection for an attack by the Canadians. Although 57th Division did not participate in the attack, they were on the edge of the battlezone. The 2/6th had three men killed and four wounded. On 1 September, it was 57th Division's turn to take part in the offensive

At 4.40am 2/7th and 8th King's advanced and captured Hendescourt Chateau; then, in the evening, the 2/6th and two companies of the 2/7th, with 52nd Division on their right, resumed their attack, capturing Riencourt lez Cagnicourt. 2/7th King's made further advances on the morning of the 2nd. The 2/6th were forming up to cross the Hendecourt-Bullecourt Road that afternoon when they were spotted by a German aircraft, shelled and machine gunned, sustaining casualties, mostly amongst the NCOs. Then, just before zero hour, 52nd Divisional Artillery commenced its bombardment, the Germans responding with a defensive barrage, fortunately falling a hundred yards behind the 2/6th. The 57th Divisional Artillery opened fire at zero hour and the two lead companies of the 2/6th advanced, two platoons up, each moving in section 'worms'. The Germans responded with a barrage of their own, but it always fell behind the advance.

The right platoon of C Company was delayed by a German machine gun; when the supporting platoon moved to outflank the German position, the Germans withdrew into a dugout, where they were made prisoner. B Company was not delayed, although sections were detached to deal with individual German posts. Both companies occupied the village of Riencourt, on which the Germans then concentrated their artillery fire, inflicting further casualties.

The division then moved to Inchy on the Canal du Nord, five miles from Cambrai. The canal was incomplete, being dug but not filled, and was still a significant obstacle. The RAF provided assistance, with ground attack support and reporting where the Germans were retiring. On 11 September, the 8th and 2/7th King's failed to establish a post on the canal. C Company 2/6th King's succeeded; but the following day the Germans counter attacked and C Company, outflanked, withdrew. In the process, the Company Commander, Lieutenant Sage, and seven men were killed and twenty one wounded. Sage was originally from 6th Gloucesters, attached to the 2/6th. The King's were relieved on the 13th and the 52nd Division relieved the division on the 16th.[49]

57th Division rested at Barly until the 26th, when they started their move back to the front, so that by midday on the 27th the 2/6th were some 600 yards east of Moeuvres. Deploying into artillery formation, they advanced across the Canal, through a stretch of the Hindenburg Line and on

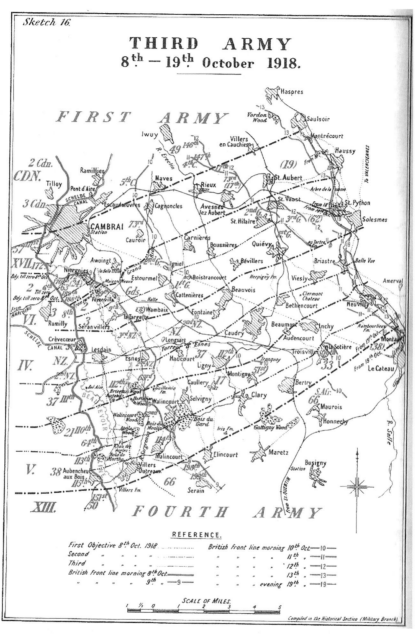

Third Army and the 57th Division, 8–19 October 1918. The 57th Division was not in combat as regularly as the 55th Division, but they did take part in the final advance as well, starting near Cambrai. (*Official History*)

to occupy high ground a mile east of Moeuvres. The plan was for the 52nd and 63rd Divisions to capture two objectives (the Red and Brown Lines), after which 171 and 172 Brigades would take a third objective (Blue Line). 170 Brigade would then seize crossings of the Canal de l'Escaut. With the Red Line captured and advances being made on the Brown Line, the 57th Division started to move on the morning of the 28th. The 2/6th King's attacked Anneux, during which the OC A Company, Lieutenant James, was wounded but carried on for eighteen hours until his CO ordered him to get aid: James received a Bar to his MC. Second Lieutenant Shirt, who had joined the battalion ten days before, was killed in action on the 28th, as was Second Lieutenant Cowman DCM, of 15 Coronation Drive, Great Crosby. Liverpool was still supporting its territorials. Patrols went forward to investigate the Marcoing Line and joined up with the Canadians, who had captured its southern section. 2/7th King's were able to cross the Canal. It was probably for bravery this action that the author's great grandfather, Corporal Fred Service, 9th King's, was awarded the Military Medal.[50]

During the night of 7/8 October the Canadians launched a general advance. 57th Division sent out small patrols, followed by fighting patrols overnight in order to keep abreast with the Canadians and then, at 7.30 am, a general advance was ordered. 171 Brigade advanced with the 2/6th left and the 2/7th right. By midday they had reached the railway line and by 2 pm had passed though Cambrai.[51]

The Battle of Bapaume had been conducted by Third Army and the left wing of Fourth Army. They advanced ten miles across the old Somme battlefield, capturing 3400 prisoners and 270 guns, and pierced the Hindenburg Line. For its part, 171 Brigade was justly proud of its achievements at Riencourt and was complemented accordingly.

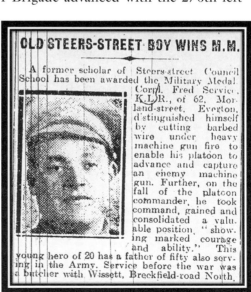

OLD STEERS-STREET BOY WINS M.M.

A former scholar of Steers-street Council School has been awarded the Military Medal. Corpl. Fred Service, K.L.R., of 62, Morland-street. Everton, distinguished himself by cutting barbed wire under heavy machine gun fire to enable his platoon to advance and capture an enemy machine gun. Further, on the fall of the platoon commander, he took command, gained and consolidated a valuable position, "showing marked courage and ability." This young hero of 20 has a father of fifty also serving in the Army. Service before the war was a butcher with Wissett, Breckfield-road North.

Although this account is a brief summary of a series of largely forgotten small actions within a larger battle, it was an achievement nonetheless.[52]

The division was soon back on the offensive, this time at Laventie, north of Béthune. At 7.30 am on 17 October 1918 the division advanced in the general direction of Lille. The outgoing division, the London territorials of the 47th, had nothing significant to tell them. Scouts went forward. The rate of German fire increased, so that lead companies moved from extended order to sections in column. The advance was so rapid that there was only just enough time to report a new position to HQ before they were off again: the CO of 2/6th King's marched at the head of his battalion, guiding the advance by use of his whistle and arms. They passed the German artillery positions that had plagued them in the Houplines positions. The road to La Marais was cratered and the way littered with booby traps. The sappers and pioneers were kept busy making safe roads and repairing them for the passage of wheeled transport.

By midday, the 57th were marching along the tramways of the suburbs. The inhabitants, when they realised it was safe, emerged with cheers, waving flags, singing songs and clutching bottles which had been buried since the arrival of the Germans. With no instructions and no real opposition, 171 Brigade decided to push on towards Flers and Annappes, about thirteen miles beyond, and then to Willems on the 19th. On the 20th, 171 Brigade was ordered to seize the bridgeheads over the Scheldt just north of Tournai, with Liverpool Irish leading off and crossing into Belgium. They were held up just beyond Blondain.

The following day, the 2/6th took the lead, with a battery of artillery, two sections of machine guns, a medium trench mortar batter and two bridging sections of Royal Engineers in support. The composition of this force looks similar to the flying column used by 55th Division at about the same time, only lacking the cavalry component.

The 2/6th experienced the problems of open warfare. They had no idea where the enemy was, whilst bridges and roads had been damaged or demolished to prevent the movement of artillery. A Company was held up by machine gun and trench mortar fire. Its Lewis guns located and neutralised one German machine gun but the weight of fire and the death of the company commander, Captain Carr (shot through the head while conducting a personal reconnaissance), effectively halted the advance at 1 pm. Other platoons came across similar machine gun nests, which were costly to destroy. The advance resumed at 7 pm. The following morning Froyennes was found to be deserted and the advance continued to the river, where the Germans kept up harassing fire from the far side.[53]

The 2/6th were relieved by the 2/7th and were billeted in Le Cornet and then Willems until 30 October. There, outside the 2/6th Bn HQ, was a map showing the progress of the allied advance, around which both civilians and soldiers crowded. Unbeknownst to the division, this was to be their last action. On the 30th, they moved back towards Hallemes and then Fives, and passed the London territorials of the 47th Division moving up to the front. The 57th Division were at Fives until the Armistice.[54]

When the telegram announcing the Armistice arrived there 'was no excitement, no wild cheering or parading of the streets'; the men became silent and thoughtful, thinking on their survival, and contemplating those who were not so fortunate. All was in contrast with the scenes of celebration in London by those who were not fighting.[55]

Chapter 6

Liverpool Territorials with other Divisions

S everal units spent the duration of the war with other formations, including: 1/1st (West Lancashire) Field Ambulance RAMC, served with the regular 29th Division in Gallipoli and then on the Western Front; 2/2nd (West Lancashire) Field Ambulance RAMC, served with the New Army 21st Division; 1/2nd (West Lancashire) Field Company RE, served with the East Lancashire Territorials (later 42nd Division), in Egypt and Gallipoli and later on in Salonika.

1/1st (West Lancashire) Field Company, RE[1]

Major Campbell, RE commanded the second Liverpool territorial unit to deploy overseas. The 1/1st had a very uncomfortable start to 1915. Ordered to embark at Southampton on New Year's Day, they did not complete the crossing to France until the 3rd, and then took a further six days to concentrate at Blendecques. Their War Diary cover page states that they were Army Troops, unattached to any division. January was taken up with training, which included regular route marches in full fighting order and engineering tasks. On the 15th, for example, Number 1 Section constructed a flying bridge over a stream using a GS wagon as a raft. Real tasks started to arrive in February, with work on trenches around Tattinghem, either by themselves or supervising an infantry battalion. The weather and work took its toll on the men. The War Diary recorded a steady rise in the number of men in hospital, rising to twenty men, or 10 per cent of the establishment, by the beginning of February.

On 11 February, orders were received for the Company to join 4th Division at Nieppe. The Company would remain with it until 27 February 1916, except for a few weeks in April 1915 when they were attached to the South Midlands Division, TF. For the next year the Company would be mostly employed in constructing trenches and strong points or repairing roads and bridges. There is nothing to show that they were employed in an offensive capacity, indeed there is no mention of any divisional attacks. So, for example, the first casualties occurred on 12 March 1915 while supervising a group of civilian workers engaged in road repairing. The first named casualty, Sapper Kingsley, was wounded in the leg on the 21st, but no circumstances are given. Otherwise, their time was busy, but safe. On 20 April, the Company received a draft of a corporal and eleven sappers, which brought the strength up to 215, just two drivers under establishment.

On their return to 4th Division, the Company found itself in the Ypres Salient; and from the beginning it was clear that this was an altogether more dangerous section of the Western Front. They arrived at Potijze Wood on 30 April and started to dig in. The Company suffered two deaths that day to German shelling. Corporal Stephen Gamble, the 31 year old son of Samuel and Mary, of Sherdley Villa, Green End, Sutton, St Helens, is buried in the Ramparts Cemetery in Ypres. The second was Sapper Peter Newcombe, who is commemorated on the Menin Gate. The shelling continued during which CSM Godfrey was compliment as he 'behaved splendidly under fire'.

In all, there would be seven deaths before the Company rejoined the West Lancashire Division in 1916, of which six occurred in the Ypres Salient. Two days later, on 2nd May, 21 year old Sapper William Garner of Club Cottage, Rigby Street, St Helens was killed. Lieutenant John Dixon-Nuttall, 24, of 'Ingleholme', Ecclestone Park, St Helens and a Corporal Kay were both killed in May. Sapper GE Dean, the 34 year old husband of Hannah, from 11 Greenfield Road, St Helens died on 4 July; but after him there would be a six month respite before the death of Sapper J Taylor on 5 January 1916. Of the fatalities where the CWGC provides biographical details, all were residents of St Helens, as one would expect from pre-war territorials or those who joined their local unit in the first months of the war, and most of those are identified by a house name (Sherdley Villa, Club Cottage, Ingleholme) rather than a house number, which would indicate a more well-to-do background – today, for example, Ingleholme is Ingleholme Gardens, an expensive development of four and five bedroom detached houses.

The Company retained its connections with the West Lancashire RE when Captain A D Murray left for England in August to command the new 2/2nd Field Company; and in September Lieutenant Bretherton left on promotion to command the 2/3rd Field Company. In return, Captain JB Hughes arrived from the Glamorgan Fortress RE. Despite his lack of Lancashire connections, his name regularly appears in the War Diary. Routine work continued, with the addition of mining and counter mining, in which Captain Hughes played a major role. On 17 August, for example, the OC spent a whole morning down a mine and reported hearing Germans a long way off.

Most of the work undertaken was routine, if dangerous and uncomfortable, but it was recognised. The GOCs of 4th Division and of 11 Brigade, for whom the Company had been working, complimented them for their work to improve a bridge while under fire.

Home leave commenced on 9 June 1915, when one officer and six men departed. Thereafter there was a regular party departing; but, with over 200 men in the company, it would take a long time for them all to get home. 'Rest' was another novelty which started four days later, on the 13th, when the War Diary simply stated 'All Sections Resting. Wet.'

At the end of July, 4th Division left the Salient for a much quieter sector of the front, at least in 1915: the Company moved to Mailly-Maillet, where its first task was to improve trenches in front of Auchonvillers, which is the village just behind what would become the Beaumont Hamel sector of the Somme the following year.

Germans used gas on two occasions at the end of January 1916. On the first occasion the report was received in the evening, so all night work was cancelled; no casualties were reported on either occasion, so they may well have been false alarms.

On 26 February, the 1/1st were ordered to rejoin 55th Division and set about handing over their stores to another territorial engineer company, the 1/1st Durhams.

1/2nd (West Lancashire) Field Company, RE – 420th Company[2]

Between June and December 1915, the West Lancashire engineers under Major Dixon-Nuttall served in Gallipoli with the East Lancashire Division.[3] On 22 June 1915, forty men under Lieutenant Bishop sailed with the transport from Avonmouth on HMT *Minneapolis*, followed a few days later by the remainder of the company (five officers and 214 other ranks) on HMT *Argyllshire*. Eleven days later the engineers disembarked at Alexandria and then moved to camp in Aboukir. On 14 July the anticipated telegram arrived from Mudros 'Field Company to Helles'. They were in the war. But not just yet. Five officers, one warrant officer and 164 other ranks took ship to Mudros, and were put to work loading and unloading ships. The Company suffered its first medical casualty there. Lieutenant Mottram was hospitalised with dysentery. He would not be the last.

Finally, at 5 am on the 28th, they took ship from Imbros, arriving at W Beach fifteen hours later. Their first task was to construct dugouts for the CRE 42nd (East Lancashire) Division, TF and build a road between Y and W Beaches. Early September saw the company taking up quarters in Gully Beach, where they were engaged in blasting rock, surveying for drainage, road building, building retaining walls, improving wells and supervising parties of a hundred infantry, who were the ones actually doing the road building and drain digging. The sappers also constructed dugouts for headquarters and their own winter quarters. There was a clear emphasis on the forthcoming winter.

On 15th July the sappers entered the front line at last. A Turkish mine had blown up about thirty five yards of Border Barricade, along with fifteen yards of an adjoining advanced sap. With only thirty minutes notice, Captain Reid and fifty one sappers were sent to clear the damage and rebuild the trenches. Fortunately, the work was completed without loss early the following morning. Mining was not the preserve of the Turks and a couple of days later Lieutenant Harris was attached to the corps mining company. Harris held a mining degree, so was an obvious candidate.

Lieutenant Mottram rejoined the company having recovered from dysentery on Mudros; but on the 19th a fellow officer, Lieutenant Simpson, was evacuated with the same ailment. The War Diary gives the strength for that day as four officers and 142 other ranks on duty, with one officer and twenty three other ranks in hospital. This means that, after less than a month at Helles, 14 per cent of the company were incapacitated, probably by dysentery, as there is no mention of any casualties due to enemy action. Neither time in the trenches on the night of the 15th/16th, nor similar work parties dispatched during the last nights of September, resulted in any casualties. Lieutenant Harris returned to duty at the end of September, just in time for Captain Reid to be sent off sick, by which time the effective strength of the company was down to four officers and 124 other ranks. The departure of other ranks to hospital had not warranted a mention in the War Diary.

The first reinforcements arrived on 9 October: Second Lieutenant Bogle from the Lancashire Fortress Engineers and Second Lieutenants Eastwood and Entwistle from the 1st and 2nd (East Lancashire) Field Companies respectively.

From the middle of October the Company was employed in the front line trenches, on sapping, constructing loopholes and generally improving the trenches. At 7 am on the 18th the Turks blew a large mine. There was no material damage to the front line trenches, but it took the sappers three hours to clear the debris. Again, there were no reported casualties, but the blast would have done nothing to help nervous soldiers, coming so soon after another mine in the same area.

By late October 42nd Division's strength was so reduced that four infantry battalions were amalgamated and two more disbanded to reinforce others. All this happened at a time when there were entire New Division armies being trained and drawing manpower from desperately undermanned formations actually in the war. Support to the division did come in the form of the (dismounted) territorial South East Mounted Brigade.[4]

Late October saw the beginning of heavy rain and frost. Over the period 15 – 17 November a violent storm raised the sea level, flooding out bivouacs and stores on the beach, while the gullies concentrated the rain into torrents that swept stores out to sea. An even more violent storm on the 26th flooded the trenches of both sides, so that Ottomans and Lancashiremen had to stand on the parapets or be drowned. Fortunately, neither side had war-like intentions under those conditions. More equipment and stores were washed away. The following day the wind changed direction to blow from the north and the rain became snow, followed by a hard frost. Men froze or lost limbs to frostbite; 10,000 were evacuated from the peninsula in four days. The resulting deep mud made movement only possible with extreme physical effort, and of course it was the role of the RE to make it all good again.[5]

Work continued in the trenches throughout late October and into early November, with a note about how moonlight interfered with work in the front line trenches. A party was engaged nightly in wiring or setting trip wires in front of the trenches and saps. The effective strength at the end of October was seven officers and ninety seven other ranks.

Ominously, Turkish shelling was noted to increase early in November, especially at night; by the middle of the month battlefield casualties are recorded. On the 9th, Second Lieutenant Archbold was wounded in the thigh by a bomb. The following night, Lance Corporal Whittingham received what was described as a 'slight' bullet wound in the left thigh while wiring around Birdcage Walk West. Then, on the 12th, Lance Corporal Williams was shot in the head and killed by a sniper while preparing a parapet. The CWGC records the death of Sapper (he was presumably Acting Lance Corporal) 6298 C Williams, son of Mr R Williams, of 64 Cholmondeley Street, Widnes, and he is buried in Twelve Tree Copse Cemetery.[6] At the end of this sombre period, the Company's effective strength was down to six officers and eighty eight other ranks.

Once again there was an exchange of sick officers – Lieutenant Simpson rejoined the Company just as Second Lieutenant Eastwood went sick. The East Lancashire RE provided a replacement for Simpson, Second Lieutenant Echlow.

Lord Kitchener visited Gallipoli in mid November to discuss the theatre commander's recommendation to evacuate the peninsula. Operations began on 8 December, but this did not mean that offensive operations ceased. On 19 December a mine was blown that allowed 7th Lancashire Fusiliers and the West Lancashire REs to enter the Ottoman positions and drive them out. The Turks counter attacked, recovered the lost trenches, but were then driven out by a Lancashire Fusilier counter attack. Then began consolidation. At the end of the day the British front line had been pushed forward. A similar operation by 9th and 10th Manchesters, supported by 5th East Lancashires and the West Lancashire REs, on the same day failed to get into the Ottoman trenches and the British withdrew with some losses. When the Turks tried to capitalise on the confusion with a bayonet charge it was checked and both sides returned to their starting positions.[7]

42nd Division was relieved by a New Army division, the 13th (Western) Division. At 5 pm on 29 December 1915, the infantry began the five mile march to the beaches and evacuation. The engineers, medics and gunners, however, remained to support 13th Division. The East Lancashire Field Companies left first, leaving the West Lancashires and a few East Lancashire officers until the final evacuation on 8/9 January 1915. During this period, especially at the end, there was a constant fear that the Ottomans, knowing that the perimeter was being weakened, would attack, summed up by an anonymous officer: 'If ever man knew terror, I knew it that night'.[8]

The Company was refitted in Egypt, where their Gallipoli uniforms were reduced to rags, not that anyone had noticed before: they had all been the same. In July 1916, when 42nd Division left Egypt for France, the West Lancashire Field Company was left at Suez and eventually returned to Mudros. They were engaged in a wide range of duties across the island, including pier repairs, water supply construction, railways, quarrying and blacksmithying. There were also huts to be built for the Royal Navy Air Service and, probably their most lasting contribution, completing the monument in the Mudros East Cemetery. From Mudros, the Company was moved to Salonika where, again, they were distributed around the garrison on specific tasks. One unusual task occurred during the night of 18/19 August 1916, when the town caught fire. Two officers and eighteen men took explosives to blast firebreaks in the town in an attempt to halt the fire, but 'owing to the confusion caused by the civilian population, little could be done'. The Company's strength was given as eight officers and 223 men.

The Company's Territorial roots were retained, even this far into the war, which is shown by an entry for 10 September 1916: Captain (Temporary Major) W F Dixon-Nuttall DSO RE TF was temporarily appointed as Staff Officer to the Director of Works, Salonika; his post was filled by Lieutenant (Temporary Captain) J H Meston-Reid RE TF as Acting Major; his post was filled by Second Lieutenant (Temporary Lieutenant) JH Mottram RE TF as Acting Captain while Company Second in Command. Three of the eight officers were certainly territorials.

During the Company's time in Salonika, there were three deaths, none of which were due to enemy action. Biographical details provided on two of them show their West Lancashire connections. Sapper W Denton, the

26 year old grandson of Ellen Troth, of 146 Knowsley Road, St Helens, died of dysentery on 24 October 1917; and the following February 21 year old Sapper Walker, the son of Mary Walker, of 241 Lily Lane, Bamfurlong, Wigan, 'died suddenly'. The third fatality occurred as a result of a quarrying accident. On 6 June 1917 Acting Lance Corporal Glover and Sapper Myers were severely burned following a blasting accident and Myers died of his injuries ten days later.

Probably as a result of this being a relatively quiet theatre, leave to the UK commenced, with ten other ranks departing on 4 October 1917. This would have been the first opportunity to get home and see their families since the Company left in June 1915. Leave to the UK continued, even though it was no longer mentioned in the War Diary, because, when demobilisation commenced in December 1918, those who were already on leave in the UK were 'struck off strength'. The first to be sent home were a police constable and twelve miners, plus two regulars who resumed their career. On 1 April 1919 the ten remaining '1914 men' were demobilised. They would represent the last of the pre-war territorials of those who joined their local unit at the outbreak of hostilities. Fifteen days later the remaining cadre of two officers and seven men were sent home for demobilisation, ending the Company's war service.

1/1st (West Lancashire) Field Ambulance, 29th Division – 87th Field Ambulance[9]

The 29th Division was created from units that were collected from various imperial garrisons and were commanded by Major General Hunter-Weston. Most famously, the division included 1st Battalion, The Lancashire Fusiliers, who would win 'Six VCs before breakfast' during the initial Helles landings; and who would again suffer heavily at Beaumont Hamel on the first day of the Somme.

Gillon's divisional history pays compliments to the three field ambulances, all territorials, from Liverpool, Aberdeen and Ipswich, noting that 'all the officers were in civilian practice before the war'. He might have mentioned that the men were also all civilians before the war.

The Field Ambulance's War Diary commenced in March 1915 while still in its mobilisation phase. Two Old Crosbeians were early members. Private Thomas Dykes originally joined 2nd (Welsh) Field Ambulance while studying medicine in Cardiff, but transferred on his return to Liverpool. He does not appear to have completed his studies as he was never commissioned as a Medical Officer and in fact was discharged as unfit to serve on 16 October 1914. He died, probably of tuberculosis, in June 1916. Another medical student who did not complete his studies was Lieutenant Edgar Golding. He enlisted as a driver but on 1 January 1915 was commissioned as an 'Honorary' lieutenant in the Army Service Corps and transferred to the 3rd Field Ambulance. He subsequently transferred to the Royal Flying Corps, was shot down and died of wounds in September 1917.[10]

Another pre-war member was IWM interviewee Driver Richard Yorston, who, like so many that summer of 1914, remembered going to Cumbria on annual camp on Saturday, returned on Sunday and was mobilised on the Monday. Cecil Tomkinson's interview is also held by the IWM. He joined after war was declared but before Kitchener's call for volunteers because he felt he should do something and because a lot of business dried up with the outbreak of war. He recalls moving from Tranmere Road to Croxteth Park, where the men lived in tents, but were moved to Canterbury before they were issued with tents and boots. Both Yorston and Tomkison enjoyed their time in Rugby before deploying to the Mediterranean.[11]

As with all territorial units, the Field Ambulance had to separate those who volunteered for overseas service from those who would not. Although there would undoubtedly have been a lot of informal pressure at this time, Richard Yorston's interview provides the only example of what may be called foul play during my research for this book. He and an unnamed medical student, who later became a consultant surgeon in Liverpool, gave white feathers to those who would not volunteer.[12]

On 12 March 1915, members of the Field Ambulance received a new set of boots and clothing: 'The sizes not in accordance with the indents sent in the case of the clothing but the sizes of boots were satisfactory'. A second suit and boots arrived on the 15th. The County Associations had struggled to provide soldiers with two suits of service dress. Whatever suit they were mobilised in would have worn thin by the following March and they may not have had a second suit.

The Field Ambulance was supported by the Second Line unit, as was common. Bugler Pothill arrived from the 2/1st on 5 May, and seven days later another fifteen men arrived 'to complete establishment'. Lieutenant JC Class 're-joined' the 1/1st from a 'Reserve unit', which may have meant that he has been assisting with the recruiting and training of the 2/1st.

Lieutenant Colonel Fagan TD, commanding, led the Field Ambulance to embarkation for Alexandria. En route, a case of appendicitis required surgery but, 'owing to the fact that our wagons were left behind at the port of embarkation, we were without surgical equipments – a most serious state of affairs which handicapped the operator'. Enough instruments were collected for the operation and the patient was put ashore at Gibraltar, apparently with no ill-effects. From Alexandria, they sailed for Lemnos and arrived on Gallipoli on 25 April 1915. They were established at Gully Beach, with an Advanced Dressing Station at Geoghan's Bluff. Horse ambulances were eventually provided for the transfer of patients between the two.

This War Diary was one of the two most detailed examined for this book (the other belonging to the 98th Field Ambulance) once operations began. The entry for 1 August 1915, for example, commences with 'There has been little of interest to record' and then goes on for one and a quater pages. Following the landings, the entries are full of accounts of surgical details: 28 April 'another batch of wounded (50 arrived about 7.30 pm – began to operate at 7.45 pm..........; 1 May 'Lt. Col. Hulme 1st Border Regt died today........'; 2 May Pte Farrow Munsters with 'no less than 24 bayonet stabs inc 1 to the head none of them more than 1 inch in width & ½ inch deep'.

Gillon recounts how, on the first day, there was no space for anything other than the most basic care on the beach. Casualties had to be evacuated back to the ships from which they had disembarked. Lack of space remained a problem throughout the campaign. Dust and flies were everywhere, while fresh fruit and vegetables and drinking water were in short supply. Simple scratches quickly became septic and operations were avoided if at all possible. Dysentery was mentioned in all accounts.

It was not only wounds which had to be treated. By 23 August, the Field Ambulance was only at 75 per cent of its established strength due to disease. On that day, the remaining personnel were shipped to Imbros for a period of rest and recuperation. The daily regime of PT in the morning and bathing in the afternoon soon had a beneficial effect on the men.

One of those permanently evacuated from Gallipoli was Driver Richard Yorston. Once recovered, he was posted to 2/1st Field Ambulance, where he became the batman to a major to whom he had previously given a white feather! Quick to escape, he spent the remainder of the war as batman to the Assistant Director of Medical Services to 67th Division, which seems to have been a safe way to pass the war.[13]

Back on Helles, with the coming of winter, the weather started to deteriorate. Gillon's account gives details of the horrors of the winter conditions, 'when men froze as they walked', with every facility 'chocked to overflowing with cases of frostbite. Like Trojans, the staffs toiled to collect every tarpaulin and brazier to warm and shelter the sufferers. Cooks, orderlies, officers, all vied with one another in trying to cope with the rush. And this at a time when every R.A.M.C. unit was sadly understrength.' 1 November was a particularly stormy night, but the end was in sight and on the last day of the month the five officers and 168 men left for Mudros; and from there to Alexandria in January, where they were inspected by General Murray. Three Senior NCOs received twenty one days leave in Cairo and undoubtedly they enjoyed that far more than any compliments from Murray.

Rest in Egypt was short-lived and the division was soon on the move again. It sailed on 14 March 1916 for Marseilles and then travelled via Paris to the Western Front, where it entered the line around Auchonvilliers – Ocean Villas to the Tommy – opposite the German held village that would mean more pain for the Lancashire Fusiliers – Beaumont Hamel.

For the attack on 1 July 1916, the Field Ambulance was reinforced by four General Service wagons for sitting cases, three two-horse ambulances and ten motor ambulances, and an officer and thirty eight men from 89th Field Ambulance. The first walking wounded cases arrived at 8.15 am from the 2nd Royal Fusiliers, 1st Dublin Fusiliers and 16th Middlesex. More serious cases started to arrive at 8.40 am. Once these were dressed they were put into groups of fifteen to twenty five under an NCO and sent to the VIII Corps

Clearing Station at Acheux. Horsed ambulances and lorries were needed for those who could not walk the distance. It would be 8 pm before they were all despatched. For the effective provision of medical care, it was essential that casualties were removed from the front areas as soon as possible to prevent congestion.

It was clear, however, that there were casualties in front of Beaumont Hamel, so the stretcher bearers, all the GS wagons and all the horsed ambulances, plus four motor ambulances were sent there. That night, the OC was able to visit the Regimental Aid Posts of the Newfoundland Regiment, 16th Middlesex, and the Dublin, Royal and Lancashire Fusiliers and his own Advanced Dressing Station. The RAPs each had an average of four cases only, and these were being evacuated by his own lorries faster than they were arriving from the front. This does not give the impression of a medical system that collapsed under the weight of casualties, although by this point they would have been working for over twelve hours.

On 2 July we see evidence of the medical evacuation chain beginning to break down. The stretcher bearers were exhausted, while help promised was not forthcoming and the cases coming in were increasingly the stretcher cases, 'men being got in from the ground in front of our trenches'. By the end of the day, the horses were exhausted as well and had to be rested. Four motor ambulances from 1/1st (South Midland) Field Ambulance arrived to replace them. It also provided an officer and twenty one men. From 11 am, stretcher bearers were able to get into No Man's Land to recover the remaining casualties, and there were more to be evacuated back from the RAPs: between 1.15 pm and 3.30 pm there were 682 stretcher and sitting cases. Two cases were noted as having had their wounds dressed by the enemy. The aim now was to get all of the casualties in by nightfall, which may well have meant that they had spent thirty six hours in the open, wounded. When the artillery warned that it was to bombard the enemy trenches at 3.20 pm, the stretcher bearers had to be withdrawn and the search for casualties abandoned.

On 4 July medical procedures returned to their normal routine, with only twenty six cases remaining. 2111 cases had been treated. Gillon's sole reference to its role on 1 July was how, having been refitted in Egypt, they 'were ready for the work when it began in earnest on July 1, 1916'.

29th Division continued to play a major part in the fighting until, on 14 December 1918, the division was chosen as part of the British Army of the Rhine: 'Weather wet. March continued. Unit crossed the frontier at STAVELOT-MALMEDY road at 10:20 am arriving at ELSENBORN. Well billeted in a German Base Camp.' This Field Ambulance was the only Liverpool territorial unit to reach Germany.

The War Diary continued until September 1919, by which time entries were limited to 'Patients Remaining'.

1/2nd (West Lancashire) Field Ambulance, 32nd Division then 30th Division – 98th Field Ambulance[14]

On mobilisation, the 1/2nd were initially sent to the New Army's 32nd Division, before joining another New Army division, the 30th, with which they would spend the rest of the war. 30th Division included the Liverpool, St Helens and Manchester 'Pals' battalions, so at least the Field Ambulance was with units raised in the same locality. Unlike the infantry, the other arms were not given the 'Pals' title and, from the beginning of the War Diary, the signature stamp used is always 98th (County Palatine) Field Ambulance. You have to look hard to find evidence of their territorial origins. On 3 June 1915, for example, the territorials who were Army Service Corps drivers were all given 7th Rate Corps Pay, a pay rise in recognition of their length of service over the New Army volunteers; the following day a reinforcement from 3/1st (West Lancashire) Field Ambulance was received. So again we see this pattern of the reserve or Home Service territorial units supporting those which were preparing for Overseas (Imperial) Service; in this case, the reserve territorial units were supporting territorial units deployed to support the New Armies, once again showing just how vital the TF was to the war effort.

Private Norman Ellison was killed on 30 July 1916; the CWGC records his unit as being the 98th (1/2nd West Lancashire) Field Ambulance, a mix of the old and new titles. As Ellison was from Pemberton, Wigan, he was unlikely to have been a pre-war territorial. Finally, on 7 March 1918, Staff Sergeant Loughlin was awarded the Territorial Efficiency Medal. The criteria for this was twelve years' service, with war service counting as double. With three and a half years' war service counting as seven years, Loghlin would have had five years' pre-war territorial service.

The Field Ambulance was at Larkhill when it deployed to France in November 1915. The winter was spent continuing its training before entering the line on the Somme. Although the Field Ambulance was one of only two Liverpool territorial units to be directly involved on 1 July 1916, the battle is barely mentioned in the War Diary, which reflects 30th Division's successful advance and the relatively light casualties experienced that day.

As late as 28 July 1916, the entries were short: 'Usual routine carried out in Rest Station. The work of the bearer Sub-Division was actually the same as on the preceding day.'

Then came the fighting of 29–31 July. At 6 pm on the 29th, A and C Sections of the Bearer Sub-Division were sent to the Advanced Dressing Station at Maricourt under the command of 98th Field Ambulance, while B Section, commanded by Lieutenant Dobers, established a collection point on the Aricourt-Briqueterie Road. By 9 pm casualties were sustained by the infantry moving up that road and B Sub-Division was busy collecting and evacuating them by horse or motor ambulances 'which were able to run up and down the road in the intervals of shelling' – which does not sound very healthy even before the battle commenced. The shelling continued overnight, and at 2 am the following morning gas shells were fired too. The stretcher bearers were forced to work in gas helmets, which would have made their work in caring for casualties and in carrying them doubly difficult. Only three stretcher bearers were gassed, and then only slightly, so they were able to return to their duties soon afterwards.

The infantry attacked at 4 am. Lieutenant Roberts and some of stretcher bearers moved up to Maltzhorn Trench to two Regimental Aid Posts so that they could provide better medical support. The evacuation chain was a regimental responsibility to the RAPs, then RAMC stretcher bearers were responsible to the collection point and then by ambulance to the ADS. However, German shelling of Maltzhorn Trench was so severe that Roberts ordered his men to take shelter in the trench and in doing so Private Ellison (mentioned earlier) was killed and two more wounded. As a result of the shelling, the remaining stretcher bearers were withdrawn further down the trenches. Roberts and Sergeant O'Connell remained at the RAPs until the withdrawal was completed;

but then a shell exploded overhead, mortally wounding Roberts and injuring and partially burying O'Connell. When Roberts and O'Connell did not rejoin the bearers, Lance Corporal Goodman asked for a volunteer, Private Byrne, to look for them. When they found the pair, Byrne remained with them while Goodman went to the collection point for assistance. Byrne later reported that Roberts had died without regaining consciousness.

Lieutenant Benjamin Richard Roberts was the 41 year old son of George and Jemima of Athlone, County West Meath, so unconnected with Liverpool or Manchester, unless he had moved to one of those cities to work. He represents another of the Irishmen who volunteered for the British Army. His body was recovered and buried by the Reverend Wilcox on 31 July at Corbie Communal Cemetery Extension. There was even the opportunity to organise a gun carriage to carry his coffin, with all of the officers and men of the tented sub section in attendance.

Heavy shelling continued so that on the morning of the 30th casualty evacuation had to be abandoned and shelter taken in Casement Trench. Three more of the stretcher bearers were buried but were recovered alive, although suffering from shell shock. By 8 am, another section of stretcher bearers had been sent up and evacuation resumed. The unfortunate side effect of this break in evacuation is that a casualty's chances of survival increases with the speed of their access to medical care. Evacuation was later resumed and continued uninterrupted throughout the day. Another section was sent to Bernafray Wood to evacuate the RFA and RE casualties and stragglers making their way through that area. The third section was kept at the ADS; the three were rotated to relieve each other periodically.

Early on the 31st, Lance Corporal Goodman reported that there were a number of casualties in shell holes in front of Guillemont and asked for volunteers to recover them; Private Bryne and two others did so. By midday all of the casualties were brought in. Evacuations continued all afternoon until they were relieved by fellow West Lancashire territorials, the 2/1st Field Ambulance from 55th Division.

After that battle, the Field Ambulance continued to support the 30th Division. Those experiences are explored in greater detail than is possible here in Graham Maddock's *Liverpool Pals* and Michael Stedman's *Manchester Pals*.

The next incident of note occurred during the Arras campaign of April 1917 when a stretcher bearer, 339245 Private G Pearce, was tried by court martial. It was alleged that, on 12 April, 'while under enemy fire & engaged in collecting wounded, refused to carry a stretcher when ordered to do so, stating that he was shaken or words to that effect' and, secondly, that when ordered to 18th Manchester's RAP, he 'left his squad & ran away'. For this, Pearce was sentenced to death but, as was far more common than is generally accepted, GOC Third Army commuted his sentence to ten years penal servitude, suspended. The sentence was read out to all ranks on parade on 19 May; but what happened to Pearce with his suspended sentence is not recorded.

The Armistice was mentioned in the War Diary, followed by a line that it was business as usual. They were at Armentières in December and in January they were sent to Boulogne, where they were to run a delousing facility at a demobilisation camp there. Over 40,000 men were processed each month in February and March, falling to 20,000 men in April and May until, on 28 June 1919, the field ambulance was abruptly disbanded and sent home.

2/2nd (West Lancashire) Field Ambulance, RAMC 21st Division – 63rd Field Ambulance[15]

The early days of the 2/2nd Field Ambulance's history are taken from Westmore's *Story of the 63rd Field Ambulances*, which tells of the raising of the 'Harper Street Boys', the physical training they undertook in Blackpool and medical training back in Liverpool.

The War Diary commenced when they arrived in Witley, Surrey on 28 August 1915. The officers are listed as Lieutenant Colonel KB Barrett and eight lieutenants, of whom three held territorial commissions, one was a member of the Special Reserve and four were unspecified, indicating wartime commissions. Barrett held both the Volunteer Decoration and the Territorial Decoration. At the end of the month he was placed on the sick list with influenza and was replaced by a regular officer, Major R Storrs RAMC.[16] The period until the 7th was filled with drawing stores and supplies in preparation for embarking for France.

The Field Ambulance sailed for France in September 1915. The first medical incidents occurred on the 15th, with a number of scabies cases, and the following day, when Lieutenant Woodhouse, 12th Northumberland Fusiliers, was admitted for gas poisoning. They were in the war.

21st Division's first action was the Battle of Loos on 26th September. A dressing station was established and processed some 500 casualties. Some of the stretcher bearers reached Loos, while the tented sub sections handled some 1,500 casualties in 48 hours. It was within range of the German guns and one Army Service Corps soldier was wounded. At the beginning of October, the divisional commander complemented them on their work but, at the end of the month, the OC lectured his officers on 'the work performed by this unit during the recent action near Loos, with criticisms'.[17]

The first fatalities – 1809 Corporal Frank Jeffreys and 1636 Private Herbert Robinson – plus three wounded occurred on 5 March 1916 when a shell in the possession of Private Kennedy, one of the wounded, exploded. Thirty-eight year old Jeffreys was the son of John and Louisa Jeffreys of 174 Chatham Street, Liverpool; while 20 year old Robinson was the son of Mr HW and Elizabeth Robinson of 85 St Domingo Vale, Everton.[18] Both fatalities are sad reminders of avoidable accidents in war. They were the first of twenty eight members of the Field Ambulance to die.

There was a steady flow of casualties throughout early 1916 until, on 12 June, the War Diary notes that all patients were to be cleared within a fortnight. Over the same period, the entries grew from a single line per day to half a page each. Despite this, 1 July 1916 passed with hardly a mention: seven motor ambulances were sent to support the Advanced Dressing Station of the 65th Field Ambulance and an officer and sergeant supported the 64th. Two officers, three NCOs and thirty six other ranks were sent to the front line as stretcher bearers; this was increased by another officer and twenty-one other ranks later in the day. Further support was provided the following day. There is no evidence of the mass causalities associated with 1 July 1916 in the War Diary, but the *Story* talks of the difficulties of getting stretchers round the corners of trenches (so tarpaulins were used) and the sheer exhaustion of the stretcher bearers as they worked into the night, each journey into the shattered German trenches becoming longer and longer.[19] August saw more casualties recorded but by early September there were daily single line entries again.

The division fought alongside 55th Division at the Battle of Flers (15–22 September 1916), which brought in another 1000 casualties per day; the bitterly cold nights and hot days did not help. The casualties overwhelmed the Field Ambulance and, in the words of Westmore, 'Something, somewhere had broken down'.[20]

March and April 1917 saw an increase in casualty evacuation, but without mentioning that a battle was raging. This is followed by a five page typed summary of the war diary, which is subtitled

> Phase "B" Battle of Arras – April – May 1917.
> 1st Period Attack on Vimy Ridge April.
> 2nd Period Capture of Siegfried Line May.

This was an unusual acknowledgement that a major battle was going on in the background. Three Military Medals were awarded on 30 April.

The Third Battle of Ypres commenced in a rainstorm and, understandably, is a tale of mud, death and exhaustion. A single shell hit a bearer post, killing fourteen of sixteen present and wounding Privates Ellacott and Martindale.

> To reach the aid post it was necessary to cross a small creek, which, owing to the heavy rains, resembled a sea of mud. Bearers with their loaded stretcher became bogged and had to be pulled out with stretcher slings. Stretchers were sunk to make some kind of a footing, and over their precarious bridge, tripping over the bodies of men lying beneath the surface, the men staggered with their burdens. For 24 hours, wallowing in ooze and slime, the work continued with few intervals. Food here consisted of what could be picked up. Here and there, by the side of dead men, one found begrimed rations which helped to give fresh strength.[21]

Most of the War Diary was taken up with routine business of casualties and postings. American medical officers were posted in from late July 1917, as has already been noted in other field ambulances. There would be a steady rotation of American officers until early 1918.

The division was caught up in the German counter attack around Cambrai, just like the 55th Division. The speed and shock of the initial advance meant that many stretcher bearers were killed or captured when the forward positions were overrun. As positions were abandoned, the *Story* recalls one bespectacled major, still in his blood spattered smock, riding his horse cross country to rejoin them; their vegetable garden was destroyed by a single German shell. As well as retiring, the medical staff also had to care for the wounded, placing a double burden on them.[22]

On 27 May 1918, the Field Ambulance was based at Jonchery, supposedly a quiet French sector, where they could recuperate' when the War Diary noted: 'German Offensive Began'. The Field Ambulance moved rapidly to Ville-en-Tardenois on the 28th, about 11 miles away; Festigny on the 29th; Boursalt on the 30th and 'Souricres' the next day. By the 1st, they had halted at Comblizy and remained there for a fortnight. They had withdrawn about 20 miles. The War Diary entries at Comblizy became more detailed, which suggests Field Ambulance was regaining the initiative; on the 2nd, for example, the OC conducted a reconnaissance of the front to make evacuation arrangements; by the 5th, normal entries resumed.[23]

August was spent at Acheux, but on the 27th they moved to Miraumont and then there were moves every few days; on 8 October, for example, they were based at Bantouzeele, were the War Diary noted: 'Division attacked. Casualties rapidly evacuated. Visited RAPs & relay posts.' As usual, there are no further details.

As part of the Final Hundred Days, the division advanced some 60 miles through Bapaume and Cambrai to almost the Belgian border. 11 November 1918 came and went without mention in the War Diary; according to the *Story*, the day was commemorated by a lack of a bread ration. The following day they moved to Bachant and remained in barracks for the remainder of the month.[24]

The Field Ambulance continued to care for the sick and injured of the division throughout the winter of 1918/1919 until 30 April 1919, when they 'Marched to LONGRPÉ and entrained for LE HAVRE en route to United Kingdom'. On 7 May they landed at Southampton and moved to Catterick Camp, where they were disbanded.

West Lancashire Royal Field Artillery[25]

On 2 August 1915, Lieutenant Colonel James Reynolds, commanding 1/3rd (West Lancashire) Brigade RFA, signed a statement that summarised the brigade's positon for the month. Since being mobilised at their base at 65 Admiral Street, Liverpool, they had been based at Knowsley Park, Liverpool, and then Brasted, Kent. They were currently at Faversham, Kent, as part of 57th (Second West Lancashire) Division TF. Training was also conducted with 2nd Canadian Division. The various administrative functions were described as 'satisfactory', while discipline was 'generally satisfactory' and saluting parades had been conducted. The main problem was that they had been waiting for the approval of a rifle range since April. All but one of the soldiers had undertaken the foreign service obligation.

Lieutenant Colonel Heyward-Melly TD, commanding the 1/4th (Howitzer) Brigade, signed a similar statement, showing that since mobilisation at The Grange, Edge Lane, Liverpool, they had been based at Allerton Priory, Woolton, then Sevenoaks and Canterbury, although at the time 8th Battery was at No. 5 Artillery Training School, Wendover. The brigade was also part of 57th Division. There were further concerns about the overall training and dispositions. 8th Battery was not getting any training except on a Saturday morning, as its guns and equipment were being used by No. 5 School, while two more sights (presumable from 7th Battery) were in Salisbury and the brigade possessed just ten Japanese carbines. New equipment arrived during the month in the form of saddles for the Ammunition Column, a telephone cart for the headquarters and thirty-six new horses. Colonel Hayward considered that a motorcycle for communications was essential and requested one.

Another statement in the 1/4th's War Diary was that of 1/1st Lancashire Battery, RGA. Since being mobilised in Liverpool, it had moved to Bidston Hill, Cheshire; Prenton in Birkenhead; then Dunton Green, Kent; and finally Thanington, near Canterbury. Also part of 57th Division, its OC, Major Charles Harlowe, considered its preparations for overseas service to be complete.

At the beginning of October 1915, the Divisional Artillery sailed for France and came under command of 2nd Canadian Division. Their own brigades of Canadian Field Artillery had been training on obsolete

The 3rd West Lancs. R. F. A.
are Ready !

A greetings card printed by 1/3rd (West Lancashire) RFA. It shows an idealised image of their role in action.

12–pounder guns in Canada, a similar training problem to that experienced by the second line territorials. Artillery units which had crossed to Britain were held up there while they were equipped with modern guns. The Canadian Corps was formed in September 1915 with the arrival of its 2nd Division, but without its artillery, the division was non-effective. By borrowing the West Lancashire Divisional Artillery they were able to support the formation of what would become one of the finest Allied Corps on the Western Front.

On 4 October, the West Lancashire RFA met the Commander Royal Artillery at Kemmel, where the brigades were restructured. Lieutenant Colonel Reynolds took tactical command of No. 1 Group, consisting of 1/1st Brigade, 1/3rd Brigade less 13 Battery and 8 (Howitzer) Battery, which were attached to 6 Brigade. The first fire mission recorded by the brigade was on 8 October when, in response to an SOS, 14 Battery fired 166 rounds. Five days later, in response to another SOS, the battery fired another 197 rounds.

	No. 1 (Right) Group	No. 2 (Centre) Group	No. 3 (Left) Group
Commander	Lt. Col. Reynolds	Lt. Col. Topping DSO	Lt. Col. Brown
	1/3rd Brigade (12th, 14th less 13th Bty)	1/2nd Brigade (9th, 10th, 11th Btys)	4th Brigade CFA
	1/1 Brigade (1st, 2nd, 3rd Bty)	13th Bty (from 1/3 Brigade)	7th (How) Bty
	8th (How) Bty		

The first fatality was recorded on 14 October, when Acting Bombardier Davies died of wounds in hospital in Bailleul. He was the son of Mr and Mrs Davies, of 66 Rodney Street, Birkenhead, Cheshire. As an 18 year old he was underage for overseas service.

War Diary entries for the middle of October 1915 report the weather as being 'very misty' or 'too misty for firing'. In two years' time they would be able to conduct indirect fire missions by map, but clearly in late 1915 there was neither the technology nor the mapping to conduct such missions. It also meant that the infantry were left unsupported in just the weather conditions that made them vulnerable to a German attack.

On 1 November 1915, a report on a bombardment against Muskrat Mound highlights the difficulties experienced by the gunners in these early days. The bombardment lasted thirty minutes from 2 pm, and was immediately hampered by the collapse of some of the Canadian trenches due to the wet weather, which broke the telephone cables between the forward observation officers (FOOs) and the battery. No correction for fall of shot could be made. Fifteen rounds from 2nd Battery hit the German trenches, but another fifteen and all thirty from 3rd Battery overshot the target. The FOOs observed mud and barbed wire being thrown into the air, but no sign of timber or concrete used in the construction of the trenches. The commander of 8th Battery added that, of five direct hits, three were 'blinds', one of which may have ricocheted in the air. So, even when the gunners got their shells on target (which was not made easier when the gun positions lost contact with the FOOs), their job was almost impossible because so many 'dud' shells were supplied to them.

1/4th Brigade's War Diary commenced on 1 December 1915. Headquarters were at Locre, with 7th Battery 1000 yards south of Dickebusch, 8th at

Sketch by]   IN NO MAN'S LAND, EVENING OF JULY 31st, 1917.   [Lt.-Col. W. J. K. Rettie, D.S.O.

The Reality of Artillery in Action. A sketch from 1/4th Brigade, RFA.

Lindenhoek and the ammunition column at Croix de Poperinghe, all near Hazebrouck. The following day Lieutenant Colonel Heywood–Melly was invalided home, to be succeeded by Major (later Lieutenant Colonel) S Pelham Morton TD, commanding 8th Battery, the command of which passed to Captain AC Tod. Morton would command the brigade until it was broken up in October 1916.

December was taken up with preparations to hand over to the artillery of the Indian Lahore Division and in January 1916 the brigade moved to 55th Division for the remainder of the war.

95th (HQ) – 98th Companies, Army Service Corps, 27th Divisional Train[26]

The War Diary opens on New Year's Day 1915 at Chocques, Colonel AH Martin commanding, and, unusually, does not describe the journey to France.

On 8 January, the Train moved to Hersken, with the billets described as '<u>bad</u>' and the following day as 'much overcrowded'; five officers were in the attic of the estaminet on straw. If that was the officer's accommodation, that of the other ranks would have been worse.

The divisional railhead was at Caestre and the divisional refilling point at Westoutre. It appeared that there was only one refilling point, so the brigades were to be supplied in order of: brigade in the trenches; brigade in support; brigade in reserve; divisional troops, including the ambulances.

Martin's War Diary entries were generally negative in tone. On 14 February, for example, four new second lieutenants were posted to the Train: 'All these Officers are new and inexperienced and joined ASC 28 Jany last. A very poor substitute for my own Officers.' Three days later he wrote 'privately' to a Major Gibb at GHQ about the quality of replacement officers with only one month's service. At that stage of the war there was probably little else available.

April began with the concentration of all four companies at Busseboom, on the Poperinghe-Ypres road, which Martin had advocated as a more efficient system.[27]

Lieutenant Colonel AR Liddell took over command of the Train on 26 April.

Unusually for a corps War Diary, on 24 May the impact of the Second Battle of Ypres was noted and all companies were 'warned for eventualities' in response to 'an action by the enemy on a large scale developing east of Ypres'. More significantly, the effects of 'noxious gases' were felt as far back as the Train HQ. The 25th was quiet, but on the 26th the Train was ordered to move to Locre, where the division was transferred to III Corps; and from there to Croix-du-Bac by 1 June, where it settled. They were sufficiently close to the River Lys (a regular feature in the lives of the other Liverpool territorials) for the horses to be watered there from the following day.

Their first fatality occurred on 30 June 1915, when Driver Robert Copas was killed by shell fire, together with Lance Corporal G Matthews of Princess Patricia's Canadian Light Infantry, who was described as a 'loader of supply wagon'. Both are buried in Cité Bonjean Military Cemetery, Armentières, very close to each other – IX C 49 and IX C 47. Copas was a 23 year old from Woking, Surrey.[28]

The only other mention of any other ranks occurred on 28 June. On that occasion the GOC 27th Division issued cards stating his appreciation for 'distinguished services' by Captain Allen ASC, Sergeant A Daborn and Driver E Bristow. The nature of their service was not recorded, but it is exceptional amongst the War Diaries for there to be only three mentions of other ranks in a year.

Interpreters are rarely mentioned in the War Diaries, perhaps surprisingly for an army operating in a non English speaking country. As with everything else, there was a shortage and on 3 October the Train lost one of its four interpreters. Presumably there had originally been one interpreter per company.

On 3 November 27th Division received orders to move to 'the East' (it would spend the rest of the war in Salonika) and the rest of the month was taken up with preparing the division for the new theatre. Although the Train would not go to the East, it was stated on the 16th that all ASC officers under the age of 25 went East with the division. In January the Train left to join 55th Division.

The Lancashire Hussars

Although a pre war member of the West Lancashire Division, the Lancashire Hussars were attached to the Welsh Border Mounted Brigade in August 1914. In April 1915 they became the divisional cavalry for the 57th Division, but were broken up later in the year. RHQ and B Squadron joined 31st Division, which sailed to Egypt. It returned to France in April 1916 and joined the 2nd Indian Cavalry Division, then VIII Corps Cavalry on 11 May 1916. C Squadron was posted to the 35th Division and sailed to France with them and rejoined the regiment as VIII Corps Cavalry. D Squadron joined the 30th Division, with the Liverpool Pals, so at least they were in good company. They rejoined RHQ and B Squadron in the 2nd Indian Cavalry Division.

W R McLeish was a pre war territorial who had enlisted in November 1911, having previously served as a bugler in the old Volunteers. He and his friends, including his future brother-in-law, joined the Hussars together and remembered riding lessons in a riding school owned by a Hussar officer. There were on annual camp at Lowther Park when war was declared, but unfortunately 'there was nothing to do for the cavalry'. He was still in the Hussars when they were dismounted and trained as infantry and survived the war.[29]

The regiment was dismounted and began training as infantry in July 1917. This training was completed in September 1917 and the Hussars were sent to 18th (Service) Battalion, The King's (Liverpool Regiment), the 2nd Liverpool Pals; the former D Squadron rejoined 30th Division. 18th King's was renamed the Lancashire Hussars Yeomanry and passed out of the realm of the territorials to become Pals. Their history from then on is covered in Graham Maddock's *Liverpool Pals*, where he notes that the Hussars' capbadge was still being worn.

However, there is evidence that this process started sooner. Percival Fry transferred to 1/5th King's in December 1916. There may have been an unofficial policy to transfer those who wanted a more active war to join the infantry before the official dismounting and re-training.[30]

Conclusion

For an organisation that was only ever intended to defend the British mainland against invasion after a period of mobilisation training, Liverpool's territorials had a war record that must have exceeded all of Haldane's expectations of ten years earlier. They fulfilled the original Home Defence role through the 57th Division until the invasion threat receded, while also supplying overseas units with desperately needed drafts of trained men; they supported and then fought alongside the regulars of the British Expeditionary Force, the Old Contemptibles.

At first, its infantry provided carrying parties, secured the trenches during attacks, and provided fire support to the regulars. Throughout 1915, they took increasingly important roles in the battles. From late 1916 they launched divisional level operations as part of Corps level battles in the most difficult operating conditions imaginable. They suffered the ignominy of defeat but, crucially, learnt from their failings to become better and stronger. Finally, they were able to stand alone as divisions, corps and even armies fell back, thereby helping to derail part of the German Spring Offensive which the latter had to win or lose the war. With the German offensive unsuccessful, it was then a matter of the Allies rebuilding their strength and returning to the offensive. 55th and 57th Divisions advanced some 50 miles in the last eighty days.

Meanwhile, apart from the infantry, which so often dominates military histories, the other arms were active in their own right. Some were permanently detached and could be found on Gallipoli, at Salonika, or supporting the regulars of 29th Division and the Pals of 30th Division on the Somme. Other units supported the BEF in France or 57th Division in the Home Defence role until January 1916, when they were brought back together with 55th Division.

These were the men of the RAMC, who struggled throughout the battle zone to recover and save the wounded; the RE Field Companies, who accompanied attacks and whose expertise worked to make the trenches safer; the RE Signal Service, who would leave the relative safety of the dugouts to ensure communications worked; the RFA, whose artillery support the infantry sought to lead their attacks and to break up German counter attacks; the logisticians of the ASC, who brought forward everything needed to survive and fight; the veterinarians, who looked after the horses that were essential for this massive effort. Finally, there were the often maligned staff officers, without whose planning critical achievements, like the Defence of Givenchy, would not have been possible.

Although it is recognised that the 'localism' behind the Territorial Force was diluted as the war progressed, these units retained a core connection with their peace time locations, which Major General Jeudwine, for the 55th

"Out of the North Parts".

Division at least, was able to capitalise upon; unfortunately, less is known about 57th Division. Perhaps more importantly, the idea of 'localism' extended throughout the city. Territorials joined units based on their school, profession, social background or the nearest drill hall – these were men who lived, worked, studied and fought together.

The descendants of those territorials remain in Liverpool to this day, training and deploying on operations, to Iraq or Afghanistan, to Olympic and Commonwealth Games or when floods threaten local communities.

OUT OF THE NORTH PARTS – A GREAT COMPANY AND A MIGHTY ARMY[1]

Notes

Chapter 1

1. Maddocks, *Liverpool Pals*, pp. 23–4. The very first Service battalion with the Pals characteristics was the Stockbrokers Battalion of the Royal Fusiliers, but Lord Derby was the first to use the term 'Pals' for recruiting.
2. *A Short History*, pp. 42–3; see also R. Westlake, *The Territorials 1908–1914*, pp. 29, 30, 60–1, 188.
3. Westlake, *The Territorials*, p. 30; Hildrey, *To Answer Duty's Call*, pp. 52, 205–6. See 1/2nd (West Lancashire) Field Company RE – 420th Company, below, for Bogle.
4. *Official History 1914*, II, p. 7.
5. Gillon, *29th Division*, p. ix; Wadsworth, *1st West Lancashire Brigade*; Westmore et al., *The Story of the 63rd Field Ambulance*.
6. The TF was reformed in 1920, and was renamed the Territorial Army in 1921, by which name it was known until 2014, when it became the Army Reserve.
7. D. Langley, "British Line Infantry Reserves of the Great War" Part 1, *Stand To!* Vol. 100 (June 2014) pp. 23–7; Part 2, *Stand To!* Vol. 101 (Sept 2014), pp. 27–31; M. Gillott, "British Line Infantry Reserves of the Great War" Part 3, *Stand To!* Vol. 102 (January 2015), pp. 14–20; Mitchinson, *Gentlemen and Officers*, p. 51.
8. Beckett, 'Territorial Force', p. 132; *Official History 1914*, II, p. 4.
9. See Beckett, *Riflemen Form* (Barnsley, 1987).
10. For example, the uniform and equipment was overhauled, from the soldier's khaki serve service dress of 1902 through to the infantry officer's sword and tunic in 1912.
11. Beckett, *Riflemen Form*, pp. 232, 234, 236.
12. Mitchinson, *England's Last Hope*, pp. 185–6; Beckett, 'Territorial Force', pp. 128, 129; *Official History 1914*, II, pp. 2–4: the five units were the Northumberland Yeomanry, the Dorset Fortress Company RE, 6th East Surreys, and 7th and 8th Middlesex.
13. For convenience, the infantry will be referred to by the battalion number and either King's Own, Loyals, King's or South Lancs, e.g. 5th King's or 4th South Lancs.
14. WO95/2915/2.
15. McCartney, *Citizen Soldiers*, pp. 17, 20, 30–1; Mitchinson, *Gentlemen and Officers*, Ch. 1, esp. p. 50; Ellison Papers quoted in McCartney, *Citizen Soldiers,* p. 29; Beckett cited the London Irish, with only the CO and one Patrick MacGill as being the only genuine Irishmen in the 18th London Irish, 'Territorial Force', p. 146; Hildrey, *To Answer Duty's Call*, pp. 9, 19, 34–5, 72–4, 123–4, 127.
16. Gregson, *1/7th Battalion*, pp. 38–45, 56, 57–8; Beckett found similar class differences when the Westminster Dragoons and 1/9th Manchesters shared a transport to Gallipoli; the latter were apt to spit and swear. 'Territorial Force', p. 145.
17. Roberts, *9th King's*, p. 2; www.9thkings.co.uk.
18. Westlake, *Territorials*, pp. 15, 31; W.R. McLeish interview, IWM 24531.

19. Westlake, *Territorials,* p. 60; Toosey was a pre-WW2 Liverpool Territorial who served in the Dunkirk campaign before being captured at Singapore. For a more accurate account of his career (rather than the 1957 film) see *The Man behind the Bridge* by HRH Price Philip and Professor Peter Davies.
20. Westlake, *Territorials,* p. 61.
21. Ibid, p. 61; www.liverpoolremembrance.weebly.com accessed 6th August 2014.
22. Westlake, *Territorials,* p. 61; Beadon, *Royal Army Service Corps,* vol. II, pp. 16–18; Young, M., *Army Service Corps, 1902–1918* (Barnsley, 2000), p. 213, 297; Westlake, *Territorials,* pp. 1, 61. Westlake give an establishment of 516 all ranks.
23. The two Army Troops battalions were the 4th and 5th Bns the Border Regiment, which did not belong to divisions like the West Lancashire Territorials; the three drivers for the Cable, Airline and Wireless Companies were the RE Signal Service Companies; but as these were based in Liverpool and St Helens, it is unclear why they were part of the North Lancashire Brigade, rather than the Liverpool or South Lancashire Brigades.
24. Mitchinson, *England's Last Hope,* pp. 57, 59, 62–3, 187; *Official History 1914,* II, p. 5.
25. Ibid, pp. 19–22; Beckett, 'Territorial Force', pp. 128–9.
26. Ibid, pp. 71–73, 83; Quoted in Sherson, E., *Townshend of Chitral and Kut,* p. 235 and Nash, *Chitral Charlie,* p. 156; Clayton, *Chavasse,* p. 56.
27. Ibid, pp. 106, 107, 108, 110; Beckett, 'Territorial Force', p. 129.
28. Ibid, pp. 116–7; Beckett, 'Territorial Force', p. 129; Clarke, *Field Army Artillery,* pp. 4, 17–8, 19–20, 24–35, 36–7, 39; Clarke, *Heavy Artillery,* pp. 3–4, 6–7.
29. Ibid, p. 168. For the ASC, see Beadon, *RASC,* ii, p. 17; Young, *ASC,* p. 40.
30. Ibid, pp. 138–9; www.kingsownmuseum.plus.com
31. Batten, S., 'A School for the Leaders', pp. 25–43; *The Times* 7 Sept 1912 p. 6 quoted in Batten; Haig, *War Diary and Letters 1914–1918,* p. 55; Beckett, 'Territorial Force', p. 143.
32. Ibid, pp. 31, 36–7.
33. *LDPM* 5 Aug 1914.
34. Mitchinson, *England's Last Hope,* pp. 183–5, 201–2; Mitchinson, *Territorial Force,* p. 52; *Official History 1914,* II, p. 5 explains the decision not to send the two Lancashire divisions to Ireland because of the 'altered political situation'.
35. Beckett, 'Territorial Force', p. 128.
36. Gregson, *1/7th Battalion,* pp. 59–60; *Official History 1914,* II, p. 5.
37. Roberts, *9th Kings,* p.62.
38. Roberts, *9th Kings,* pp. 2–3; The Newsboys' Home was a charitable institution which provided accommodation for sixty five 'street boys'.
49. Mitchinson, *England's Last Hope,* pp. 91, 99, 199.
40. Gregson, *1/7th Battalion,* p. 45; see also Mitchinson, *Gentlemen and Officers,* p. 165, for a London example.
41. Clayton, *Chavasse,* pp. 55–6, 61; McGilchrist, *Liverpool Scottish,* pp. 13–14.
42. Wyrall, *King's Regiment,* i, p. 72

Chapter 2

1. For further details, see Beckett, 'Territorial Force', p. 133; *Official History 1914,* II, p. 6 gives the figure as 60 per cent of volunteers, provided the unit could recruit to 125 per cent, which was not a problem.
 2. The East Lancashire Division sailed on 10 September 1914, about five weeks into the war and well within the six months mobilisation period. As it was the first TF division to

deploy overseas complete, it became the senior division when numbers were allocated in 1915. The army in the north west of England today is still the 42nd but is now reduced to a brigade.

3. Mitchinson, *Gentlemen and Officers*, p. 31; Beckett, 'Territorial Force', p. 131.

4. Beckett, 'Territorial Force', p. 132.

5. Beckett, 'Territorial Force', pp. 130, 131, 132–3.

6. McGilchrist, *Liverpool Scottish*, p. 14.

7. Ibid, pp. 14–5.

8. NGC to EJC 27 Sept 1914, BL 6/9 quoted in Clayton, *Chavasse*, p. 63.

9. Clayton, *Chavasse*, pp. 65–6; McGilchrist, *Liverpool Scottish*, pp. 15, 16. One of the three hundred left behind was Private Geoffrey Hawsley-Hill who sailed on 23 January 1915, but was killed at the Battle of the Hooge, Hildrey, *To Answer Duty's Call*, p. 93.

10. NGC to FJC 31 Oct 1914, BL 6/15–16 quoted in Clayton, *Chavasse*, p. 66.

11. NGC to DC 31 Oct 1914, BL 6/17 quoted in Clayton, *Chavasse*, p. 68; WO95/2918/2.

12. Clayton, *Chavasse*, p. 68; McGilchrist, *Liverpool Scottish*, p. 16.

13. McGilchrist, *Liverpool Scottish*, pp. 16–7; *Official History 1914*, II, p. 378n.

14. Clayton, *Chavasse*, pp. 74–5. While in Edinburgh the Liverpool Scottish had provided an honour guard for the burial of Lieutenant General Sir James Grierson, who was GOC II Corps, but who died unexpectedly in his train at Amiens. McGilchrist, *Liverpool Scottish*, pp. 15, 18.

15. McGilchrist, *Liverpool Scottish*, pp. 17–18.

16. J.C. McLeavy interview, IWM 24552.

17. Clayton, *Chavasse*, pp. 75–6, 135–6, 180, 195; McGilchrist, pp. 19, 60, 117; Mitchinson, *Gentlemen and Officers*, p. 95.

18. Clayton, *Chavasse*, pp. 79–80; NGC to FJC 5 Dec 1914, BL 6/9 quoted in Clayton, *Chavasse*, p. 80; NGC to FJC 11 Dec 1914, BL 6/9 quoted in Clayton, *Chavasse*, p. 83; McGilchrist, *Liverpool Scottish*, pp. 20–1, 25–6.

19. NGC to FJC 11 Dec 1914, BL 6/33 quoted in Clayton, *Chavasse*, p. 82.

20. McGilchrist, *Liverpool Scottish*, pp. 22–3, 26; Pegler, *Lee-Enfield Rifle*, pp. 17–28.

21. Ibid, p. 31.

22. Clayton, *Chavasse*, pp. 92–3; *Liverpool Post* 19 Jan 15.

23. McGilchrist, *Liverpool Scottish*, p. 31.

24. Ibid, pp. 33–36, 40–41.

25. Ibid, pp. 39–40.

26. *Official History 1915*, II, p. 100.

27. Clayton, *Chavasse*, pp. 117–23, 125, 126; NGC to FJC 20 June 1915, BL 6/33 quoted in Clayton, *Chavasse*, p. 82; McGilchrist, *Liverpool Scottish*, pp. 42–50.

28. McGilchrist, *Liverpool Scottish*, pp. 51–54; 5th Londons, the London Rifle Brigade, was another 'class' battalion whose CO considered that 95 per cent of his battalion was commissionable; while 28th Londons (Artists Rifles) became an Officer Training Corps. Mitchinson, *Gentlemen and Officers*, pp. 85–6.

29. Wyrall, *King's Regiment*, i, pp. 210–1; Roberts, *9th King's*, pp. 17–19; McGilchrist, *Liverpool Scottish*, pp. 55–61.

30. Ibid, p. 62.

31. Clayton, *Chavasse*, p. 143. See also p. 182. Coop's private papers are held by the IWM, Documents 1696.

32. Wyrall, *King's Regiment*, i, pp. 107–8.

33. Ibid, i, pp. 110, 111, 115.

34. Ibid, i, pp. 135, 138.
35. Ibid, i, p. 142.
36. Ibid, i, p. 144.
37. Ibid, i, pp. 107, 147–9, 151.
38. He was the divisional commander's senior RE officer and his Engineer advisor.
39. Mitchinson, *Gentlemen and Officers*, pp. 92–3.
40. Wyrall, *King's Regiment*, i, pp. 171, 184, 189–90.
41. Ibid, i, pp. 197–9.
42. Ibid, i, pp. 205–6.
43. Ibid, i, p. 206.
44. WO95/1572/3.
45. Wyrall, *King's Regiment*, i, p. 108; Hildrey, *To Answer Duty's Call*, p. 19. www.cwgc.org accessed 4 May 2015.
46. Quoted from Wyrall, *King's Regiment*, i, p. 118.
47. WO95/1572/3; www.cwgc.org accessed 4 May 2015.
48. Wyrall, *King's Regiment*, i, p. 118–9.
49. Ibid, i, pp. 119.
50. Ibid, i, pp. 124–131; www.cwgc.org accessed 4 May 2015; *Official History 1915*, I, p. 304–6; Hildrey *To Answer Duty's Call*, p. 20–1 records four killed with the Liverpool Rifles, making it possibly the worst single day for the school in the war.
51. WO95/1572/3.
52. Wyrall, *King's Regiment*, i, pp. 163, 194–5, 209.
53. WO95/1575/3.
54. Wyrall, *King's Regiment*, i, p. 109.
55. Ibid, i, p. 135; Gregson, *1/7th Battalion*, p. 79.
56. Gregson, *1/7th Battalion*, p. 83.
57. Ibid, p. 86; Kearsley, *1915*, pp. 10–11; *Official History 1915*, II, pp. 56–7, n. 56.
58. Gregson, *1/7th Battalion*, p. 88; Wyrall, *King's Regiment*, i, p. 142.
59. Wyrall, *King's Regiment*, i, pp. 142–5, 150; Gregson, *1/7th Battalion*, p. 89–97.
60. Ibid, i, p. 145; Gregson, *1/7th Battalion*, p. 103–4; Hildrey, *To Answer Duty's Call*, pp. 59–60; *Official History 1915*, II, pp. 77–8, 257n.
61. Wyrall, *King's Regiment*, i, p. 171.
62. Ibid, i, p. 189.
63. Ibid, i, pp. 206–7.
64. Roberts, *9th King's*, p. 3.
65. Ibid, pp. 3–5; Hildrey, *To Answer Duty's Call*, pp. 193–4; William Marshall interview, IWM 10686.
66. Ibid, p. 5.
67. Ibid, pp. 7–9.
68. WO95/1269/3 6 and 9 April 1915.
69. Ibid 16 April; 21 July; 29 July; 20 Aug; 23, 28, 29, 30 Aug; 28 Sept; 3 Nov 1915.
70. WO95/1269/3 8 and 9 May 1915, gives 14 killed and 69 wounded all ranks, with two missing who reported later.
71. Wyrall, *King's Regiment*, i, pp. 135–8; Roberts, *9th King's*, pp. 9–11; www.cwgc.com accessed 27/12/14.
72. Ibid, i, p. 176; Roberts, *9th King's*, pp. 11–2; Richard Trafford interview, IWM 11218.
73. Ibid, i, p. 177, Roberts, *9th King's*, p. 12.
74. Ibid, i, pp. 182–3; *Official History 1915*, II, p. 209–10.

75. Ibid, i, pp. 187–8; Roberts, *9th King's*, pp. 13–17; *Official History 1915*, II, pp. 217, 220–1; Richard Trafford interview, IWM 11218.

76. Wyrall, *King's Regiment*, i, pp. 197, 199–20; Roberts, *9th King's*, pp. 13–5; WO95/1269/3 7 & 8 October 1915; Hildrey, *To Answer Duty's Call*, pp. 138–9; *Official History 1915*, II, p. 372–3; William Marshall interview, IWM 10686.

77. Quoted from Wyrall, *King's Regiment*, i, Appendix II and Robert *9th King's*, pp. 15–6. The above compliments are taken from the two accounts. Wyrall's is an edited version. However, the message to 3rd Infantry Brigade is identical in content to one in Roberts addressed to 2nd Infantry Brigade, with the file number 1st Div. No. 604/2(G) and signed by Lt Col H. Longridge. Setting aside this discrepancy, the compliments to 1/9th King's remain the same.

78. Roberts, *9th King's*, p. 17.

79. WO95/1269/3 7 Nov 1915.

80. Roberts, *9th King's*, pp. 17–20; WO95/1269/3 28 and 29 Nov 15; Wadsworth, *1st West Lancashire Brigade*, p. 24 described them as 'monstrous heavy things', but they got used to them.

81. Wyrall, *King's Regiment*, i, p. 135.

82. Ibid, i, pp. 153–5; *Official History 1915*, II, p. 96.

83. Ibid, i, pp. 175, 209–10.

84. Clark, *Donkeys*, p. 11.

85. McGilchrist makes the same point, *Liverpool Scottish*, p. 22.

Chapter 3
1. *Official History 1916*, I, p. 24.

2. LRO 356 FIF 7/9/5; Clayton, *Chavasse*, pp. 177, 214; McCartney, *Citizen Soldiers*, pp. 83–5; www.cwgc.org accesses 18 Dec 15; Wadsworth, *1st West Lancashire Brigade*, pp. 68–9.

3. LRO 356 FIF 7/5/1.

4. Ibid FIF 2/1/16, 4/1/13.

5. Coop, *55th Division*, pp. 22–25, 28–29, 30–31; Wryall, *King's Regiment*, ii, pp. 240n, 242–4.

6. Clarke, *Artillery Tactics*, pp. 36–7.

7. Coop, *55th Division*, pp. 25–28, 168; Wyrall, *King's Regiment*, ii, pp. 248–50, 251–2, 253–5, 442; Hildrey, *To Answer Duty's Call*, pp, 138–9; William Marshall, IWM 10686.

8. Coop, *55th Division*, p. 29.

9. Wadsworth, *1st West Lancashire Brigade*, pp. 24–7.

10. Stedman, *Guillemont*, p. 70; Taylor, B., ed., *Absolute Hero*, University of Liverpool Archives, A332.

11. *Official History 1916*, II, p. 178.

12. Ibid, p. 177.

13. Stedman, *Guillemont*, pp. 73–4; Coop, *55th Division*, pp. 169–70; www.cwgc.org accessed 21 September 2015; Wadsworth, *1st West Lancashire Brigade*, pp. 35–6; *Official History 1916*, II, pp. 166, 175–6.

14. Richard Trafford interview, IWM 11218.

15. See also Laudan, S., "'Not a Single Blade of Grass…' Guillemont, 3 September 1916 – Tactics and Insights", pp. 69–79, *Stand To!* Vol. 106 (June 2016).

16. Coop, *55th Division*, pp. 30–36; Clayton, *Chavasse*, pp. 159, 160, 161; Wyrall, *King's Regiment*, ii, pp. 292–322, 422–3; Hildrey, *To Answer Duty's Call*, pp. 32–3, 63–5; *Official History 1916*, II, pp. 177–181, 184n, 387; Jünger, *Storm of Steel*, "Guillemont".

17. Coop, *55th Division*, pp. 37–41; Wyrall, *King's Regiment*, ii, pp. 322–7; Wadsworth, *1st West Lancashire Brigade*, pp. 40–1; Clarke, *Artillery Tactics*, pp. 20–1; Strong and Marble, *Artillery in the Great War*, pp. 92–3, 125, 136–7, 139–40.

18. Lt J.A. Evans quoted in Wadsworth, *1st West Lancashire Brigade*, p. 42.

19. 21 Division included 63rd Field Ambulance, another West Lancashire TF unit, whose history is described in Chapter 6.

20. Coop, *55th Division*, pp. 41–45; Wyrall, *King's Regiment*, ii, pp. 332–7; *Official History 1916*, II, p. 389n gives the casualties suffered in late September as another 1555 all ranks.

21. Griffiths, *Battle Tactics*, pp. 82–3.

22. Coop, *55th Division*, pp. 46–7; Wyrall, *King's Regiment*, ii, pp. 357–61, 370, 423–6, 491–2; Wadsworth, *1st West Lancashire Brigade*, pp. 48–55.

23. Wadsworth, *1st West Lancashire Brigade*, p. 79.

24. Coop, *55th Division*, pp. 47–55; Wadsworth, *1st West Lancashire Brigade*, pp. 80–88; Wyrall, *King's Regiment*, ii, pp. 497–508; *Official History 1917*, II, pp. 158, 167, 171–2, 174n, 178n, which gives the casualty figures slightly higher at 3447 all ranks.

25. *Official History 1917*, II, p. 266.

26. Coop, *55th Division*, pp. 55–60; Wyrall, *King's Regiment*, ii, pp. 514–20.

27. Coop, *55th Division*, pp. 60–64; *Official History 1917*, II, pp. 267–8, 276, 279.

28. LRO 356 FIF 2/2/48, 2/2/49, 2/2/65, 2/2/72, 2/2/74.

29. Coop, *55th Division*, pp. 65–66; LRO 356 FIF 3/1/3; Wadsworth, *1st West Lancashire Brigade*, pp. 96–9; *Official History 1917*, I, p. 44.

30. Coop, *55th Division*, pp. 66–71; LRO 356 FIF 3/1/2; LRO 356 FIF 3/1/3; Wyrall, *King's Regiment*, ii, pp. 546–50; Wadsworth, *1st West Lancashire Brigade*, pp. 99–100; *Official History 1917*, I, pp. 94–6.

31. Coop, *55th Division*, pp. 72–82; Wyrall, *King's Regiment*, ii, pp. 553–61; *Official History 1917*, I, p. 177.

32. Ibid, pp. 82–83; Wadsworth, *1st West Lancashire Brigade*, pp. 100–5.

33. Quoted in Coop, *55th Division*, p. 84.

34. Griffiths, *Battle Tactics*, pp. 80–1; Sheffield, *Douglas Haig*, pp. 261–2; *Official History 1917*, I, pp. 184–5, see also pp. 295–6 and 302.

35. Jünger, E., *Storm of Steel*, "The Double Battle of Cambrai."

36. Coop, *55th Division*, pp. 85–87.

37. Ibid, pp. 87–92.

38. Wyrall calls this the Battles of the Lys (which became the official title) and the Battle of Estaires, 9–11 April 1918, although the division's actions are usually referred to as the Defence of the Givenchy Craters. See also Tomaselli, *Lys*, p. 9 who extends the fighting to 12 April, and Baker, *Flanders*, Appendix I.

39. Evans, *1918*, pp. 42, 44, 63, 71; Wyrall, *King's Regiment*, ii, pp. 640–5; Baker, *Flanders*, p. 6.

40. Stevenson, *With Our Backs to the Wall*, p. 70.

41. Evans, *1918*, p. 74; LRO 356 FIF 3/2/1; Wadsworth, *1st West Lancashire Brigade*, p. 114. See also Tomaselli, *Lys*, p. 18; William Marshall interview, IWM 10686.

42. Evans described the 2nd Portuguese Division as a 'sorry formation, understrength, and with men denied home leave and consequently suffering from low morale… holding a line some seven miles long…. inexperienced and only partly trained and, indeed, the

British had small confidence in them'. They were due to be relieved on the night of 9/10 April. *1918*, pp. 72–3; Tomaselli, *Lys*, pp. 27–8; Baker, *Flanders*, pp. 29–35. Colonel Rettie's diary, quoted in Wadsworth, *1st West Lancashire Brigade*, p. 118; *Official History 1918*, II, p. 175; William Marshall interview, IWM 10686.

43. For a portrait of Eills, see Tomaselli, *Lys*, p. 52, where he wears the Territorial 'T' below his collar badges and the 55 Division insignia on his left shoulder; Wadsworth, *1st West Lancashire Brigade*, p. 120; www.cwgc.org accessed 20 Dec 15.
44. Stevenson, *With Our Backs to the Wall*, p. 72.
45. Ibid, p. 74.
46. Coop, *55th Division*, pp. 92–97, 99–102; LRO 356 FIF 3/2/1, 2/25; Tomaselli, *Lys*, pp. 49–53; Baker, *Flanders*, p. 76; Wadsworth, *1st West Lancashire Brigade*, pp. 118–127; William Marshall interview, IWM 10686.
47. Coop, *55th Division*, pp. 102–103.
48. Ibid, pp. 103–105; Tomaselli, *Lys*, pp. 133–5; Baker, *Flanders*, pp. 118–9.
49. www.army.mod.uk/firstworldwarresources/archives/1455/special-order-of-the-day-field-marshall-sir-douglas-haig accessed 7 Dec 15; Baker, *Flanders*, pp. 94–5; *Official History 1918*, II, pp. 161–74.
50. Coop, *55th Division*, pp. 105–107.
51. Quoted in Coop, *55th Division*, p. 108.
52. Evans, *1918*, p. 80; Wadsworth, *1st West Lancashire Brigade*, pp.
53. Coop, *55th Division*, pp. 109–117.
54. Quoted in Coop, *55th Division*, p. 117.
55. Evans, *1918*, p. 74.
56. Coop, *55th Division*, pp. 119–120.
57. Ibid, pp. 124–127.
58. LRO 356 FIF 3/3/2.
59. Coop, *55th Division*, pp. 127–132; LRO 356 FIF 3/3/1.
60. Ibid, pp. 124–132; Wyrall, *King's Regiment*, ii, pp. 687–8.
61. Ibid, pp. 133–134.
62. Ibid, pp. 134–135.
63. Ibid, pp. 135–136; *Official History 1918*, V, p. 125.
64. Coop, *55th Division*, pp. 136–141; LRO 356 FIF 3/3/1; *Official History 1918*, V, p.408.
65. Ibid, pp. 141–143.
66. Ibd, pp. 143–147; *Official History 1918*, V, p. 412.
67. Ibid, pp. 148–151.
68. Ibid, pp. 151–157.
69. Ibid, pp. 157–158.
70. Ibid, pp. 158–159.
71. Wyrall, *King's Regiment*, iii, pp. 699–700.

Chapter 4
1. WO95/2916/4, 5–23 June 1916.
2. Coop, *55th Division*, p. 13. WO95/2916/1 2 Sept 16, 19 Nov 17 for Lt Milne of 419 Company, marked out a trench for the pioneers to dig.
3. WO95/2916/1 3 and 16 May 16; WO95/2916/2 26 Jul 16
4. Ibid 10 Mar 16.
5. Ibid 24–28 Jun 16; WO95/2916/2 28 Jun 16.
6. WP95/2916/2 7, 8 Aug 16; *Official History 1916*, II, p. 379n.

7. WO95/2916/1 27, 29 Nov 16.
8. Ibid 16 Jun 17.
9. WO95/2916/1, WO95/2916/2, WO95/2916/3 31 Jul–4 Aug 17;
10. WO95/2916/2 20–23 Sept 17; www.cwgc.org accessed 20 Oct 15.
11. Awards for all three field companies WO95/2916/1 24 Nov 17.
12. WO95/2916/1 30 Nov–3 Dec 17; WO95/2916/2 30 Nov–3 Dec 17.
13. WO95/2916/1 11 Mar–24 Apr 18; WO95/2916/2 9–11 Apr 18.
14. Ibid 9, 24 Jun 18; WO95/2916/2 1 Jun 18.
15. WO95/2916/1 24–25 Aug 18, 16 Oct–11 Nov 18; WO95/2916/2 3 Oct–11 Nov 18.
16. WO95/2916/1 17–19 Jul 16; WO95/2916/2 24 Aug 16, 18 Aug 18; WO95/2916/3 4 Apr 16, 7 Dec 16.
17. Ibid 11 Mar 16; WO95/2916/2 22, 24, 30 Mar 16; Beckett, 'Territorial Force', p. 135.
18. WO95/2916/1 25 & 31 Jul 16; 8, 11, 16, 29 Aug 16; 26, 27 Dec 16; 28–30 May 17; Coop, *55th Division*, p. 13.
19. WO95/2916/3 6 Dec 1916, 7–10 Jan 17. www.cwgc.org accessed 8 May 2015.
20. Welti, *Signals*, p. 34.
21. Mitchinson, *England's Last Hope*, p. 168.
22. Coop, *55th Division*, p. 182; WO95/2916/4.
23. R. Westlake, *The Territorials*, p. 61; *Field Service Pocket Book, 1914* reprinted Naval and Military Press, p. 64.; Hall, 'British Army Communications', pp. 42–8.
24. Welti, *Signals*, makes the same point on 4 May 1917: 'this was never possible in forward areas in France and Belgium except during the Somme retreat, and the last days of the War in Oct 1918', p. 33. 55th Division, of course, did not participate in the Somme Retreat.
25. Wadsworth, *1st West Lancashire Brigade*, p. 113.
26. *Field Service Pocket Book 1914*, reprinted Naval and Military Press, p. 64.
27. WO95/2916/4; Coop, *55th Division*, p. 14.
28. Ibid, pp. 3–8. On 2 Mar 16 Pioneer Pinkstone of J Carrier Pigeon Service from 7 Corps Signal Company and on 17 Mar 16 Pioneer Birchall of W Carrier Pigeon Service arrive with their teams. The electric plant was supplied by 17 Corps.
29. Ibid, pp. 3, 6, 8, 10.
30. Ibid, p. 6.
31. Ibid, pp. 8, 96; www.cwgc.ord accessed 14 Sept 2015
32. Ibid, pp. 18, 21, 22, 23.
33. Ibid, pp. 24, 27.
34. Ibid, pp. 40–4.
35. Ibid, pp. 45–63.
36. Ibid, p. 63.
37. Ibid, pp. 68–74.
38. Ibid, pp. 83–4.
39. Ibid, pp. 104–5.
40. WO95/2916/4, p. 121.
41. WO95/2914/3 17, 23 and 24 Apr 16; WO95/2915/1 22 Apr 16.
42. WO95/2915/2 9 Mar 16, 4 Apr 16, 15 May 16; Wadsworth, *1st West Lancashire Brigade*, pp. 21–2.
43. WO95/2915/2 1, 9, 13 Jan 16, 2 Feb 16. See also Wadsworth, *1st West Lancashire Brigade*, p. 21.
44. WO95/2914/3 55 Divisional Artillery Order No. 2; No.4 23 Feb 16.

45. WO95/2915/1 May 16.
46. WO95/2914/3 3, 5, 8 Mar 16.
47. WO95/2915/1 3 Sept 16; www.cwgc.org accessed 28 May 2016.
48. WO95/2914/3 17 Apr 16; Report on Wire Cutting Experiment, 17 Apr 16.
49. WO95/2914/3 15, 24–29 Jun 16; WO95/2914/4, 24 Jun 16; WO95/2915/1 18–30 June 16.
50. WO95/2914/3 8, 9 Aug 16; WO95/2914/4 7 Aug 16; WO95/2915/1 5, 7, 8, 9 Aug 16; Strong and Marble, *Artillery in the Great War*, pp. 57, 62, 108.
51. WO95/2915/1 5, 8 Oct 16; WO95/2915/2 19 Oct 16; Wadsworth, *1st West Lancashire Brigade*, p. 49.
52. WO95/2914/3 15–30 Sept 16; WO95/2915/1 15 Sept 16; Strong and Marble, *Artillery in the Great War*, p. 169.
53. WO95/2914/4 20 Dec 16; WO95/2915/1 5 Aug 16; WO95/2915/2 5 Mar 16. 1 Apr 16.
54. WO95/2914/3 1–6, 11–14 Sept 16, 15 Oct 16, 4–6, 29 Nov 16, 4 Mar 17; WO95/2914/4 24 Jun 17; WO95/2915/1 23 Dec 16.
55. WO95/2914/3 April 17 and Appendices; Strong and Marble, *Artillery in the Great War*, p. 44.
56. Wadsworth, *1st West Lancashire Brigade*, pp. 79, 84–86.
57. WO95/2914/3 29 Nov–3 Dec 17; WO95/2914/4 30 Nov 17; Wadsworth, *1st West Lancashire Brigade*, pp. 100–6; *Official History 1917*, I, pp. 187n, 211.
58. Coop, *55th Division*, pp. 173–4; Gliddon, *Cambrai 1917*, pp. 167–172; Strong and Marble, *Artillery in the Great War*, p. 152.
59. WO95/2914/3 25–31 Jan 18.
60. See Strong and Marble, *Artillery in the Great War*, pp. xviii–xxiii on different the artillery deployments at Le Cateau.
61. Wadsworth, *1st West Lancashire Brigade*, pp. 118–127.
62. WO95/2914/3 February–April 18; WO95/2914/4 20, 26 Feb 18, 9 Apr 18; Wadsworth, *1st West Lancashire Brigade*, pp. 135–144; www.cwgc.org accessed 20 Dec 15.
63. For example WO95/2914/3 19 Sept 18; 30 Sept 18; 1, 2 Oct 18; WO95/2914/4 2 Oct 18, Oct–Nov 18; Wadsworth, *1st West Lancashire Brigade*, pp. 153–6.
64. WO95/2914/3 22, 26 Oct 18; 7–9 Nov 18; Wadsworth, *1st West Lancashire Brigade*, pp.156–7.
65. Wadsworth, *1st West Lancashire Brigade*, pp. 157–9; WO95/2914/3 11–18 Nov 18; WO95/2914/4 11–30 Nov 18.
66. Wadsworth, *1st West Lancashire Brigade*, pp. 32, 63–4, 139, 142; www.cwgc.org, accessed 18 Dec 15.
67. WO95/2915/4; www.cwgc.org, accessed 28 May 2015.
68. SAA – Small Arms Ammunition, .303 rifle ammunition.
69. Wadsworth, *1st West Lancashire Brigade*, pp. 33–34, 44–5, 52–3, 65, 74–7, 90–1; www.cwgc.org accessed 19 Dec 15.
70. For ease, I have referred to the RAMC throughout, but it includes the role of the nurses, VADs, dentists and the ASC who drove the ambulances throughout. Clayton, *Chavasse*, pp. 169–71.
71. Finn, 'Local heroes', p. 527.
72. In the Appendix to Aug 16 War Diary, Wood is the only one of ten officers to be annotated 'RAMC TF'.
73. WO95/2918/2 November and December 1916, see Coffey's end of month signatures.
74. See also Mitchinson, *Gentlemen and Officers*, p. 55, for cases of CSM in early 1915.

75. www.cwgc.org accessed 31 May 15.
76. WO95/2918/1 6–10 Aug 16; www.cwgc.org accessed 31 May 15.
77. www.cwgc.org accessed 31 May 2015; Clayton, *Chavasse*, pp. 199–203.
78. www.cwgc.org accessed 1 June 2015.
79. WO95/2918/1; WO95/2918/2; www.cwgc.org accessed 31 May 2015.
80. WO95/2919/2; WO95/2918/2 7 Apr 18, 5 Aug 18.
81. WO95/2919/4.
82. Young, *ASC*, pp. 69, 71–2, 213, 252, 274, 335; WO95/2919/4 Dec 15 and Jan 16.
83. WO95/2975/5; WO95/2975/6.
84. Young, *ASC*, p. 238.
85. WO95/2919/4; www.cwgc.org accessed 28 May 2016.
86. WO95/2919/3 for 14, 19 and 21 Jan 16; 27, 28 and 29 Mar 18; 15 Feb 19.
87. Ibid 19 Mar 17, 23 Aug 17, 23 Mar 18.
88. Ibid 3 Sept 17; 7 Jan and 20 Mar 18, 1 Feb 19; Coop, *55th Division*, p. 184; www.gwgc.org accessed 6 May 2015.
89. Ibid September to November 1918.
90. Ibid 3, 13 and 31 Jan 19, 30 April 19.
91. Wadsworth, *1st West Lancashire Brigade*, p. 132.

Chapter 5
1. McGilchrist, *Liverpool Scottish*, p. 189.
2. Wurtzburg, *2/6th*, p. 1; McGilchrist, *Liverpool Scottish*, pp. 14–5.
3. Ibid, p. 2; McCartney, *Citizen Soldiers*, p. 32.
4. www.1914–1918.net accessed 10 May 2015.
5. Wurtzburg, *2/6th*, p. 3.
6. Formed at the same time as the TF, the OTCs were common in public schools rather than being limited to universities as today. For their experiences, see Lewis-Stemple, *Six Weeks*.
7. Wurtzburg, *2/6th*, pp. 3–5, 7; McCartney, *Citizen Soldiers*, p. 31; Hildrey, *To Answer Duty's Call*, p. 175.
8. William Marshall interview, IWM 10686; Richard Trafford interview, IWM 11218.
9. McGilchrist, *Liverpool Scottish*, pp. 189–90, 191; *Obituaries from the Queen's Own Cameron Highlanders*, Inverness, May 1957.
10. J.C. McLeavy interview, IWM 24552.
11. Wurtzburg, *2/6th*, pp. 3, 5–6.
12. Ibid, pp. 7–9; McGilchrist, *Liverpool Scottish*, pp. 190–1.
13. Ibid, pp. 9–10, 14.
14. Ibid, pp. 10–11, 19; McGilchrist, *Liverpool Scottish*, pp. 189–91, 200; McCartney, *Citizen Soldiers*, p. 47.
15. Ibid, p. 12–3.
16. McGilchrist, *Liverpool Scottish*, pp. 191–2; McCartney, *Citizen Soldiers*, p. 62; Beckett, 'Territorial Force', p. 137.
17. Wadsworth, *1st West Lancashire Brigade*, pp. 11–12.
18. Wutzburg, *2/6th*, p. 13.
19. Ibid, pp. 15–6. Also see McGilchrist, *Liverpool Scottish*, p. 191.
20. Ibid, pp. 17–20; McGilchrist, *Liverpool Scottish*, pp. 192–3, 194.
21. Ibid, pp. 21, 27.
22. Ibid, pp. 27–8; McGilchrist, *Liverpool Scottish*, p. 194.

23. Ibid, pp. 44–7; 2/9th War Diary 23 Feb 17; McGilchrist, *Liverpool Scottish*, pp. 196, 197; Wyrall, *King's Regiment*, ii, pp. 428–41.
24. Ibid, pp. 48–9; Wyrall, *King's Regiment*, ii, pp 428–30.
25. Ibid, pp. 52–3.
26. Ibid, pp. 70–71, 79.
27. Ibid, pp. 83–4, 93, 312. Garrod is listed as 'invalided to England' in August 1917, and it is to be hoped it was not serious enough to prevent him returning to the Philharmonic.
28. Ibid, pp. 96–7.
29. Ibid, pp. 98–111, 325; Wadsworth, *1st West Lancashire Brigade*, p. 74.
30. Ibid, pp. 121–4, 126; WO95/2985/4 27 May 17, 1 Jun 17; McGilchrist, *Liverpool Scottish*, pp. 207–8; Wyrall, *King's Regiment*, ii, p. 437.
31. Ibid, p. 191.
32. Ibid, pp. 128–9, 30; McGilchrist, *Liverpool Scottish*, p. 209.
33. Ibid, pp. 130–5; see also Mitchinson, *Gentlemen and Officers*, pp. 130–5 for the controversy of diluting 'localism' in London.
34. Ibid, pp. 138–142.
35. Ibid, pp. 142–3.
36. McGilchrist, *Liverpool Scottish*, pp. 211–3.
37. Wutzburg, *2/6th*, pp. 148–54.
38. Ibid, p. 155.
39. Ibid, *2/6th*, p. 157; McGilchrist, *Liverpool Scottish*, pp. 213–4.
40. Ibid, p. 159.
41. Ibid, pp. 159–60. See Chavasse and RAMC earlier.
42. WO95/1269/3 1–6 February 18.
43. McGilchrist, *Liverpool Scottish*, p. 216; McCartney, *Citizen Soldiers*, p. 72. See also McCartney, p. 60 where the impact of the merger of the 10th and remaining independent for 1/6th and 2/6th is discussed.
44. Wutzburg, *2/6th*, pp. 167–170; McGilchrist, *Liverpool Scottish*, pp. 214–5.
45. Baker, *Flanders*, pp. 45, 107, 124, 131; *Official History 1918*, II, pp. 105, 113.
46. Wutzburg, *2/6th*, pp. 178–79.
47. Ibid, pp. 179–80.
48. Ibid, pp. 180–1, 184, 194, 196–200, 203.
49. Ibid, pp. 216–8; *Official History 1918*, IV, pp. 404, 456; V, 51–2; www.cwgc.org accessed 14 Nov 15.
50. Ibid, pp. 219–225; see Lewis-Stemple, *Six Weeks*, which was the average life expectancy for an infantry platoon commander on the Western Front; www.cwgc.org accessed 14 Nov 15.
51. Ibid, pp. 229–30.
52. Ibid, pp. 204–7, 210–4; *Official History 1918*, IV, p. 381–2.
53. Ibid, pp. 233–45.
54. Ibid, pp. 247–50.
55. Ibid, pp. 250–1.

Chapter 6

1. WO95/2975/6; www.cwgc.org accessed 16 August 2015.
2. WO95/4314; *East Lancashire Royal Engineers*, pp. 27, 28, 29; Gibbon, *42nd Division*, pp. 58–63.

3. See the reporting death of Lieutenant Dixon-Nuttall with 1/1st Field Company. It has not been possible to confirm if they were related, but it seems plausible.

4. Gibbon, *42nd Division*, pp. 48, 54.

5. Ibid, pp. 54–55.

6. www.cwgc.org accessed 4 April 2015

7. Gibbon, *42nd Division*, pp. 56–57.

8. Ibid, p. 62.

9. Gillon, *29th Division*, pp. 41, 42.

10. Hildrey, *The Answer Duty's Call*, pp. 68–9, 80–1.

11. Richard Yorston interview, IWM 24554; Cecil Robert Tomkinson interview, IWM 7497.

12. Richard Yorston interview, IWM 24554.

13. Richard Yorston interview, IWM 24554.

14. WO95/2325/1.

15. TNA WO95 2147/1; Westmore, Thomson and Allison, *the Story of the 63rd Field Ambulance*; www.21stdivision1914-18.org

16. Westmore, *Story*, p. 33.

17. Ibid, p. 23.

18. www.cwgc.org accessed 2 May 2016.

19. Westmore, *Story*, pp.37–40.

20. Ibid, p. 47.

21. Ibid, p. 64.

22. Ibid, pp. 71–2, 75–76.

23. Ibid, pp. 84–92.

24. Ibid, p.96.

25. WO95/2915/1 and WO95/2915/2; www.cwgc.org accessed 28 May 2015; Nicholson, *Canadian Expeditionary Force*, p. 110; Wadsworth, *1st West Lancashire Brigade*, pp. 11–17.

26. WO95/2259/6.

27. See Appendix I after Feb 15.

28. www.cwgc.org accessed 30 June 2015.

29. W.R. McLeish interview, IWM 24531.

30. Hildrey, *To Answer Duty's Call*, p. 79.

Conclusion

1. From the Cenotaph, taken from Ezekiel 38:15 'And thou shalt come from thy place out of the north parts, thou, and many people with them, all of them riding upon horses, a great company, and a mighty army.'

Bibliography

Unpublished Sources:
Imperial War Museum
Canon J.O. Coop private papers, IWM Documents 1696.
William Marshall interview, IWM 10686.
J.C. McLeavy interview, IWM 24552.
W.R. McLeish interview, IWM 24531.
Cecil Robert Tomkinson interview, IWM 7497.
Richard Trafford interview, IWM 11218.
Richard Yorston interview, IWM 24552.

The National Archives War Diaries

WO95/1269/3	1/9th King's (Liverpool Regiment)
WO95/1469/3	1/1st (West Lancashire) Field Company, RE
WO95/1572/3	1/6th King's (Liverpool Regiment)
WO95/2147/1	2/2nd (West Lancashire) Field Ambulance, RAMC
WO95/2259/6	27th Division Train, ASC
WO95/2296/1	1/1st (West Lancashire) Field Ambulance, RAMC
WO95/2325/1	1/2nd (West Lancashire) Field Ambulance, RAMC
WO95/2914/3	1/1st (West Lancashire) Brigade, RFA
WO95/2914/4	1/2nd (West Lancashire) Brigade, RFA
WO95/2915/1	1/3rd (West Lancashire) Brigade, RFA
WO95/2915/2	1/4th (West Lancashire) (Howitzer) Brigade, RFA
WO95/2915/4	55th Divisional Ammunition Column, ASC
WO95/2916/1	1/1st (West Lancashire) Field Company, RE
WO95/2916/2	2/1st (West Lancashire) Field Company, RE
WO95/2916/3	2/2nd (West Lancashire) Field Company, RE
WO95/2916/4	1/1st Divisional Signal Company, RE
WO95/2918/1	2/1st (West Lancashire) Field Ambulance, RAMC
WO95/2918/2	1/3rd (West Lancashire) Field Ambulance, RAMC
WO95/2919/2	55th Divisional Sanitary Section, RAMC
WO95/2919/3	1/1st (West Lancashire) Mobile Vety Section, AVC
WO95/2919/4	55th Divisional Train, ASC (from 27th Division)
WO95/2975/5	57th Divisional Train, ASC
WO95/2975/6	57th Divisional Train, ASC
WO95/2985/4	2/9th King's (Liverpool Regiment) Feb 1917–Jan 1918
WO95/4314	1/2nd (West Lancashire) Field Company, RE

Liverpool Record Office
Records of the 55th (West Lancashire) Division 356 FIF
A short history of the Units, administered by the West Lancashire Territorial & Auxiliary
    Forces Association (1952) 356 (72) WES
University of Liverpool Archive
Taylor, B., ed., *Absolute Hero*, A332
PhD Thesis
Gregson, A.S., *The 1/7th Battalion King's Liverpool Regiment and the Great War – the
    experience of a Territorial Battalion and its Home Town*, University of Coventry, 2004.

Published Sources:
Anon., *A History of the East Lancashire Royal Engineers* (Manchester, 1921, reprinted 2003).
Anon., *History of the 359 Medium Regiment RA (4th West Lancashire)(TA) 1859–1959*
    (Liverpool, 1959).
Baker, C., *The Battle for Flanders* (Barnsley, 2011).
Batten, S., 'A School for the Leaders', JSAHR, Vol. 93 No. 373 Spring 2015
Beckett, F.W., 'The Territorial Force' in I.F.W Beckett and K. Simpson (eds.), *A Nation in
    Arms: a social study of the British Army in the First World War* (Manchester, 1985).
Becket, F.W., *Riflemen Form* (Barnsley, 1987).
Beadon, R.H., *The Royal Army Service Corps* (Cambridge, 1931).
Clark, A., *The Donkeys* (London, 1961).
Clarke, D., *British Artillery 1914–19 Field Artillery* (Oxford, 2004).
Clarke, D., *British Artillery 1914–19 Heavy Artillery* Oxford, 2005).
Clarke, D., *World War I Battlefield Artillery Tactics* (Oxford, 2014).
Clayton, A., *Chavasse Double VC* (Barnsley, 1997).
Coop, J.O., *The Story of the 55th (West Lancashire) Division, 1916 – 1919* (Liverpool, 1919).
Davies, P., *The Man Behind the Bridge: Colonel Toosey and the River Kwai* (1991).
Edmonds, J.E., ed., *Official History, Military Operations France and Belgium*, 1914, II, (London,
    1925).
Edmonds, J.E., ed., *Official History, Military Operations France and Belgium*, 1915, I (London,
    1927).
Edmonds, J.E., ed., *Official History, Military Operations France and Belgium, 1915*, II (London,
    1928).
Edmonds, J.E., ed., *Official History, Military Operations France and Belgium, 1916*, I (London,
    1932).
Edmonds, J.E., ed., *Official History, Military Operations France and Belgium, 1916*, II (London,
    1938).
Edmonds, J.E., ed., *Official History, Military Operations France and Belgium, 1917*, I (London,
    1938).
Edmonds, J.E., ed., *Official History, Military Operations France and Belgium, 1917*, II (London,
    1948).
Edmonds, J.E., ed., *Official History, Military Operations France and Belgium, 1918*, II (London,
    1937).
Edmonds, J.E., ed., *Official History, Military Operations France and Belgium, 1918*, I (London,
    1935).
Edmonds, J.E., ed., *Official History, Military Operations France and Belgium, 1918*, V (London,
    1947).
Evans, M., *1918, the Year of Victories* (London, 2002).

Field Service Pocket Book, 1914 (1917 reprint; Naval and Military Press reprint).

Finn, M, 'Local Heroes: war news and the construction of 'community' in Britain, 1914–1918' in *Historical Research*, vol. 83, no. 221 (August, 2010).

Gibbon, F.P. *The 42nd (East Lancashire) Division 1914–1918* (1920).

Gillon, S., *Story of the 29th Division A Record of Gallant Deeds* (London, 1925).

Gillott, M., "British Line Infantry Reserve of the Great War" Part 3, *Stand To!* Vol. 102 (January 2015).

Gliddon, G., *VCs of the First World War: Cambrai 1917* (Stroud, 2004).

Grant, N., *The Lewis Gun* (Oxford, 2014).

Griffiths, P., *Battle Tactics of the Western Front: the British Army's Art of the Attack*, (London, 1994).

Hall, B.N., 'Technological Adaption in a Global Conflict: The British Army and Communications beyond the Western Front, 1914–1918', *Journal of Military History*, 78 (January 2014).

Hildrey, T.W., *To Answer Duty's Call* (Oxford, 2015).

Jünger, E., *Storm of Steel*.

Langley, D., "British Line Infantry Reserves of the Great War" Part 1, *Stand To!* Vol. 100 (June 2014).

Langley, D., "British Line Infantry Reserves of the Great War" Part 2, *Stand To!* Vol. 101 (Sept 2014).

Laudan, S., " 'Not a Single Blade of Grass…' Guillemont, 3 September 1916 – Tactics and Insights", *Stand To!* Vol. 106 (June 2016)

Lewis-Stemple, J., *Six Weeks* (London, 2011).

Nicholson, G.W.L., *Canadian Expeditionary Force, 1914–1919* (1962).

Maddocks, G., *Liverpool Pals* (Barnsley, 1991).

McCartney, H., *Citizen Soldiers* (Cambridge, 2005).

Welti, A., ed., MacGregor, A., *Signals from the Great War* (Brighton, 2014).

McGilchrist, A.M., *Liverpool Scottish 1900 – 1919* (Liverpool, 1930; Naval and Military Press reprint)

Mitchinson, K.W., *England's Last Hope: the Territorial Force, 1908–1914* (Basingstoke, 2008).

Mitchinson, K.W., *Gentlemen and Officers* (Uckfield, 1994).

Mitchinson, K.W., *The Territorial Force at War, 1914–1916* (Basingstoke, 2014).

Nash, *Chitral Charlie* (Barnsley, 2010).

Obituaries from the Queen's Own Cameron Highlanders, Inverness, May 1957.

Pegler, M., *The Lee-Enfield Rifle* (Oxford, 2012).

Roberts, E., *The Story of the "9th King's" in France* (reprinted Litera, 2014).

Sheffield, G., *Douglas Haig: from the Somme to Victory* (London, 2011).

Sherson, E., *Townshend of Chitral and Kut* (London, 1928).

Stedman, M., *Guillemont* (Barnsley, 2012).

Stevenson, D., *With Our Backs to the Wall: victory and defeat in 1918* (London, 2011).

Strong, P., and Marble, S., *Artillery in the Great War* (Barnsley, 2013).

Tomaselli, *The Battle of the Lys* (Barnsley, 2011).

Wadsworth, M.C., Capt. W.W., *War Diary of the 1st West Lancashire Brigade, RFA* (Liverpool, 1923).

Westlake, R., *British Territorial Units, 1914–18* (Oxford, 1991).

Westlake, R., *The Territorials 1908–1914* (Barnsley, 2011).

Westmore, A.W., *The Story of the 63rd Field Ambulance (2/2nd West Lancashire Field Ambulance TF) 1914–1919* (Liverpool, ND).

Wurtzburg, C.E., *The History of the 2/6th (Rifle) Battalion "The King's" (Liverpool Regiment) 1914–1919* (Naval and Military Press reprint).
Wyrall, *King's Regiment*, vol. I (London, 1927).
Wyrall, *King's Regiment*, vol. II (London, 1930).
Wyrall, *King's Regiment*, vol. III (London, 1935).
Young, M., *Army Service Corps, 1902–1918* (Barnsley, 2000).

Websites
www.army.mod.uk/firstworldwarresources/archives/1455/special-order-of-the-day-field-marshall-sir-douglas-haig
www.cwgc.org
www.kingsownmuseum.plus.com
www.liverpoolremembrance.weebly.com
www.1914-1918.net
www.9thkings.co.uk
www.21stdivision1914-18.org

Index